Psychology

and

Health Care

For my wife, Daryl and my children Bonnie, Bradley, Ross and Brandon

PSYCHOLOGY AND HEALTH CARE

Robert W. Oliver
BSc(Hons), RGN, RSCN, CertEd FE
Freelance Lecturer
Formerly Nurse Tutor at
Cambridgeshire College of
Professional Health Studies

Baillière Tindall
LONDON   PHILADELPHIA
TORONTO TOKYO SYDNEY

Baillière Tindall
W B Saunders

24–28 Oval Road
London NW1 7DX

The Curtis Center
Independence Square West
Philadelphia, PA 19106–3399, USA

1 Goldthorne Avenue
Toronto, Ontario M8Z 5T9, Canada

Harcourt Brace Jovanovich (Australia) Pty
Limited
32–35 Smidmore Street
Marrickville, NSW 2204, Australia

Harcourt Brace Jovanovich Japan Inc.
Ichibancho Central Building, 22–1
Ichibancho
Chiyoda-ku, Tokyo 102, Japan

A catalogue record is available from the British Library

ISBN–7020–1601–2

Typeset by Columns Design and Production Services Ltd., Reading
and printed in Great Britain by Butler and Tanner Ltd, Frome, Somerset

CONTENTS

PICTURE CREDITS

ACKNOWLEDGEMENTS

It is said that writing a book is a lonely endeavour, and so it has proved, but it cannot be done without the support, help and advice of others. First, I really have my wife, Daryl, to thank, not only for giving me the confidence to write in the first place, but also for her help with the clerical work, her comments on some of the text, providing many of the quotes that head the chapters and sections, and perhaps most difficult of all, being such a super mother and keeping our four energetic children occupied when Dad was tearing his hair out!

I would very much like to thank the tutors who have influenced my thinking over the years, and especially Sonia Reynolds, formally lecturer at Tottenham College of Technology who was the first person to arouse my interest in psychology and teaching by her energetic and lively approach. To friends and colleagues who have been kind enough to take an interest in the subjects I was teaching (and the methods I used) I wish to give my grateful thanks. To these individuals I owe some of the credit for the format of the book.

I thank my close friend and business partner, Colin Endersby for his support throughout the project, in particular for his invaluable comments on each chapter, and for keeping our business, Presentation Skills Consultants, ticking over so smoothly whilst I was buried under a pile of books and articles. Whilst on the subject of books and articles, I would like to express my gratitude to Debbie Fisher, Senior Librarian at the Charles West School of Nursing, Great Ormond Street.

Finally, I wish to thank the editorial and production staff at Baillière Tindall, principally Sarah James (Senior Editor) for her support, inspiration, expertise and tolerance towards a neurotic author. Latterly my thanks go to Gill Robinson and to Jackie Curthoys who kept me on an even keel towards the end of the project. To the battery of proof readers, reviewers and other experts, I also send my thanks.

March, Cambridgeshire, November 1992

PREFACE

The writing of any textbook which attempts to introduce the reader to a subject such as psychology is a far from simple task. This is not necessarily because of volume – time and perseverence help this along, but rather the choice of material that is to be included, and that which is to be excluded. Naturally, although such decisions are largely objective, the experiences of the author play a major role, and this text is no exception. This is not to say, however, that I am expressing a preference for one school of thought or another, but rather that some approaches to certain subjects are perhaps traditionally utilised in preference to others, and hence a more complete account of them will help the reader to decide for themselves whether or not they are appropriate. In addition to this, I have attempted to present the reader with some of the 'classic' works which have contributed to our understanding of behaviour. It is my belief that such classic theories together with the inclusion of more up to date research will enable the reader to form a more complete picture of how psychology and health care interact.

As a nurse, it would have been tempting to have written a highly specific text for nurses, but as the project developed it became apparent that the majority of health professionals in contact with patients and clients face the same dilemmas and problems, and hence a more 'patient centred' approach was needed. I hope that this has been achieved, and that I have managed to 'talk' to more than just nurses!

I think that at this point that it would benefit the reader if I revealed some of my personal observations that led to the writing of this book.

Firstly, psychology is seen by some as taking a secondary place to the more physical sciences which are sometimes seen as playing a more direct role in curing disease. In fact, the correct psychological approach to the patient, when, for instance, discussing medication and treatment, may well prevent the patient being readmitted.

Secondly, many people have told me that psychology is taught in a very dry way, and have difficulty in learning it. This is a desperate shame, as psychology is a science in which we all can participate with our own experiences and emotions and can hopefully discover better ways to understand ourselves and others.

Finally, many of the theories expounded by both teachers and authors are not put into the context of health care, and hence their relevance is lost. It was principally this last reason that finally led to the writing of this text. There are of course many admirable texts available, a few of which look at psychology from the point of view of individuals who spend their days caring for people, and of course personal experience and beliefs lead to the conclusion that those that are applied effectively could have had additions; and I have no doubt that future authors will feel the same about this text. This leads me to briefly discuss the origins of the book and the topics covered.

The book is divided into three sections, all of which are related, to a greater or lesser extent, to patient care. The first section 'Individual Differences' examines those factors which make us different from 'the crowd' and I begin with a brief overview of upbringing in Chapter 1; as with every other chapter, more material could have been included, but it is intended to give the reader an idea as to the extent that childhood influences have over health in later life.

In the book, probably the most contentious chapter is chapter 2 which deals with personality. Personality as a subject inspires heated debate on the part of some psychologists, and it was therefore rather difficult to present the reader with a fair representation of the theories. I have to say that I have probably (almost definitely) failed to achieve this if it is seen as the intention to present the reader with all points of view. I have written the chapter with the view that our understanding of the subject of personality is largely based on the works of a few principal theorists and that many other theories have emerged from them. As such, I have attempted to present some of these theories, even though some are rarely used in this 'raw' form. The theories of Sigmund Freud are such a case, but the direction that Freud gave to succeeding generations cannot be ignored, and many of the cornerstones of his theories are very much alive and well today. I feel that I should stress that, although I have endeavoured to present as wide a scope of theories as possible, their inclusion in no way indicates my preference for one or another.

The subject of physiological psychology is briefly covered in chapter 3, principally because of the massive strides forward in this field in recent years, and because of its possible implications for the future treatment of a whole range of psychiatric disorders. The thought that the stigma of mental illness may one day be eradicated because of advances in treatment is an exciting one. The everyday activities of individuals such as eating and sleeping, are covered in this chapter and will hopefully stimulate the reader to consider the implications for care.

Motivation, both in terms of health care and work, is covered in chapter 4. It has been one of the saddest aspects of my professional life to observe how appallingly we treat each other at times, so, for this and other reasons, a significant part of this chapter is concerned with dealing with people in the occupational setting.

Possibly one of the most significant psychological factors involved in patient care is how we communicate with our clients; this is covered in chapter 5. Numerous cross references are made later in the book to this chapter, reflecting the growing body of research that indicates that individuals receiving health care feel that, in one way or another, they have been poorly communicated with. From learning the individuals' fears to helping them to understand their treatment, effective communication is essential, but research has shown that more often than not, it does not happen.

An understanding of learning and cognition are essential if we are to provide effective health education, and especially if we are to enable the individual to understand their illness and treatment. A significant part of the chapter is devoted to the theories of Jean Piaget which continue to attract the attention of researchers into cognitive development. A significant body of research continues to be produced using Piaget's theory as a foundation, and certainly the readers are presented with the ideal opportunity to form their own opinions by observing children of different age groups carrying out certain activities originally described by Piaget. I felt it essential to include a significant amount of material on the factors affecting learning, and I confess that the amount of material generated tempted me on more than one occasion to put it into a separate chapter, but in the end I decided to trust to my instincts and leave it as it now appears. Only time will tell whether I was right or wrong! I felt it essential to include a small section on educating both staff and patients as the latter, especially, have been the subject of considerable debate in recent years.

The 'Humanistic Psychology' of both Allport and Rogers forms a large part of the section on 'the Self', although other theorists who have made contributions in this area are included. The cornerstone premise of the Humanistic School is that we are all individuals, and indeed this approach has been extensively utilised in education and clinical psychology for some time. I felt it important to present this point of view, partly in order to add another important dimension to the text overall, and partly to help the reader to consider the wider implications of individualised patient care. Naturally, one of the important aspects of individuality is our attitudes; these are discussed in chapter 8. The inclusion of such a chapter probably comes as little surprise to anyone but I have included it for a couple of specific reasons. First, the term *attitudes* is a highly misused one and I felt that an understanding of the formation and components of attitudes might lead to a more productive use of the term. More realistically, the subject has been included because of its relevance to health care in terms of, for instance, seeking treatment and how we treat those with certain diseases in our community. Changing attitudes is an integral part of health education, but little can be achieved if we do not understand the 'mechanics' behind such a mechanism.

It can be seen, therefore, that Section 1 acts as a sort of reference section for the rest of the book, although the relevance to health care does at times stand independently of the other sections. As with the rest of the book, suggested reading is included in the chapters in order to help the reader to pursue individual subjects in more depth, and I hope that what they read in this text will stimulate them to do so.

The second section, which examines our reactions to life events, comprises three chapters which cover such material as anxiety, stress and bereavement. The understanding of such reactions contribute to our understanding of our reactions to illness in ourselves and in others. Certainly an understanding of coping strategies is essential if we are to facilitate a return to normal life of those individuals in our care. I was concerned that the reader could view different approaches to the subject areas, such as anxiety. An alternative to this could have been to produce a highly prescriptive account of how to deal with various situations, and I was determined to avoid any such path that would lead to health professionals failing to respond as individuals to unique situations that they may encounter. On the other hand, I was similarly determined to present information in such a way as to provoke an analytical approach to the subject areas, and hence go at least some way towards preventing a stereotypical approach to clients.

The final section of the book deals specifically with health care intervention and is in part an extension of the previous section in that it deals with two major groups of life events, namely illness and hospitalisation. This section has been arranged in age groups, and as such, chapters 1 and 6 are particularly relevant, although the chapter on attitudes to illness should be read in conjunction with chapter 8. A vast amount of literature is currently being generated in these areas, and I hope the reader will forgive the omission of so much of it, but as with other chapters, I have attempted to develop themes in a meaningful way and some selectiveness was required.

My overall aim for the book, as may already have been gleaned, is to present the reader with numerous viewpoints which have contributed to our understanding of psychology in relation to health care, and which will stimulate thought and debate in a constructive way. Moreover, I fervently hope that this printed collection of theories, thoughts and discussions will be translated into effective and thoughtful patient care.

INDIVIDUAL DIFFERENCES

CHAPTERS

Everything, insofar as it is itself, endeavours to persevere in its own being . . .

SPINOZA

INTRODUCTION TO SECTION ONE

It is a virtual impossibility to give a complete account of all the concepts, past and present, that have contributed to the body of knowledge that is relevant to this text, however, in this section an overview of some of the more important concepts is given.

It is perhaps the most challenging aspect of psychology that we are all individuals, and as such, will react in different ways to different situations. In this section, some of the differences between individuals will be examined, although, as always, the reader is directed to the source texts for a more in-depth account.

The choice of topics covered in this section reflects certain assumptions. Firstly, certain theories have contributed to our current knowledge, even if they have been developed and diversified by other theorists; secondly, that an overview of some of the more famous theories may serve to help the reader to understand some of the major approaches to the subject; and thirdly, that some theories are more applicable to health care than others.

Commencing with patterns of upbringing, the possible origins of some behaviours that affect our health are discussed. Moderating factors such as personality (Chapter 2), motivation (Chapter 4), the self (Chapter 7) and attitudes (Chapter 8) are explored in some depth and form the basis of discussions in later sections. 'Cognition and learning' (Chapter 6) is concerned not only with how the individual learns, but also how education may be facilitated. Chapter 5 looks at communication, which has been suggested by many researchers as one of the most crucial aspects of patient care. 'Physiological psychology' (Chapter 3) briefly examines this ever-expanding speciality that explores physiological correlates of behaviour.

CHAPTER 1

UPBRINGING AND
HEALTH

'He that would know what shall be must consider what has been'

T. FULLER (1732) *Gnomologia: Adagies and Proverbs.*

INTRODUCTION

We are probably all aware of the importance of keeping fit and avoiding those factors that could damage our health. Eating a high cholesterol diet, not taking enough exercise, smoking, and drinking excessive alcohol will rank highly as health hazards for many people. There are some who would add to the list considerably, conversely others will choose to ignore all warnings.

Many of us actively attempt to change our lifestyles in order to reduce risks to our health, in the hope that we will live longer. There is no doubt that such changes in many cases are successful in achieving this objective, particularly with regard to activities such as smoking. However, instead of accepting that poor lifestyles need to be changed, a more critical and in-depth analysis needs to be carried out. If successful health education is to be instigated then the origins of disease need to be identified. We are all aware of the remarkable progress made towards identifying the pathological causes of disease and we can readily relate some physiological changes to lifestyle, but we have to consider whether the factors leading up to a poor lifestyle could have been avoided, and in order to do this we need to understand how they arose in the first place.

In considering the origins of poor health habits, consideration must be given to both the physical and mental shaping of the individual with regard to the implication for health in later life, not least in terms of the equality of individuals in our society. That some individuals are more advantaged than others is an unfortunate fact of life that few of us could dispute, and it is evident that finances, housing, education as well as many other factors within our society will all affect our future patterns of health. Add to this list the complexities of our relationships in early life and the influences brought to bear on us throughout our formative years and we begin to see a picture emerging in which the influences on us are not only vast in number, but also at times in their interactions.

Many of these factors will emerge in the following discussion, but regardless of the number of factors which may be present in the life of any child, the most significant variable of all will always be that we are individuals, and will contribute in a variety of ways to the development of our offspring. Not least we must consider those influences which are genetic in origin that will have a fundamental bearing on future health, such as inherited disorders, e.g. cystic fibrosis.

The effects of the family on our health and our attitudes towards it are considerable. A search through both psychology and sociology literature yields vast amounts of research regarding the effects our parents, siblings and others have on us in our formative years. Erikson (1963), for instance, attributes considerable amounts of responsibility for our psychological status first to the principal caregiver, who is usually the mother, who may or may not enable the infant to trust. The father is seen as the major relationship to facilitate autonomy, and the family as a whole to help the child to develop initiative (for a full account of this theory, refer to Chapter 2).

THE ECOLOGICAL ENVIRONMENT

Bronfenbrenner (1979) puts forward the argument that children are affected in their development by virtue of several interacting systems to which they belong. Primarily, children live within a **microsystem**, which Bronfenbrenner describes as: 'A pattern of activities, roles and interpersonal relations experienced by the developing person in a given setting with particular physical and material characteristics'. The microsystems of, for instance, a 7 year old would normally be school and family. A microsystem in which the child lives will naturally include other individuals, who in their turn will relate to and interact with others in one of the child's other microsystems (e.g. parents and teachers), and hence a system of microsystems is formed, which is termed a **mesosystem**. The examples that Bronfenbrenner gives are 'the relations among home, school and neighbourhood peer group'. In addition to these systems are those settings in which the individual is not an active participant, but which will nevertheless have an effect upon him or her, and these are termed **exosystems**. Examples of exosystems are the parent(s)' place(s) of work, and the parents' friends.

These systems are all encompassed by the culture in which we live. The existence and interactions between the systems can serve as a valuable reminder that for any given effect that we may observe in the individual, a

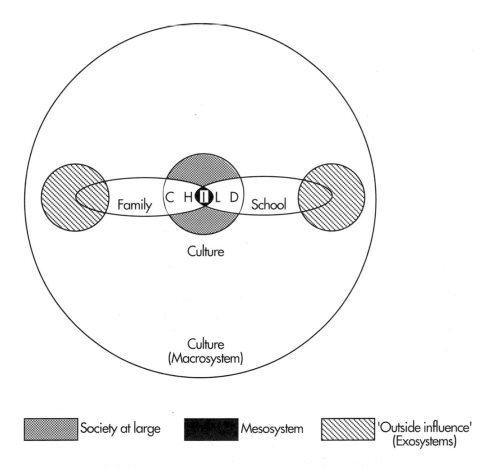

Fig. 1.1 The ecological system proposed by Bronfenbenner.

significant amount of interactions may have taken place in order for them to occur. It will be seen during the following discussion that many different factors may be responsible for producing a particular behaviour.

Just about everything, from our sexual habits and problems to our patterns of eating, smoking, alcohol abuse or even drug abuse, have at some time or other been attributed to childhood or adolescent influences, and it is unusual to find a psychologist or sociologist who ignores childhood experiences when considering the future status of the adult.

EARLY RELATIONSHIPS

The relationships which we form as adults, which will comprise such a major part of our life, and the quality of such relationships will contribute greatly to our psychological well-being. To a large extent they owe their origins to the pattern of relationships in early life, and the possible consequences of disturbed early relationships is well documented. Horney (1945, 1950) describes many patterns of behaviour that parents may exhibit towards their offspring, such as neglect, favouritism to another sibling, overindulgence, physical abuse, humiliation etc., which may give rise to severe neurosis in later life. The neurosis arises out of a profound insecurity (**basic anxiety**), and may be apparent not only in personal relationships but also in work life. Parental behaviour, principally a lack of genuine emotional warmth, is also cited by Fromm (1976) as a major cause of later problems, principally a fear of love, and hence difficulty in forming and maintaining relationships. Fromm believes that pathogenic parental behaviour is so common that normal behaviour is the exception to the rule!

Murray (1938) shares the Freudian view of pleasurable infantile experiences, and the potentially traumatic effects associated with weaning, toilet training etc. Murray maintains that such effects endure into adult life as 'complexes', but only if extreme will abnormal behaviour emerge. For example, toilet training, if traumatic, may lead to a '**urethral complex**' which is manifested by bedwetting (**enuresis**) or bedsoiling (**encopresis**). '**Claustral complexes**' may result from natal frustration, and could be manifested in adults as a fear of open spaces, fear of suffocation and fear of falling.

According to Freudian thought, the child will develop strong feelings for the opposite sexed parent, and resentment for the same sex parent who they see as a competitor, particularly in the case of boys (the **Oedipus complex**). A strong, caring relationship between father and son will normally reassure the child that he is not under threat from such rivalry, and friendship with his same-sex peers in later life should be relatively stable, as should his relationships with the opposite sex. The converse is likely to be true if the father has been overbearing and strict. It is also more than feasible that he will role model his father's characteristics in some way, thus extending the influence to future generations.

As far as girls are concerned, once again the attraction is to the opposite sex parent, but the attachment to the mother is such that strong guilt feelings may emerge as a result of her perception that she has taken her father away from her mother. The flirtatious behaviour towards her father is a normal part of her development, and can be viewed as her way of 'sharing' her father with her mother. Resentment may be the result of the deep disappointment at realising that her father wholly 'belongs' to her mother, and this in turn may lead to a resentment towards men in later life.

The implications for both boys and girls for sexual relationships in adult life are fairly obvious, and may account for a wide range of sexual problems. For a more complete account of Freudian theory, please refer to chapter 2.

There does appear to be significant differences between the ways in which men and women socialise with their children, for instance:
— fathers tend to discourage aggressive behaviour in daughters but not in their sons (Block, 1978);
— fathers more than mothers tend to reinforce dependent behaviour in their daughters but not in their sons (Osofsky and O'Connell, 1972);
— both sexes are less restrictive of girls' behaviour than of boys' (Fagot, 1974);
— mothers tend to supervise daughters more than sons (Block, 1978);
— mothers tend to talk more to their daughters than to sons in the first 3 months (Lewis, 1972);
— both sexes touch newborn males more than newborn females (Parke, 1976).

These are just a few examples of how adults behave towards their offspring, but we must also recognise that race, culture, social class (or, in Bronfenbrenner's terminology, **exosystems**), personality of the parents and the physical attractiveness of the child will all affect the parent–child interaction. The last factor is particularly important when considering the child following major surgery, or those with disfiguring diseases. Naturally, strange and stressful environments such as hospital wards may also disturb the normal pattern of interaction.

Many factors may intervene in the pattern of health and illness that emerges with children, and certainly early relationships cannot be ignored. There may be some circumstances when it is tempting to infer links between certain family circumstances and illness, for instance an increased occurrence of ill health in children from single parent families (e.g. Jennings and Sheldon, 1986), although such inferences should not be at the expense of other factors (such as economic ones).

INTRODUCTION OF STEP PARENTS

It goes without saying that, although the roles of the biological parents are usually thought of first, one should also consider that for various reasons, a step parent may have been introduced into the family. Children usually form strong bonds with their biological parent, and if we examine the possible consequences of, for instance, maternal deprivation (Chapter 10), it can be gleaned that the child may undergo considerable trauma, hence compounding the problems associated with the introduction of a step parent, although in many cases the problems may be minimal.

The reason for the step parent being introduced is usually death or divorce, and each may present its own problems. Following bereavement, the child's grief may stand in the way, either temporarily or permanently, of the formation of a relationship with the step parent. Naturally, a parent cannot be replaced, particularly with children who had formed strong attachments to the deceased parent, and the difficulties appear to be worst in the school child and the adolescent.

Where one parent has remarried following divorce, the child's reaction may be somewhat different. The biological parent is not only still alive, but will usually have fairly regular access to the children. The child is usually able (albeit in a modified form) to maintain bonds in a physical as well as in an emotional way. The grief caused by the breakup of the parents' marriage, may result in great anxiety for the child, possibly leading to disturbed behaviour, enuresis or worse. The converse may actually be true however, with the child being much happier and emotionally more stable, if for instance she or he has had to endure the traumas of an unhappy and unstable environment.

Regardless of the reasons for the introduction of step parents, if difficulties do arise, they may due to:
(1) Not enough allowance being made for the child's suspicions and fears.

(2) The step parent tries to adopt a predetermined role too quickly, instead of learning about the child gradually and acting accordingly.

(3) The child may be expected to renounce his affections for the biological parent in favour of the step parent.

The early relationships have implications for later mental health, particularly with regard to the repression of unpleasant experiences, and their later emergence which may take many different forms.

ILLNESS AND HOSPITALISATION

Long term hospitalisation will naturally cause considerable disruptions to the child's home life in the purely physical sense, but may also cause disruption of relationships with the family. The effects of separation will be examined in Chapter 10, but another factor needs to be considered here, and that is behaviour of parents, in particular within the hospital setting, but more generally during periods of illness. It is not difficult to identify at least some of the factors which may cause disruption to the normal parent–child interactions.

Firstly, the young child sees his or her parents as having certain qualities. The child may view the parents as protectors from harm, with 'harm' being construed by the child as anything that is painful or unpleasant. This point will be further developed later in the text, but for now it should be remembered that the trust which the child invests in the parents may be disrupted as the parents apparently sanction 'harm' to be done to her or him (in the form of treatment).

The hospital setting may also give rise to the feeling on the part of the parents that they are being watched and/or judged by the health professionals around them, and this may lead to the parent behaving in a way which they think others will find acceptable. The need for privacy for the parent and child to interact as normally as possible should be recognised and ensured wherever feasible.

Thirdly, the child's parameters of exceptable behaviours may alter during illness and even more during hospitalisation, as parents 'make allowances' for certain outbursts that would normally merit some form of reprimand, and this may lead to feeling of insecurity and confusion, particularly when the parameters are 'redrawn' yet again following recovery. The reader is referred to Chapters 12 and 14 for a more in-depth discussion of the effects of illness and hospitalisation on the child.

ROLE MODELLING

One of the key ways in which a child learns is imitation of parents or those who the child is in closest contact with. We have already examined the possible implications on future relationships and this type of effect extends not only to this aspect but also to the more generalised areas of attitudes, perspectives, and more importantly, actions.

It should be remembered that the effects are not only to be seen in childhood, but rather extend into adult life with the individual perhaps not fully understanding why they do the things they do. Naturally, such **role modelling** extends to health behaviour, and although it would be ridiculous to assume that we copy our parents in everything, and that other influences have no part to play, significant aspects of health behaviour are nevertheless evident. It will be seen later in the chapter that dietary and smoking behaviour can both be considered as having been role modelled, and it may be possible that relationships can be viewed in the same light.

That **role modelling** is not merely the province of parents is an important consideration when planning health education programmes, and also general education programmes, for the child.

THE EFFECTS OF PARENTAL DEPRESSION

The profound importance of the child–mother relationship, which has been the subject of so much research, takes on a different emphasis if there is evidence of a psychological disturbance on the part of the mother or if the security of the relationship is threatened.

The incidence of depression amongst young mothers is now emerging as a major contributing factor in the occurrence of psychiatric disturbance in childhood (Angold, 1986), although the occurrence of such behaviour is considerably less if at least one adult within the household, usually the father, is supportive. Where there is no father, in other words if there is a female-headed single-parent family, the situation is usually compounded by diminishing household income, often to the point of poverty, and this may well be linked with psychiatric disorder in the parent (Swanson *et al.*, 1989). A further discussion regarding the relationship between life events and depression can be found in Chapter 9.

Separation experiences, particularly before the age of 3 years, have long been known to cause a depression syndrome in some children (Bowlby, 1954), although if the separation is short lived (such as for a hospital admission where mother cannot stay with the child) the effects have been seen by some as short lived (Heinicke and Westheimer, 1965). Depression in adult life, however, may well be linked with prolonged separation from maternal care in childhood (Rutter, 1971).

Another aspect of this theory needs to be examined, for although considerable research has been carried out, attempting to examine a possible link between mental disorders in parents and mental disorders in children, and indeed into the results of separation and **maternal deprivation**, alternative and sometimes simpler explanations may be found. A genetic link, for instance, may emerge as a determining factor in mental disorder, which would, if proven, cast the whole subject in a different light.

It may be, however, that a fundamental flaw in our reasoning could emerge, namely, that we tend to expect children and adults to react differently in a given set of circumstances, whereas this may in fact not be the case. Let us consider for instance a young family, with poor housing and no spare cash beyond what is needed for food, and perhaps other conditions such as evictions, failing accommodation and marital discord. The mother of the family is found to be suffering from depression, and the father, who is unemployed and wondering how he can provide the basic needs of his family, is unable to provide the emotional support his wife needs. The young children of the family, who are both under 7 years of age, are also found to be depressed. What could be the possible reasons for this phenomenon? Are the children reacting to their mother's depression? Are the children reacting to **stimulus privation** because their mother finds it so hard to provide the stimulation her children need because of her own depression? Are the children suffering as a result of a maternal deprivation effect because they perceive that their mother's character and actions have changed so much?

It is, of course, possible that any one of these explanations could apply here, but we need to ask an additional question; are the children depressed as a result of the same factors (albeit perceived in terms of results of hardship, discord, etc.) that are depressing the mother? Certainly a child, from a very early age, may become upset if the mother and father argue, but perhaps more obviously she compares her life with that of her peers (most commonly observed when children are comparing toys).

In addition to these questions, as mentioned earlier, we need to consider whether the mental disorder is genetically determined. Regardless of the answers we give to the questions posed above, one fact appears to be abundantly clear, and that is mental disorders of parents, and in particular mothers, may have a profound effect on the children.

ECONOMIC FACTORS AND HEALTH

The relationship between diet and health has been briefly reviewed at the beginning of the chapter. The connection between what we eat (and also give to our children) and our economic status is a clear one, with fresh high-protein foods such as meat and fish being amongst the most expensive, and food of much lower nutritional value being less expensive.

The clear inference here is that poverty and poor nutrition are natural partners, although at this juncture it is worth noting that malnutrition in industrial countries usually has psychological causes (not only financial) whereas malnutrition in developing countries is often associated with frequent illness (Pradilla, 1984).

POOR HOUSING AND HEALTH

The accommodation occupied by the family also has an affect on the health of the children. The effects of living in blocks of flats, for instance, go

Fig. 1.2 Poor housing is a major contributing factor in determining health.

beyond the known safety hazards and can present such problems as isolation and by their very construction and design may lead to deteriorating
health (Lowry, 1990). It is not only the type of accommodation that affects
health but also such factors as the quality of life produced by overcrowding. From a purely practical point of view, poor housing is usually associated with poverty, which may obviously be compounded by the family being
large, hence implying that the income to the family will be proportionally
less per head.

Research appears to indicate that the poorer families in the community in
the United Kingdom are getting poorer (Roll, 1988), and if this is the case a
deterioration in living conditions, and standards of living generally, must
invariably follow. The medical effects of poor housing and overcrowding
will include the hazards associated with communicable diseases as well as
the effects of damp and lack of basic amenities. The added pressures of
financial difficulties which affect interpersonal relationships are magnified
when people are forced together in close, maybe claustrophobic proximity
(Heyward Jones, 1988).

EARLY DIETARY HABITS

As far as our health is concerned, we are influenced directly and indirectly by our experience in early life, primarily by our principal caregivers. Naturally, one of the obvious factors is what we are given to eat (more often what we are not discouraged from eating) and its relation to obesity in both childhood and in later life. Following on from this is the known relationship between persistent (usually learned) poor eating habits (principally fried foods and high-cholesterol diets) and subsequent cardiovascular disease (Roy and Galeano, 1985).

Poor eating habits have been found to be particularly prevalent in adult males who live in inner cities (Wilson, 1989). Sociocultural factors must be considered as a major influence on our eating habits as children, although the genetic 'preprogramming' of the hypothalamus also plays a large part in determining body weight (see Chapter 3). Maternal eating disorders could also be responsible for abnormal eating habits amongst children (Stein and Fairburn, 1989).

From a psychoanalytic point of view, overeating is often viewed as a comfort in times of anxiety, which has been learnt in early life and becomes a ready response in later years. Although the response appears to be an unconscious one at the time, many people will readily admit to overeating on such occasions, even perpetuating the practice by feeding their own

infants in order to pacify them, or giving their older children sweets perhaps following an upsetting experience, or minor accident. Solace may be sought through eating particularly during the 'emotional minefield' of adolescence, during which possible conflict with parents may lead to considerable tension.

A seemingly endless amount of publications regarding the dangers or benefits of various foods and eating habits are brought to our attention every year, and these must undoubtedly affect how we feed ourselves and our children. Many of our habits, though, are passed down from generation to generation, such as increasing the concentration of, or adding sugar to feeds in order to help the baby to sleep, both of which may lead to obesity with all its implications.

SMOKING

Smoking has long been known as a predisposing factor in heart and lung disease, claiming the lives of thousands of people each year, and yet many young people continue to take up the habit. Parental opposition to smoking would seem to be, in many cases, an important indicator to a young person's intention to smoke (Eiser *et al.*, 1989) when compared to a parent's smoking behaviour, insofar as it is more probable that a child will remain a non-smoker if their parents are non-smokers themselves.

Parental (and child) smoking behaviour has also been investigated in terms of its effect on school absenteeism (Charlton and Blair, 1989). In a survey of 2885 12 and 13 year olds it was observed that there was a higher rate of minor ailments amongst those who smoked and in children whose mother smoked. In the same study if was found that regular smoking was significantly more common amongst boys.

Smoking, from a psychoanalytic view may be construed as an oral fixation, which could relate to the oral stage of development, and the individual's sublimation of instinctual urges (breast feeding, thumb sucking, etc.) in order to satisfy the norms of society.

THE EFFECTS OF THE MASS MEDIA

Peer pressure, not only in adolescence but much earlier, as **role modelling** is occurring, is a strong motivator for many behaviours including eating, drinking and smoking. This, combined with advertising through the media, particularly television, for low-nutrition, high-calorie foods, increases the amount of consumption of these foods in children. Most interestingly, the reverse does not appear to be true. Advertisements for health foods produce little increase in their consumption (Jeffrey *et al.*, 1982).

Tobacco advertising has, in many countries, been severely curtailed whilst in others it has a relatively high profile. One reason for concerns over such advertising is its effects on children and adolescents. Television is the most available source of entertainment in most homes, and therefore the possible effects may be relevant to the discussion. The reasons why children watch so much television must, for the most part, be due to its availability, but also due to the attitudes of the parents to their children's viewing habits.

Investigating the effects of television advertising on the health beliefs of American adolescents (10–13 years), Lewis and Lewis (1974) revealed that 47% of the subjects accepted all commercial messages, related to health beliefs and behaviours, with 70% of television messages overall bein– believed. The effects of advertising were found to be 20–30% greater on subjects from lower socioeconomic backgrounds. Unfortunately, when these messages were analysed by a panel of experts, it was found that 70% were inaccurate.

Advertising on television, by inference, may actually have a beneficial effect, although this will almost certainly depend on how often it is repeated, and the extent to which the individual can identify with it.

ADOLESCENT BEHAVIOUR AND HEALTH

Much of what we would normally term as 'deviant' behaviour occurs in adolescence, during the search for self-identity (see Chapter 2). Most of us can remember, usually with extreme embarrassment, our own forms of deviant behaviour in adolescence, such as smoking the illicit cigarette behind the bicycle sheds, being the first to enter a pub within our circle of friends or going through bizarre rituals in order to be accepted as a member of a group. Quite where normality ends and deviancy begins is, at times (particularly when considering the adolescent), difficult to identify, although such behaviour becomes easier to identify when it becomes prolonged and obsessive.

There has been considerable research regarding the consequences of a broken home, institutionalisation, child abuse and cultural deprivation on the child's future development, but what we should also remember is that a child from an apparently happy home may engage in seemingly inexplicable deviant behaviour and the reasons for this should be considered.

Firstly, as we have discussed, the adolescent is frequently considered to indulge in deviant behaviour, although this may be seen as an attempt to find a **role identity**, and in order to form such an identity several different roles and behaviours are being tried out. Frequently, the adolescent will identify with a group and indeed this is seen as part of normal development, but in reality this merely delays individual identity formation, provides breathing space and enables the adolescent to see the reaction of his or her peers towards various behaviours. Whilst most parents and indeed society in general find adolescent behaviour disturbing at times we should all remember that older generations for many centuries have been complaining about the apparent strange habits, rowdy behaviour and inexplicable 'goings on' of the younger generation.

It is quite normal for the adolescent to try out various behaviours and indeed those behaviours which they know parents may find disturbing such as taking drugs, solvent abuse, engaging in frequent sexual activity, smoking, etc., but in the vast majority of cases the adolescent is just experimenting. There are occasions, however, when the child or adolescent or even adult may have been pressurised to such an extent in early life (usually during school years) that they rebel purely because it will be totally against the parents' wishes, and may continue to do so with sometimes disastrous consequences.

The difference between what is seen as a normal psychological adjustment and an abnormal psychological adjustment seems, at least to the parents of the adolescent, to be indistinguishable, but the adolescent who is merely experimenting (although inadvertently may form addictions) will move on quite quickly, and the parents may know little of the illicit activities, whereas the activities of the adolescent who is adjusting abnormally may persist so as to make the individual both a danger to herself or himself and possibly to society also.

The persistent failure to form affectionate bonds is sometimes seen as a contributing factor to deviant behaviour, and although his work has since been evaluated by many researchers, John Bowlby has postulated that there has been a higher incidence of juvenile delinquency in children brought up in institutions and who have failed to form affectionate bonds throughout their lifetime.

Delinquent behaviour is seen by many as an attention-seeking device both in the child and in the adolescent in order to draw attention to themselves from their parents, and is also seen as a plea for recognition for them as individuals and also as a plea for clearer controls and restraints.

It has already been said that the child may rebel against pressures which have been brought upon her or him, usually during school life, although many parents have not directly brought pressures to bear. The adolescent or child may nevertheless rebel against the mother's or father's achievements and may feel that they are being pressurised to live up to the parents' achievements as distinct from forming an individual life and identity.

The peer group that the adolescent may join may also be a source of deviant behaviour, inasmuch as the adolescent may persistently try and prove himself or herself within that group by either constantly surrendering to their demands or, in order to gain some self-esteem, by performing acts from which he or she will be considered to be the leader of the group. For a more complete account of identity, the reader is referred to the account of the work of Erikson in Chapter 2.

DRUG ABUSE

Drug abuse is common among adolescents, although rather disturbingly it is also found in younger age groups. Frequently the euphoria and elation felt with some drugs produces an escape for the adolescent or younger child from the insecure world in which they may be living and it is arguable that, especially with the so-called 'soft drugs' such as cannabis, it may be this escapism which is the addiction rather than the drug. Although this is certainly very debatable, many drugs are addictive in their own right.

It has already been mentioned earlier in the chapter that role modelling is a contributing factor in abnormal health behaviour, and it may be that this could be one such case, with at least one study showing the incidence of drug abuse higher in those adolescents who had parents with drinking problems (Johnson *et al.*, 1989). Although the correlation is not immediately obvious (as there is no significant difference between this group of adolescents and the control group in drinking behaviour), the dependence aspect is apparent (has the adolescent **role modelled** poor coping strategies?).

ALCOHOL ABUSE

The consumption of alcohol is, within modern society, seen as a social activity and therefore we do not consider that it is a drug, however this is a misconception. Alcohol abuse in the adolescent, particularly, is common and the escape from insecurity that alcohol may give, no matter how temporarily, is appealing to many, bearing in mind its easy availability. Alcohol abuse will occur for all the above reasons when considering deviant behaviour, but may also occur as part of the adolescent's endeavour to gain the status of an adult in their own right.

Occasionally in later life the adolescent who has abused alcohol may become an alcoholic, although it is far more likely that more harm will come to him due to its short-term intense abuse, which will cause perceptual distortion, inhibitions and lack of judgement which may lead to road traffic accidents, petty crime or even violence. The ability to drink large quantities is to many adolescents a form of status within peer groups, and this is hardly surprising as we observe adults who take great pride in the amount they can drink.

DISCUSSION

The development of the child is to an extent dependent on his interactions with the world around him, and restriction of that interaction could do as much harm as good. It should be remembered (with the possible exception of adolescence) that many behaviours are learnt from others with whom the child has a trusting relationship, and much can be done to shape a child's future health behaviour merely by acting as a role model.

This appears to be most vividly illustrated in the pre-school age group who, when compared to their parents' responses to questions regarding the child's illness, demonstrate significant accuracy (Maheady, 1986). Naturally as the child grows, other influences become important in their lives, and will influence the child's concepts of illness. Maheady ventures to suggest that nurses are uniquely placed to help pre-school children to develop accurate health concepts, and suggests the following action that may be taken:

(1) Provide pre-school children with accurate information about their health.
(2) Encourage parents to do the same.
(3) Involve the child in the history taking process.
(4) Support pre-school education programmes.

When attempting to plan care using a problem-solving approach, the perceptions of the child (and the parents) are absolutely vital, and naturally will direct the care that is given. Although this does appear to be stating the obvious, the implications of not establishing the existing concepts of the child's illness (and also possible treatments) may lead not only to considerable anguish, but conceivably a reduction in compliance with medical/nursing regimes.

As we have seen in this chapter, relationships play a vital role in forming the child's concept of health, but other factors are also important. Certainly, if health education is to be successful, then the child's environment needs to be taken into account in a much wider sense.

CHAPTER SUMMARY

The individual develops, through a number of ways, behaviours towards and patterns of health. Our genetic make-up will, to an extent, determine our predisposition to certain illnesses, but environmental influences will largely determine our patterns of health behaviour and may even determine the nature of illness in later life.

Both mental and physical health can be determined by a variety of factors, which would normally be a result of interactions between several factors. Influences in childhood, according to most theorists, may affect us in adult life.

The relationships we form in early life may determine the pattern of relationships in the adult years, and may give rise to sexual problems as well as an inability to form meaningful relationships altogether. Physical symptoms such as enuresis may also result from aspects of the parent–child relationship.

The mental health of the parents has been shown to have an effect on the child, particularly in the case of maternal depression. A link has also been established between separation experiences and depression.

The child may learn behaviours by using the parents as **role models**, and hence a major source of potential problems may be at least in part reduced by the behaviour of the parents. Poor eating habits emerge through the home environment, peers and advertising.

The economic status of the parent may influence health patterns, particularly in the case of poor housing, with some immigrant groups being particularly at risk.

The adolescent, whilst being susceptible to all the aforementioned influences, may also engage in potentially hazardous activities as a normal part of their identity formation.

REFERENCES

* indicates a standard text or article

Angold, A. (1986) Parents who are depressed. *The British Journal for Nurses in Child Health* **1** (5).

Block, J.H. (1978) Another look at sex differentiation in the socialisation behaviours of mothers and fathers. In: Sherman, J. and Denmark, F. (eds), *Psychology of Women: Future Directions of Research*. Psychological Dimensions, New York.

Bronfenbrenner, U. (1979) *The Ecology of Human Development: Experiments by Nature or Design*. Harvard University Press, Cambridge, Mass.*

Charlton, A. and Blair, V. (1989) Absence from school related to children's and parental smoking habits. *British Medical Journal* **298**, 90–92.

Eiser, J.R., Morgan, M., Gammage, P. and Gray, E. (1989) Adolescent smoking: attitudes, norms and parental influence. *British Journal of Social Psychology* **28**, 193–202.

Erikson, E.H. (1963) *Childhood and Society*. Norton, New York.

Fagot, B.I. (1974) Sex differences in toddlers' behaviour and parental reaction. *Developmental Psychology* **10**, 554–558.

Fromm, E. (1976) *To Have Or To Be*. Harper and Row, New York.*

Heinicke, C.M. and Westheimer, I.J. (1965) *Brief Separation*. Longman,

Heywood Jones, I. (1988) Home Is Where The Hurt Is. *Nursing Times* **84**, 48–49.

Horney, K. (1945) *Our Inner Conflicts: A Constructive Theory of Neurosis*. Norton, New York.

Horney, K. (1950) *Neurosis and Human Growth: The Struggle Towards Self-Realization*. Norton, New York.*

Jeffrey, D.B. *et al.* (1982) The development of children's eating habits: the role of television commercials. *Health Education Quarterly* **9**(2,3): 78, 174–193.

Jennings, A. and Sheldon, M.G. (1986) The health of pre-school children and the response to illness of single parent families. *Health Visitor* **59**, 337–339.

Johnson, S., Leonard, K.E. and Jacob, T. (1989). Drinking, drinking styles and drug use in children of alcoholics, depressives and controls. *Journal of Studies on Alcohol* **50**, 427–431.

Lewis, M. (1972) Parents and children: sex role development. *The School Review* **80**, 229–240.

Lewis, C.E. and Lewis, M.A. (1977) The impact of television commercials on health related beliefs and behaviour of children. *Pediatrics* **53**, 397–404.

Lowry, S. (1990) Housing and health: families and flat. *British Medical Journal* **300**, 245–247.

Maheady, D.C. (1986) Health concepts of pre-school children. *Pediatric Nursing* **12**, 195–197.

Murray, H.A. *et al.* (1938) *Explorations in Personality.* Oxford University Press, New York.*

Osofsky, J.D. and O'Connell, E.J. (1972) Parent–child interaction: daughters' effects on mothers' and fathers' behaviours. *Developmental Psychology* 7, 157–168.

Parke, R.D. (1976) Family interactions in the newborn period: some findings, some observations and some unresolved issues. In: Riegel, K. and Meacham, J. (eds), *The Developing Individual in a Changing World*, Vol. 2, Mouton, The Hague.

Pradilla, A. (1984) Nutrition: facts and hopes. *World Health* **Oct.**, 2–4.

Roll, J. (1988) Measuring family statistics: a recent controversy in the use of official statistics. *Social Policy and Administration* **22**, 134–149.

Roy, C.C. and Galeano (1985) Childhood antecedents of adult degenerative illness. *Pediatric Clinics of North America* **32**, 517–583.

Rutter, M. (1981) *Maternal Deprivation Reassessed*, 2nd edn. Penguin, Harmondsworth.*

Stein, A. and Fairburn, C.G. (1989) Children of mothers with bulimia nervosa. *British Medical Journal* **299**, 777–778.

Swanson, W., Holzer, C.E., Canavan, M.M. and Adams, P.L. (1989) Psychopathology and economic status in mother only and mother–father families. *Child Psychiatry and Human Development* **20**, 15–24.

Wilson, G. (1989) Family food systems, preventative health and dietary change: a policy to increase the health divide, *Journal of Social Policy* **18**, 167–185.

SUGGESTED READING

The following presents the reader with an interesting perspective on the developing child.

Bronfenbrenner, U. (1979) *The Ecology of Human Development: Experiments by Nature or Design.* Harvard University Press, Cambridge, Mass.*

CHAPTER 2

PERSONALITY

'Every individual is the exception to the rule'.

C.G. JUNG (1921)

INTRODUCTION

In Chapter 1 is was noted that amongst many other factors the individual's personality to an extent determines his reaction to and even the nature of his illness or health. In this chapter a general overview will be given of the major personality theories as well as their possible implications in health care. The number and diversity of such theories is such that only an overview is possible. However, the main salient points have been extracted from each, so that the reader may gain an overall impression as to the major approaches to personality, rather than gaining an in-depth exhaustive knowledge of the subject.

It is only to be expected that many of the theories have considerable applications within the realms of clinical psychology, particularly with reference to psychiatric disorders, although the link between certain mental states and physical disorder is also present in many theories. It will be seen that certain inferences can also be made, such as how the individual views his or her illness and how such views may lead to certain patterns and behaviours in response to the illness.

The very diversity of the field of personality study may lead the reader to confusion, and this indeed has been the verdict of many previous students. The path to the resolution of this problem is strewn with obstacles, usually put there by theorists who have consistently been unable to relate or integrate their models of personality with any others. It may well prove necessary at some stage in the future for us to gain an overall impression of personality, by the concerted integration of not only the theories mentioned below, but also many others, in order to give an overall picture and understanding of the subject. There can be no doubt that certain theorists have had some success in the application of their theories in clinical practice, though the major problem remains that many aspects of theories remain abstract, and unsubstantiated in the scientific sense (as in psychoanalytic and neo-analytic theories to name but two).

The fact remains absolutely certain, however, that the central core of our very psychological being, i.e. the personality, is the difference between individuals which cannot be ignored in virtually any sphere of interaction, and we should all be cautious about any approach in health care which assumes any uniform approach to treatment and care and ignores the individual. It has been the dilemma of many students and teachers of health care, that whereas the physical aspects of a patient's care can, at least in part, be generalised, for virtually all patients (aspects of post-operative care, investigations, etc.) the psychological aspects cannot. In particular we have difficulty in predicting how someone will react to bad news, bereavement, surgery, disability, or even just visiting their G.P.

Pre-determined prescriptions for what to say to someone following the death of a close relative would only be possible if we could be certain exactly how an individual would react at any given time. This is clearly impossible, and it must inevitably lead to apprehension and anxiety on the part of the student who encounters this sort of situation for the very first time.

We must reach the conclusion that although personality theory may help us to understand why someone has reacted in such a way and, in a minor way, after a period of observation, enable us to come to some form of restricted prediction as to how they may react, it must by its very essence remain unreliable.

Quite a gloomy picture emerges therefore, for the accurate prediction of behaviour within the clinical setting. There is nevertheless some hope on the horizon. A person's responses can be predicted to a large extent by the use of an ever-increasing battery of personality assessments, which have been used extensively in clinical psychology and occupational psychology, and have had various degrees of success. As time goes by, these are becoming more refined and sophisticated.

With these cautionary notes in mind, a possible path to take could be to combine the essence of some theories with the care we give to individuals in order to forestall possible psychological disasters, which may be encountered, for instance, by the child in hospital, or the adult embarking on self-care, during and following discharge. However we decide to use such theories (if indeed we choose to use any), the key to success must be the building of a trusting relationship between the health care worker and the patient or client, and the sustained observation of their behaviours and reactions.

THE PSYCHOANALYTIC APPROACH

The starting point for many, when studying personality, is the psychoanalytic approach attributed to Sigmund Freud (1856–1939). This is a complicated theory, or to be more precise a complicated set of theories, which Freud himself altered considerably during the latter part of his life, and only the briefest of summaries is included here. Criticised in its earliest years for its highly controversial sexual basis, and latterly by some for its apparent lack of scientific basis, psychoanalytic theory nevertheless provides us with a fascinating insight into the early perceptions of the workings and structure of the human personality. Freud believed that most of our mental activities are not at the conscious level, but rather at an **unconscious** level which is unavailable to the **conscious** mind in any direct way. Naturally we do not have all the material we need in the conscious at the same time, and this is contained in the '**pre-conscious**', being easily recalled when required. It is this intermediate state which can translate information in the unconscious to a form which is understandable and acceptable to the conscious mind. Additionally, the pre-conscious holds the residue of trivia, unsolved problems, worries, intentions etc. of our daily living which form the basis of dreams. The theory of the conscious/unconscious was further refined in later years (see below).

Fig. 2.1 Sigmund Freud.

INSTINCTS

It was Freud's belief that our total mental activity is geared towards achieving pleasure, and conversely, avoiding what he terms as 'unpleasure', and that this process is achieved through the workings of the '**pleasure principle**' (Freud, 1966). We are motivated by two major instincts:

(1) sexual
(2) destructive (aggressive).

Sexual Instinct (Eros)
One of the many controversies which Freud managed to initiate was that

sexuality covers the entire range of human experiences that are pleasurable and may extend to less obvious behaviours which we engage in. In his writings before his death in 1939, Freud maintained that not only the genitals, but the whole body can be regarded as an erotogenic zone, therefore adding sexual connotations to activities less associated with the sexual act, such as eating, smoking, etc. The sexual instinct arises from self-preservation, which in itself comes from self-love (**narcissism**). Fulfilling a need would naturally bring about a degree of gratification and this gratification is brought about by the reduction in tensions which are brought about by deficit in need fulfilment in the first place (such as hunger, thirst, etc.). Nobody would suggest that the tension brought about from hunger, thirst, sexual frustration or other such needs is a pleasant one and indeed the greater the need, then the greater the strength of the instinct (impetus) becomes, thus the degree of tension is increased.

The Destructive/Aggressive Instinct

Freud never completed his theory of the destructive instinct and some of the work on the subject has been completed by more recent theorists. Some in the neo-analytic school, such as Melanie Klien, have developed the theme of an aggressive instinct, and integrated it into their individual theories. Like the sexual instinct, the destructive instinct is innate, and without the moderating effects of society the human being would remain a killer and indeed a host of other abominations in order to ensure his survival. Quite naturally, society would not (and does not) endure such a personality and therefore we have to modify our innate instincts of untamed aggression to other more socially acceptable outlets, such as physical sports, fast cars, and other activities, which allow us to vent our natural instincts. This process is known as **sublimation**. Sublimation, according to Freud, enables the individual to divert the energy to higher asexual aims, in some instances leading to considerable cultural achievements.

PSYCHIC ENERGY

Freud likens mental activity to physical activity, inasmuch as both require energy and both are in a finite supply. The psychic energy of the sexual instinct is referred to as the **libido**, and is thought to be the energy responsible for the aggressive instinct. Psychic energy can be tied to objects (e.g. the need for food can be transformed into a desire for the mother). This process is known as **cathexis**.

PSYCHIC DETERMINISM

Virtually everything that we do, apparently by accident, such as forgetting a name, dreaming, or even the mistakes that we make, are in fact occurring for various underlying reasons which are usually unconscious.

THE STRUCTURE OF PERSONALITY

The theory of the conscious, unconscious and pre-conscious only goes a certain distance in explaining many of our actions, particularly those emotions which are repressed. In order to overcome these difficulties, Freud further hypothesised that the personality had three components and that these components were not distinct compartments, but rather an interactive structure. These three components he termed:

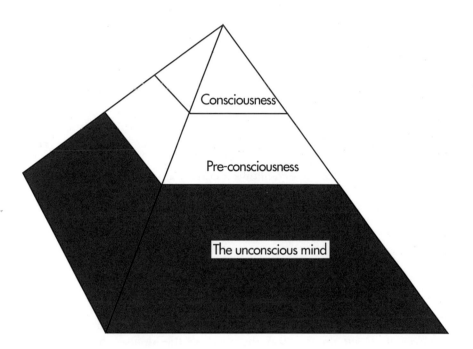

Fig. 2.2   The mind's three territories – a cornerstone of Freudian theory.

(1) the **id**
(2) the **ego**
(3) the **superego**.

The Id

Only the **id** is innate. It is composed of basic instincts only and is closely linked with biological functions. It is entirely unconscious, illogical, unaware of time and is unaffected by experience. The function of the id is to seek immediate gratification regardless of moral or social consequences, by the discharge of tensions, which have originated from biological needs. In order to achieve this, the id will form mental images of objects that will satisfy his needs (**wish fulfilment**). The discharge of these tensions, as previously discussed, is known as the '**pleasure principle**'. As a child requires immediate gratification, it can be seen that if the object of his gratification is not available then cathexes may be displaced. The child may, for instance, suck a dummy or his thumb if his feed bottle is not immediately available.

The Ego

Unlike the id, which is entirely unconscious, the **ego** spans the **conscious**, the **pre-conscious** and the **unconscious**. It is a part of the personality which is in constant touch with its surroundings, and provides the id with more realistic objects of gratification. The energy created by the id and the subsequent discharge of immediate gratification, will invariably, at times, have an adverse effect on the individual and his environment. If the child is hungry for instance, and attempts to steal food, he will be punished; there-fore a restraining factor which can delay immediate gratification so that the longer term gratification, and the avoidance of adverse affects, can be achieved, is necessary. This delay of immediate gratification in favour of long-term gratification is known as the **reality principle** and emerges from the experience of the child in comparing the images which the id creates and the actual objects which exist in reality that may satisfy his needs (**reality testing**).

The development of the ego allows a certain amount of control over the id and its effects on the child. The ego is able to curb the irrational impuls-es of the id, and therefore results in a more rational mode of gratification.

The Superego

At about 4 or 5 years of age, the **superego** begins to emerge and is a com-bination of society's norms, and parental influences, which produce ideals, which the ego will continually strive to attain.

The superego is in direct opposition to the id and whereas both are unconscious, the superego can exert no influence over the id itself. The ego, however, in its attempt to satisfy the needs of the id, also comes into con-flict with the superego, producing guilt. This guilt may affect the way we behave, as the ego may attempt to find a substitute object which the super-ego finds more acceptable.

STAGES OF PSYCHOSEXUAL DEVELOPMENT

The discharge of tensions by the id passes through stages, with outlets con-stantly being sought. At each stage, certain erotogenic zones are charac-terised.

Stage 1: The Oral Stage (Birth–1½ years)
Erotogenic zone: the mouth.
Satisfaction: pleasure sensations via the mouth, through feeding activities and general acts of oral incorporation.

Relaxed and generous treatment through feeding activities are thought to give rise to later optimistic, friendly and cooperative traits within the personality. Infants who are on the other hand deprived of these treatments, may compensate later by excessive drinking and smoking, and of course eating, which may lead to obesity.

Stage 2: The Anal Stage (1½–4 years)
Erotogenic zone: the anus.
Satisfaction: pleasure sensations from bowel activities.

Toilet training is the first activity in which children can submit to or defy their parents and, as control over sphincter muscles develops during this period, the child can determine whether she is rewarded or punished. It is at this time in the child's development that the ego makes its appearance. The anal stage is a battle ground between newly emerging ego and the innate id. On the one hand the id gains pleasure from withholding faeces and on the other hand the ego seeks a more prolonged and intense gratification through evacuation of the bowel and resulting parental approval. Fixation at this stage can result in the 'anal personality' thought to be the result, according to Freud, of harsh and strict toilet training, and this may be characterised by evidence in later life of excessive orderliness, obstinacy, fastidiousness, frugality and stinginess. Many of these children are inhibited and fail to develop self-confidence and independence.

Stage 3: The Phallic Stage (4–6 years)
Erotogenic zone: the genitals.
Satisfaction: manipulation of the sexual organs.

At this stage the pleasure-seeking activity of the id concentrates on the child's genitals. It is during this stage that the child develops the correct sex role. If complexes are not resolved in this period with adequate development of masculine or feminine identity, then possible homosexual behaviour, impotence or frigidity can result. It is during this stage of development that the **Oedipal conflict** occurs. The child is said to desire direct sexual relationships with the opposite sex parent. Fearing discovery, and resulting punishment (castration), the child attempts to resolve the conflict by identifying with the same sex parent which includes adopting ideals and values of that parent. Suppression of these incestuous desires coincides with the emergence of the superego.

Stage 4: The Latency Stage (6–12 years)
This is a stage of intellectual development and sexual activity remains dormant. Children are now less concerned with their bodies, and turn their attention to learning and coping with their expanding environment.

Stage 5: The Genital Stage
This marks the maturation of sexual activity and, according to Freud, if

previous stages have been adequately resolved, normal sexual relationships may now occur.

Despite continued attempts and experimental verification Freud's theories have never been substantially proven or disproven. However, this theory is a result of extensive clinical investigation and should not be discounted, although when first confronted by Freud and his theories, many people respond with disbelief.

Despite the incredulous nature of Freud's explanations it remains fact that stages are passed through by children whereby pleasure is obtained by the mouth, the anus, and the genitals. This can be verified by observing any small child directly. It should be noted here that we are expressing no judgement on Freud's theories. However, if we take each stage in turn, we may see the implications for the carer.

The Oral Stage

The carer should realise that feeding should be a pleasurable occasion for the child and that relaxed and generous feeding will make for a more contented baby. The carer may observe from her own empirical observations that babies derive great pleasure from sucking and placing things in their mouths. It can be deduced, therefore, that as the normal child derives much pleasure from feeding then the sick infant, who may be fed nasogastrically or by other artificial means, does not derive the same pleasure as her healthy counterpart. This fact alone should prompt the nurse to make alternative provisions, and in this instance a 'dummy' may well be beneficial.

The Anal Stage

Defaecation in babies is a pleasurable experience, as it could be argued still is in adults! Toilet training marks a significant stage in the child's development. Toilet training is a component of the continuing social interaction between the infant and its immediate caregiver. Subsequently, toilet training should not be undertaken in hospital without the parents' consent and should certainly never be started with a short-term admission.

Often the carer can see the results of hurried or badly arranged toilet-training programmes with children who are admitted with encoperesis. Carers who are involved in toilet-training programmes with children should bear in mind that the process should be unhurried and relaxed, and adequate emotional reward should be given to the infant in their care.

Toilet training can never be achieved in a matter of days and there is no place for punishment. If nothing else, badly organised toilet training will result in a nervous child. If Freud's theories are to be believed, the insertion of any foreign objects, e.g. thermometer, into the rectum during the anal stage of development may result in fixation. These theories, combined with the danger of damage to the rectal mucosa, should prompt the carer not to insert anything into the child's anus over the age of 1 year unless absolutely necessary.

The Phallic Stage

This stage of development is associated with the child's exploration of his own body, and the carer, on finding for example a young boy masturbating, should be careful not to scold the child or make him feel embarrassed as this is a normal stage of development.

The Latency Stage

Although Freud considered the latency stage and the genital stage less important to the development of the personality, both stages however have important implications for the nurse.

Because the latency period sees the child repressing sexual feelings, it is usual for them to divert their energies to games and sports. In the hospital setting this can prove especially frustrating for the child, and the carer can be of considerable help. Firstly the carer can provide games which are intellectually and competitively suitable for this age (computer games are particularly popular). It should also be remembered that children of this age prefer to mix with other children of the same sex, and effective ward management (bed positions etc.) will go a long way to making the environment more conducive to a less traumatic stay in hospital.

The Genital Stage

This stage of development brings with it an awakening of sexual feelings, and it is a time when emotional upheavals replace the stability and equilibrium of the latency stage. The carer must be aware of the adolescent's possible romantic infatuations and confusions, and must be willing to devote more of his time to listening and talking with the adolescent, whilst at the same time ensuring that she has adequate time on her own to possibly listen to records, tapes or just to sit quietly.

ANALYTICAL PSYCHOLOGY (CARL G. JUNG)

Although closely associated with Freud in his early years, Jung went on to formulate his own theory of personality. The psychic energy that Jung identified was the **libido** – regardless of the instinct involved. The greater the psychic energy expended, the greater the desire for the event or object.

The ego is described by Jung as being the centre of the personality, and is essentially conscious. Through the ego are channelled aspects of the wider 'self' which are **unconscious** to us in everyday life, but may manifest themselves through the imagination, dreams etc. As Jung, describing his approach to dream analysis, states: '. . . I gradually gave up following associations that led far away from the text of a dream. I chose to concentrate rather on the associations to the dream itself, believing that the latter expressed something specific that the unconscious was trying to say' (Jung, 1964).

THE NATURE OF THE UNCONSCIOUS

For Jung, the unconscious had two major components: the '**personal unconscious**' and the 'collective unconscious'. The personal unconscious in many ways resembles the Freudian concept with regard to its repressed and forgotten experiences, amongst the total of life experiences contained within it.

The collective unconscious, on the other hand, represents a major departure from psychoanalytic theory. Jung places great emphasis on the existence of ancestral remnants called '**archetypes**', and these, unlike the unique aspects of the personal unconscious, are common to many human beings. Jung proceeded to identify several archetypes which only become known to us in symbolic form, for instance:

(1) The **anima** — the female set of feelings of males represented as a woman figure.
(2) The **animus** — the male set of feelings of females represented as a male figure.
(3) The **shadow** — the unacceptable aspects of the self sometimes represented as a 'devil' figure.
(4) The **persona** — a protective mask (symbolic) which prevents others from seeing our inner self and also creates a specific impression. This may be symbolised as a coat or covering of some description.

The **anima** in males and the **animus** in females provides us with a balance. Denial of our opposite sex archetype can lead to conflict.

Many other **archetypes** exist according to Jung; these include the wise old man, God, the child and the great mother as well as many others. Jung warns us against trying to summarise them using mere words, as they have to be experienced to be understood (Jung, 1964).

INTROVERSION AND EXTROVERSION

Like Eysenck (see below), Jung placed great emphasis on the ancient Greek writings which attempt to describe the nature of the total being in terms of 'types', such as 'sanguine', 'choleric' etc. and used the terms '**introvert**' and '**extrovert**' to form the basis of his theory. It has to be said that the theory is rather complicated, and any attempt at simplification cannot do justice to it. With this firmly in mind a brief description of each type will suffice to give an overall picture.

The introvert is described as being reflective and hesitant, with a retiring nature, rather defensive, and will generally shrink away from social contact. Introverts derive their motivations from within. The extrovert, on the other hand, is outgoing, confident, forms attachments easily, is highly adaptive and is motivated by outside factors. The important qualification that both Jung and Eysenck make is that virtually no one will display such characteristics and that it is rather a matter of considering introversion and extroversion as a continuum, with each individual occupying a unique position on it. As Jung puts it, 'Every individual is the exception to the rule' (Jung, 1921).

Jung's work was prolific, both in its concepts and its sheer volume. It has proved difficult to quantify the soundness of his theories in terms of scientific validation, and this at least he shares with his former mentor and friend, Sigmund Freud. He does however make some important (though controversial) statements about our day-to-day conflicts and about the nature of mental illness. Jung considered that the only difference between an individual with mental illness and one without is that the sufferer from mental illness has fewer defences against his own **unconscious**. These defences can be seen 'in action' by, amongst other things, the use of word association tests. Unlike previous investigators, as well as later ones such as Kelly (see below), Jung was not so much interested in the responses that the individual gave to a particular word, but rather the delays in giving a response to certain words. By analysing such responses, Jung was able to organise them into clusters which he termed 'complexes', and this enabled him to formulate the nature of the individual's **unconscious**.

Another aspect of Jung's work was the concept of self-analysis which he believed could lead to self-expansion. Using a combination of techniques, such as dream interpretation and a dynamic approach to imagination, Jung believed that parts of the unconscious that may have been previously ignored can be communicated with, and hence are real. A consistent denial of these aspects which manifest in symbolic form, can lead to problems ranging from apparent psychological peculiarities to physical symptoms.

Perhaps one of the greatest contributions that Jung made to modern techniques of therapy was a belief in the client as the prime component in the therapeutic setting, with the analyst as a facilitator.

EGO DEVELOPMENT (ERIK ERIKSON)

Erikson has postulated a theory of psychosocial development in which he suggests that the individual passes through eight stages of ego development, which he calls the 'eight stages of man'. The theory is also psychosexual in nature (Erikson, 1963).

At each stage there is a particularly important social relationship which will largely determine the outcome of that stage of development. At each stage the individual is confronted by the alternative and opposite attitudes towards life which Erikson describes as '**self**' and 'other people'. Each stage may have a positive or negative outcome, depending on whether the crisis has been resolved or not.

Erikson's theory is closely related to that of Freud and indeed in some respects there is little difference. His work initially within the traditional psychoanalytic school in Vienna is reflected in his later theories, which to a large extent build on Freud's later modifications to his theories. The basic components of the personality, namely the id, the ego and the superego, are all considered important by Erikson, however the emphasis on each differs from the original psychoanalytic approach in some ways.

THE ID

The id is essentially considered by Erickson as similar to that of Freud's concept with the possible exception that the id is more creative than was originally thought.

THE EGO

In Freudian theory, the ego is described as a structure which is essentially in conflict with the superego. Erickson stresses the altogether more adaptive characteristics of the ego, which by implication suggests that in his theory, ego conflict is not an all-engulfing issue. This is not to say that the ego does not lie between the id and the superego, nor does it deny that it has a restraining effect on the id and a modifying effect on the superego. Rather it suggests that the defence mechanisms employed by the ego may be adaptive as well as maladaptive and as such play a constructive role in identity and mastery.

Each of the stages up to adolescence is closely related to Freud's psychosexual stages of development. Erickson does, however, go on to talk about stages beyond these (sexual maturity) and in particular offers many insights into the changes occurring during adolescence itself, especially in terms of identity formation.

STAGE 1: THE FIRST YEAR OF LIFE

Psychosocial crisis: trust vs mistrust.
Psychosocial relationship: principal caregiver.

This stage corresponds to Freud's oral stage of development. Satisfaction is derived from what Erickson terms the 'oral zone' and it is during this time that the infant not only gains satisfaction from feeding, but also experiences the warmth and nurturance of the principal caregiver (usually the mother). If the mother responds to the infant's needs, namely provides the materials whereby the baby is comforted and hunger is satisfied, then the baby will learn to trust. If, on the other hand, the baby's needs are dealt with inappropriately and badly, the baby will learn to mistrust the responses of those around her. The implications for a baby in hospital are immediately obvious, if family-centred care, principally involving the mother, is not encouraged. Certainly, the lack of time available to staff in paediatric units must suggest that there are times when the baby's needs will not be met in a satisfactory or individualised manner.

STAGE 2: THE SECOND YEAR OF LIFE

Psychosocial crisis: autonomy vs doubt.
Psychosocial relationship: the parents.

This stage corresponds to Freud's anal stage of development. In this stage Erickson stresses in particular the process of toilet training and cleanliness, and the role that the parents play in this process. Considerable reassurance must be used in this quantum leap between the complete dependence of the infant in the first stage and the emergence of some self-control over behaviours in this stage. The impulses of the id at this stage are no less strong than in the previous one, and the expulsion of faeces is a desirable action. The retaining of such faeces until a time deemed appropriate by the parents requires a firm and very reassuring approach which will lead to the beginnings of the child's autonomy. It is not difficult to see that a very strict regime at this time, or a **laissez-faire** approach to toilet training, can lead not only to the child having difficulty in reaching the goal of autonomy, but also to shattering the trust which was built up in the first stage of development. The implications in health care naturally go along the same lines as for Freud's anal stage, although it is easy to see how additional damage may be done in a hospital where toilet training is initiated in an inadequate manner.

STAGE 3: 3–5 YEARS

Psychosocial crisis: initiative vs guilt.
Psychosocial relationship: the family.

This stage corresponds to the Freudian genital stage. It is during this stage that mastery, particularly in a locomotor sense, is evident. The child will often take great delight in physical accomplishments, such as running, riding a bike, jumping, climbing, etc. It is also at this stage that the child begins to recognise the differences between the sexes, principally mother and father, and will express a desire to marry the opposite sex parent. Upon realising the impracticalities of this situation, and also identifying the strong rivalry with the same sex parent, the child will divert such urges into creative play. His previous feelings of aggression towards his rival, and the resulting guilt feelings that this may have produced, can now be replaced with an increasing initiative which has been brought about by parental approval. The investigating world of the 3–5 year old can be severely inhibited by long-term hospital admissions, particularly for orthopaedic disorders, neurological disorders, etc., and considerable imagination must be employed on the part of carers to provide the child with the facilities and opportunities to channel his drives into play.

STAGE 4: SIX YEARS–PUBERTY

Psychosocial crisis: industry vs. inferiority.
Psychosocial relationship: school.

This stage corresponds to Freud's latency period. It is characterised by learning and satisfying curiosity, and naturally at this age this will substantially take place in the school setting. A sense of industry is achieved, with the child's increasing successes in learning and creativity and encouragement in this direction further increasing this sense. Failure at this stage is largely determined by others' criteria around them, principally teachers, parents and even peers, and continual rejection and criticism of the child's achievements will lead to a sense of inferiority. Praise and encouragement at this stage, as in all others, is of immense importance and will lead to further industry on the part of the child. At this stage the child is extremely fragile regarding the opinions of others, and may cease an activity or may show deterioration in improvement.

STAGE 5: ADOLESCENCE

Psychosocial crisis: identity vs. identity confusion.
Psychosocial relationship: peers.

The positive outcome which is strived for at this stage is a well-integrated, well-balanced self-image and a clear identification of role. **Identity** encompasses four basic aspects of personality:

(1) Personal identity. This aspect is concerned with preparation for approaching adulthood, by developing an individual perspective and direction in life.
(2) Continuity of personal character. This aspect is concerned with forming a meaningful link between the developments and experiences of childhood, and future roles and aspirations of adulthood.
(3) The integration of biological development and social influences in the growth of the ego. As mentioned earlier, Erickson sees the ego in a more positive light than Freud, although he acknowledges the dilemmas with the emergence of the secondary sexual characteristics.

(4) Solidarity with the ideals and identity of the peer group. The trials and tribulations of the transition from childhood to adulthood as well as biological changes and social pressures mean that adolescence is fraught with insecurities. The adolescent will seek the security of the peer group, although such identification may be carried to extremes, to such an extent that the adolescent may appear to suffer a complete loss of individuality. Erickson describes this intermediate stage between childhood and adulthood as being typified by an **identity crisis** (Erikson, 1968) which, if not resolved, may lead to the indefinite duration of certain adolescent behaviours and may even result in the inability to decide one's own future and progressive dependence on the peer group.

STAGE 6: EARLY ADULTHOOD

Psychosocial crisis: intimacy vs. isolation.
Psychosocial relationship: sexual partners, colleagues in the competitive environment.

If the adolescent has been successful in the formation of her **identity**, then this will be put to the test in early adulthood, principally from an occupational and relationship viewpoint. The intimacy which results from close relationships, particularly of a sexual nature, can only be achieved with a well-established and secure identity, without which a one-to-one relationship with all its responsibilities and compromises would not be possible. The individual with a poorly formed identity will soon find herself isolated not only from sexual relationships (more specifically the ability to love), but also will be unable to tolerate any competitive environment which will put considerable strain on an already fragile identity.

STAGE 7: MIDDLE ADULTHOOD

Psychosocial crisis: generativity vs self-absorption.
Psychosocial relationships: the integrated household and society.

Erickson sees this stage as essentially a time for guiding the oncoming generation into adulthood (**generativity**) and being able to view contributions made to society as being valuable. Although this is a time when many will reach their peak as far as career and family life are concerned, it must also be viewed as a time of little hope for those who look back upon their early adult years with regret with regard to achievements unfulfilled and ambitions unrealised. This must lead inevitably to a state of stagnation and self-absorption. This can naturally occur in an individual whether or not they have a family, but the implications of having a parent who is not capable of generativity, in terms of the relationship with any adolescent offspring could possibly be to affect identity formation.

STAGE 8: OLD AGE

Psychosocial crisis: integrity vs despair.
Psychosocial relationship: mankind.

At this stage, if the previous stages have been resolved, the individual may look back on their lives with satisfaction that they have achieved what they set out to, or at least achieved a meaning to their life, which was important to them. Death is approaching; the individual who has achieved this ideal state of ego integrity will normally face it philosophically, and with inevitability. By now, the choice of routes that can be taken to substantially change one's life in order to compensate for past failures is very limited, and this will only add to the despair of the individual who has not achieved ego identity.

PERSONAL CONSTRUCT THEORY (GEORGE A. KELLY)

George Kelly was responsible for formulating the 'personal construct theory'. The theory suggests that 'a person's processes are psychologically channelled by the ways in which he anticipates events' (Kelly, 1955). He suggests that a person will construct theories about her or his environment, test these theories and come to a conclusion on the information thus gained. There is no wrong or right conclusion or answers as such, merely ways of interpreting events (constructs). To look at the meaning (as far as the previous personality theories are concerned) Kelly states 'the term learning scarcely appears at all (in personal construct theory). That is wholly intentional, we are throwing it overboard altogether, there is no ego, no emotion, no motivation, no reinforcement, no drive, no unconscious, no need'.

A **construct** is basically a method of predicting future events, and depending on the outcome, behaviour will manifest accordingly. Obviously, usefulness of a construct is determined by the accuracy of the predictions we make from it. All constructs involve a contrast between two opposite poles, e.g. hot and cold, and constructs arise when an individual construes two people or objects sharing a common characteristic which differentiates from a third.

It should be pointed out that constructs cannot be applied to every situation, that is, some situations will lie outside theories' range of convenience and indeed some constructs may be non-verbal. However, for the constructs which can be verbalised, various characteristics can be noted.

Firstly, a hierarchy of constructs can be established and suitably identified. For example, a very wide range in constructs 'good–bad' is termed as a superordinate construct, in contrast to other subordinate constructs which do not share its wide range of convenience.

Some of the more stable superordinate constructs are particularly important, because these in particular will give a person their sense of continuity and identity. These constructs are termed 'core' constructs.

Some of the subordinate constructs, however, are more flexible and are termed **peripheral constructs**. These may alter without a person losing her sense of identity or continuity, i.e. without disturbing or changing her core constructs. The peripheral constructs are said to be permeable, inasmuch as they are able to absorb new elements (those things or events which are abstracted by a person's use of a construct) into their range of convenience as other constructs, particularly core constructs, do not possess this ability.

As stated above, the purpose of these constructs is to be able to make predictions. Some of these predictions may be particularly rigid if certain constructs are strongly correlated with others. However, the reverse will happen if there is not a close correlation.

The first type of correlation is termed a 'tight' construct, while the second is termed a 'loose' construct. To have a too tight or too loose construct would reduce the validity and reliability of predictions, although this is sometimes necessary (water/wet; tight construct, hence very restricted prediction).

POSTULATES AND COROLLARIES

The fundamental **postulate** underlies the whole of the personal construct theory, and states that psychological processes that comprise our personality are naturally active, and are moulded into customary patterns by the ways in which we anticipate the future.

The **corollaries** (11 in all) are designed to elaborate and clarify the nature of personal constructs.

Construction Corollary
Predictions based on past events abstracting the similarities and differences between them.

Individual Corollary
This suggests that we will all construe situations differently, in other words, everyone's constructs are unique.

Organisation Corollary
This suggests that all constructs are arranged in a hierarchical system, in order to make anticipation easier.

Dichotomy Corollary
All constructs are bi-polar; occasionally a person may only be able to verbalise one pole, but in this case the other is said to be submerged.

Choice Corollary
This suggests that we value more highly that pole of a dichotomous personal construct that more readily enables us to achieve greater predictive accuracy. We strive to achieve such accuracy by choosing either the more secure course of further clarifying the constructs we already use, or the more adven-

turous path of exploring new realms and extending the range of convenience of our constructs. It should be reiterated once again that a personal construct is useful for anticipating only some types of events.

Range Corollary

Some constructs as previously mentioned have a narrow range whereas others are relatively wide. However, Kelly suggests that a construct can anticipate only a finite range of events.

Experience Corollary

Constructs must change so that we may predict events more accurately as our experience grows.

Modulation Corollary

Some constructs are far less permeable and hence less acceptable to revision than others. Generally, superordinate constructs are more permeable than subordinate constructs. Put another way, permeability refers to the ability to admit newly perceived elements into its context. Such permeabilities are necessary, in order that we may adapt to changing patterns of living.

Fragmentation Corollary

This enables us to cope with contradictory situations, employing a variety of incomplete subsystems at different times by the same individual. A person may subsume tolerance under good, but take violent exception to cowardice because he subsumes this under hateful.

Commonality Corollary

We are psychologically more like those individuals whose personal constructs have much in common with our own.

Sociality Corollary

We relate more effectively to an individual who construes the world in a way that we can understand.

These final two corollaries are concerned with interpersonal characteristics, whereas the others are concerned with individual characteristics.

ROLE CONSTRUCT REPERTORY TEST

The method used to establish the basic construct which a person uses and interrelationship between them is the **role construct repertory test**. Initially the subject is given a list of roles, such as employer, teacher, close friend, etc., and then asked to supply the name of someone who fits the role. Next, in order to establish the similarity and constrast poles of the construct, the subject is presented with three cards, each bearing one of the names supplied, and then asked to say in which way two of them are alike, but different from the third. The constructs elicited from the repertory test can be analysed in terms of their content or in terms of how the subject applies the constructs to particular individuals or events.

The **repertory grid** is a method devised from the above test. Briefly, it allows the investigator to present the subject with more variety of elements such as role titles or names, and constructs may be elicited or provided by the investigator. The subject may then be asked to assign each role title at one or other end of the construct pole, to rank order them in relation to the construct; for example, to assign the elements, mother, girlfriend, etc., to one pole of the construct, honest–dishonest, alternatively, rank order them in terms of their honesty. A matching score may be obtained from the first method (a measure of the degree of association between the constructs) and a similar technique can be used for measuring the second method.

Uses of personal construct theory include the diagnosis of schizophrenic thought disorder (Bannister *et al.*, 1971), where abnormally loose constructs are found. Fixed role therapy is a relatively new type of therapy, once again still in its embryonic stage. It consists of therapists drawing up the most important constructs of a patient, using the repertory test. The therapist draws up a role sketch, which the client is required to act in her daily life. This sketch is totally different to her own constructs. After some time, and after repeated sessions to help her act out her role, her original role sketch is returned and discussed. The principle is that if the constructs are changed, then so will the behaviour be changed.

TRAIT THEORY (R.B. CATTELL)

A **trait** can be considered as a characteristic in our actions, thoughts or feelings. Traits are either inherited or acquired, but remain relatively stable and hence predictable. Cattell's theory evolved by the use of a statistical method known as **factor analysis**, and a very brief explanation of this method is required before an overview of trait theory is given.

FACTOR ANALYSIS

The number of descriptive words that can be used to describe aspects of our personality is vast, and any theory which attempts to use this amount of data without some form of 'statistical distillation' would lead to countless problems both in the theory itself as well as any testing procedures which may evolve from it.

The starting point therefore of Cattell's theory, and also of Eysenck's 'type' theory, is to reduce the amount of data originally obtained by administering a variety of tests to a large amount of subjects. In Cattell's own words: 'The strategy of research in this area has therefore been to sample the total personality sphere and thus gradually to distill, so to speak, from an enormous amount of variables, the major dimensions of personality which crop up repeatedly in different researches and situations' (Cattell and Butcher, 1968).

The first step is to analyse which correlations exist between a wide variety of measures which have been taken from a large number of subjects, and these correlations are then arranged in a 'correlation matrix'. The purpose of factor analysis is to enable us to group together various correlations by the determination of a small number of factors/dimensions which can summarise the data. The degree to which a particular factor is related to a test is demonstrated by the correlation between them, and this is known as the test's '**loading**' on the factor.

The factors produced by an initial factor analysis are known as 'first order factors' or 'traits'. A further factor analysis on the 'first order factors' will yield 'second order factors', or '**types**'. One type of factor analysis will produce factors which are unrelated (orthogonal factor analysis), whilst with another (oblique factor analysis), the factors emerging may be in some way correlated. Cattell used oblique factor analysis and it is the 'first order factors' that he is predominantly associated with.

MOTIVATIONAL ASPECTS OF PERSONALITY

Cattell recognises that motivational factors play an important part in personality. 'Dynamic' traits not only direct us towards our goals, but provide

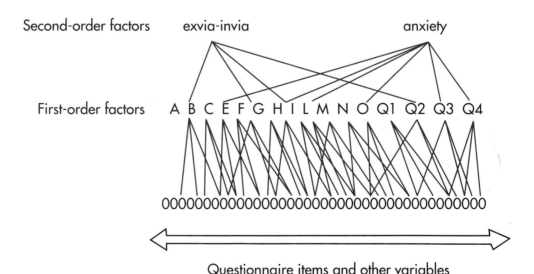

Fig. 2.3 Cattell's levels of factors. In contrast to Eysenck, Cattell stresses the importance of first order factors (traits). (Reproduced with permission from Cattell, R.B., *The Scientific Analysis of Personality*, Penguin, Harmondsworth (1965)).

the drive or energy for us to achieve them. Some of these motives are innate ('**ergs**'), and some are acquired.

STRUCTURAL ASPECTS OF PERSONALITY

In all, sixteen first-order factors have been identified by Cattell and his co-workers, and these are the basis for the Sixteen Personality Factor Questionnaire (16PF). It is these factors which are the enduring components of personality, and are referred to as '**source traits**', made up of fifteen '**temperament' traits** and one 'ability' trait. A temperament trait will determine how actions are carried out, whereas the ability trait (intelligence) determines how well it is carried out.

It can be seen that Cattell also identified two major second-order factors: exvia–invia and **anxiety**. These equate with Eysenck's **introversion–extroversion** and neuroticism (see below), although Cattell attributes little accuracy to them in terms of predictors of behaviour, saving this attribute for first-order factors. Second-order factors do however influence our behaviour, but only through the first-order factors.

The interaction between two or more source traits determines an individual's 'surface' traits, which are readily observable to the onlooker, and may indeed appear to be basic components of the personality, while in fact they are mere manifestations rather than basic personality elements.

A summary of the personality traits measured by the 16PF is given below.

Trait designation by letter	Title of trait
A	Affectothymia vs sizothymia
B	General intelligence vs mental defect
C	Emotional stability or ego strength vs dissatisfied emotionality
E	Dominance or ascendance vs submission
F	Surgency vs desurgency ('enthusiasm vs melancholy')
G	Superego strength vs lack of internal standards
H	('Adventurous' vs 'timid') Technical names: parmia vs threctia
I	Protected emotional sensitivity vs tough maturity. Technical names: premsia vs harria
L	Protension vs alaxia ('suspecting vs accepting')
M	Autia (autistic temperament) vs practical concernedness
N	Sophistication vs rough simplicity (or 'shrewdness vs naivete')
O	Guilt-proneness vs confident adequacy ('insecure vs confident')
Q	Radicalism vs conservatism
Q2	Self-sufficiency vs lack of resolution
Q3	Strong self-sentiment vs weak self-sentiment
Q4	High ergic tension vs low ergic tension

(From Cattell and Butcher, 1968.)

Cattell has since reported seven further factors which are less well defined. The following extract from the 16PF Questionnaire should clarify the characteristics of each trait mentioned above.

Low score description	Factor	High score description
Reserved, detached, critical	A	Outgoing, warmhearted
Less intelligent, concrete thinking	B	More intelligent, abstract thinking
Affected by feelings, easily upset	C	Emotionally stable, faces reality
Humble, mild, accommodating	E	Assertive, aggressive, stubborn
Sober, prudent, serious	F	Happy-go-lucky, impulsive, lively
Expedient, disregards rules	G	Conscientious, persevering
Shy, restrained, timid	H	Venturesome, socially bold
Tough minded, self-reliant	I	Tender-minded, clinging
Trusting, adaptable	L	Suspicious, self-opinionated
Practical, careful	M	Imaginative
Forthright, natural	N	Shrewd, calculating
Self-assured, confident	O	Apprehensive, self-reproaching
Conservative	Q1	Experimenting, liberal
Group-dependent	Q2	Self-sufficient
Undisciplined, self-conflict	Q3	Controlled, socially precise

(From Cattell and Eber, 1963.)

By virtue of the strong mathematical basis of Cattell's theory, its uses to the casual observer of personality are almost completely non-existent. The most that we could deduce from casual observation is a rough outline of the individual's surface traits and this would constitute a most unsatisfactory approach. It does, however, have major applications, particularly for education, and probably most famously as part of a psychometric testing procedure for selecting candidates for certain types of occupation (most commonly used in the health care professions for selecting managers). Cattell claimed to have identified certain scores on some factors which appeared to be common in certain occupations.

TYPE THEORY (H.J. EYSENCK)

Fig. 2.4 H. J. Eysenck.

Type theory also uses factor analysis as outlined above. The principal difference is that orthogonal factor analysis was employed, thus producing a small number of independent factors. There are considerable similarities between the second-order factors identified by Cattell and those identified by Eysenck (Eysenck and Eysenck, 1969), although little agreement on first-order factors. Eysenck places considerable emphasis on second-order factors (unlike Cattell), pointing out that, psychologically, they are far more meaningful than first-order factors (Eysenck, 1976).

The biological basis of personality features strongly in this theory, inas-

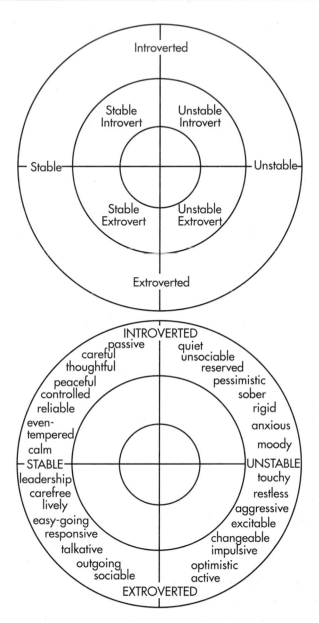

Fig. 2.5 Dimensions of Personality. Based initially on the work of Wundt at the beginning of this century. Eysenck, through the application of factor analysis, has developed a 'type' theory of personality.

much as Eysenck considers that 'possibly as much as three quarters of the total variance for differences between individuals with respect to extroversion and neuroticism, is due to hereditary factors' (Eysenck, 1956). In many ways the starting point of the theory emerged from Eysenck's interest in abnormal psychology (as did Jung's) and on first inspection bears a certain resemblance to some aspects of Jung's theory. It must be pointed out that much of this similarity is semantic rather than structural (e.g. the use of the terms **introversion** and **extroversion**).

Eysenck's research has led him and his associates to identify four dimensions of personality. The majority of his research has been carried out with two dimensions, namely extroversion/introversion and neuroticism/stability. Of the two other dimensions, intelligence is not considered as a pure dimension, and the psychoticism/stability dimension has, compared to the rest of Eysenck's work, received little attention except in the last few years.

Eysenck points out that the dimensions that he has described bear a close relationship to those identified by Galen almost two thousand years ago (melancholic, choleric, phlegmatic and sanguine) and a system of identifying the four temperaments, unchangeable, changeable, emotional and non-emotional (Wundt, 1903), has been adapted to illustrate the individual's appropriate space on a two-dimensional diagram.

It will be noted that around the rim of the diagram are some of the traits characteristic of each quadrant. These are the results of studies carried out of the intercorrelations between traits identified by Guilford, Cattell, Eysenck and others.

As stated earlier, Eysenck uses a biological basis for his theory and accordingly, the individual's position on the neuroticism scale would be dependent upon the degree of excitability of the nervous system. The individual's position on the extroversion–introversion scale is dependent upon the balance between the excitatory and inhibitory processes in the cortex.

Once again, as with Cattell's theory, type theory has been utilised in the occupational sphere (using the Eysenck Personality Inventory). Investigations have also been carried out to examine the possible correlations between certain psychiatric disorders and personality **types** (which

indeed was the starting point of the theory). Certain associations are also found between some physical phenomena and personality types. Barnes (1975), for instance, is just one researcher to conclude that there is an association between extroversion and pain thresholds, with introverts having a low pain threshold and extroverts having a high pain threshold.

EVALUATION

Any subject in this book could fill a textbook in its own right, and the study of personality is no exception. The major theorists quoted above have written several hundred books and major articles between them, and consequently only a fraction of each theory could be included here. Other theories which have helped to mould our understanding of personality have not been included, principally because they do not relate specifically to a general study of health care or because they are an 'off-shoot' of theories already mentioned. Some theorists, such as Maslow and Allport, are mentioned elsewhere in the text.

The diversity of personality research makes it difficult to summarise the findings effectively, but certain aspects can be taken from each for the purposes of this discussion.

Generally speaking, most theorists accept the concept of an unconscious which, for the most part, is not accessible to our conscious mind, but nevertheless is capable of playing a significant part in the way we behave, particularly when we are under stress. It is frequently a part of us that we are not consciously acquainted with, and as a result our behaviour in response to some situations may even shock the person who exhibits the behaviour. The instinct to survive is a strong one, and may manifest in a number of ways, even during times of debilitating illness. This will be examined further in later chapters.

Kelly's assertion that we all form theories of the world in which we live, has strong implications for how we not only view our illness, but also how we view subsequent treatments. There can be little doubt that many patients can create, quite unintentionally, their own private hell by virtue of the theories they have formed, perhaps several decades previously. Concepts such as cancer, leukaemia or even diabetes may, for an elderly patient especially, form part of a construct which usually has death as one of its components, and a great deal of time may be required to allow new information to permeate in order for the construct to be of more benefit. Often the patient may need to meet other patients who have similar problems in order for this to be resolved.

The developmental aspects of personality have, in part, been discussed especially with regard to children. Family-centred care is well established in some units, although its utilisation in terms of caring for adults is rather less prolific. This is not necessarily a criticism, as many aspects of our personality are not geared to illness, and it is conceivable that frictions may occur if, for instance, a husband and wife are attempting to adjust to new (albeit temporary) roles by coming to terms with dimensions of their personalities which have previously been ignored or repressed, whilst at the same time attempting to maintain control over domains in which, due to their illness, they are no longer able to play a part. Conversely most people will need the support of those people closest to them because they will have a greater understanding of their psychological plight.

The scientific analysis carried out by Cattell and Eysenck points us in the direction of being able to predict behaviour, albeit following a sophisticated testing procedure, although perhaps Jung was the most astute when he stated that everyone was the exception to the rule! Putting the theories under the 'microscope' reveals directions and basic facts which can be utilised by careful observation, and the prediction of behaviour of a highly neurotic patient in particular can be roughly gauged in a given situation, such as reactions to pain. Work continues on these highly sophisticated theories, and one is left with the impression that they will always need to be revised in the light of new **traits** or even **types** which have been uncovered.

REFERENCES

Bannister, D., Fransella, F.G. and Agnew, J. (1971) Characteristics and validity of the grid test of thought disorder. *British Journal of Social and Clinical Psychology* **10**, 144–51.

Barnes, G.E. (1975) Extraversion and pain. *British Journal of Social and Clinical Psychology* **14**, 303–308.

Brome, V. (1978) *Jung*. Macmillan, London.

Cattell, R.B. (1965) *The Scientific Analysis of Personality*. Penguin, London.

Cattell, R.B. and Butcher, H.J. (1968) *The Prediction of Achievement and Creativity*. Bobbs Merrill,

Cattell, R.B. and Eber, H.W. (1963) *The 16 Personality Factor Test and Handbook*, 3rd edn. Institute for Personality and Ability Testing, Illinois.

Erikson, E.H. (1963) *Childhood and Society*, 2nd edn. Norton, New York.

Erikson, E.H. (1968) *Identity: Youth and Crisis*. Norton, New York.

Eysenck, H.J. (1956) The questionnaire measurement of neuroticism and extraversion. *Rivista di Psicologia* **54**, 113–140.

Eysenck, H.J. (1976) *The Measurement of Personality*. Baltimore University Park Press, Baltimore.

Eysenck, H.J. and Eysenck, S.B.G. (1963) *The Eysenck Personality Inventory*, San Diego Educ. & Indust. Testing Service, London.

Eysenck, H.J. and Eysenck, S.B.G. (1969) *Personality Structure and Measurement*. Routledge & Kegan Paul, London.

Freud, S. (1966) *Introductory Lectures on Psychoanalysis*. Norton, New York (orig. publ. 1916).

Jung, C.G. (1921) *Psychological Types*. Princeton University Press, Princeton, NJ.

Jung, C.G., ed. (1964) *Man and His Symbols*. Aldus Books, New York.

Jung, C.G. (1976) *Personality Types*. Princeton University Press, Princeton, NJ (orig. publ. 1921).

Kelly, G. (1955) *The Psychology of Personal Constructs*. Norton, New York.

Sulloway, F.J. (1979) *Freud, Biologist of the Mind.* Fontana.
Wundt, W. (1903) *Grundzüge der Physiologischen Psychologie*, Vol 3 (5th edn). W. Engelmann, Leipzig.

FURTHER READING

Apart from the above texts, which have become standard texts in their own right, the following is strongly recommended as an excellent account of the theories covered 0in this chapter.

Ewen, R.B. (1980) *An Introduction to Theories of Personality.* Academic Press, New York.

CHAPTER 3

PHYSIOLOGICAL PSYCHOLOGY

'The deficiencies in our description (of mind) would probably vanish if we were already in a position to replace the psychological terms by physiological or chemical ones'

SIGMUND FREUD

INTRODUCTION

The search for links between the physiological functioning of the individual and their behaviour is far from new. Sigmund Freud, to name but one, was convinced that physiology and psychology were linked in some way. Today, 'physiological psychology' is a major subject area which has yielded, and continues to yield, vast amounts of research.

The study of the physiological basis of behaviour is an enormous subject which involves, for those wishing to pursue it in depth, an extensive know ledge of, amongst other things, neurophysiology. The subject areas which underpin physiological psychology are covered admirably in other texts, a selection of which is included in the reference section of this chapter.

For the purposes of our discussion in this chapter, the subject has been approached from a highly selective standpoint, from two points of view. Firstly, there is a minimal amount of anatomy and physiology included, although at the same time it has not been ignored and a brief description of some structures and mechanisms involved has been given. Instead, a more 'practical' discussion regarding the implications of research findings has been pursued. In many cases, the research findings are still confusing, insofar as much of the research is carried out on animals, and further, that the areas being investigated are still in their 'research infancy' in many cases, sometimes leading to the discovery of a plethora of apparent physiological changes, the relevance of which requires further work.

Secondly, the aspects of the subject which will be discussed should have implications for health care, and hence, some areas have more prominence than others. Topics such as eating, drinking, sleeping, learning and memory are included, because of the importance to the health professional in understanding the possible mechanisms which underlie, for instance, obesity, as well as those that have a bearing on mental disorders. It will be noticed that many of the headings correspond to chapters found elsewhere in the text, and these, it is suggested, should be considered together.

Firstly, we need to consider some daily activities which are commonly assessed by the health professional in an attempt to gain an understanding of their physiological background, in order that we may understand the potential problems that the individual may have. Secondly, we will examine some of the more common phenomena observed in the health care setting such as fear, stress and pain, and finally the subject of psychopathology will be examined.

EATING

Eating is a behaviour well known to all of us and whether we eat to live, or live to eat, it occupies a central role in our lives which cannot be ignored. This is of course stating the obvious, but if we then consider dieting to lose weight, obesity, and other changes which may occur in our weight following neurosurgery, and even the psychological aspect of eating, we may see that it is rather more than just a basic survival function.

Eating behaviour, and more especially how we become hungry and how we respond to it, is something that as health professionals we tend to take for granted, and in the more extreme aspects of practice we tend to compare individuals' body weights with pre-determined tables (usually prepared by insurance companies), which tell us how much we should weigh according to how tall we are or how large or small our frames are. Anyone who has ever attempted to give advice as far as dieting to lose weight is concerned, in order to meet the requirements of such tables or graphs, will readily admit that they are beset with far more problems than first anticipated, with the individual having extreme difficulty in losing weight, or losing too much weight at once, but most commonly being able to reduce their weight to a certain level and then no further followed by increases of weight when the diet is stopped. It does in fact seem that some people can get away with eating exactly what they like when they like without having to suffer dire consequences, whereas others will, it seem, merely have to walk past a bakery in order to put on weight!

There are two major approaches to the study of eating behaviour. The first is the investigation into the role of the hypothalamus and the second considers the role of the peripheral mechanisms (gastrointestinal tract, endocrine systems, mouth etc.). Firstly, we should discuss the possible role of the hypothalamus.

HUNGER AND THE HYPOTHALAMUS

Ventromedial Hypothalamus
First described in 1942 by Hetherington and Ranson, studies into the parts of the **hypothalamus** known as the **ventro-medial hypothalamus** (VMH) and the **lateral hypothalamus** (LH) have been vast.

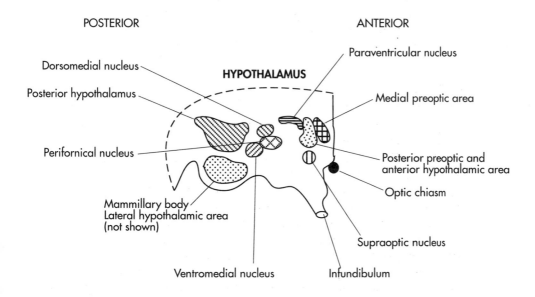

Fig. 3.1 The hypothalamus.

Lesioning of the VMH has been found to produce hypophasia (overeating) leading to gross obesity over a period of time (Hetherington and Ranson, 1942). The mechanisms whereby this is effected are still a matter of some debate, although some factors have been identified. Grossman (1960) found that if noradrenaline was injected into the hypothalamus, then feeding and drinking were elicited in a satiated rate, and further work by Leibowitz (1970) suggested that two different types of noradrenaline receptors exist in the hypothalamus, one with excitatory effects (causing feeding) and the other with inhibitory effects (inhibiting feeding).

Other evidence (e.g. Gold, 1973) points to 'VMH obesity syndrome' being due to the severing of the ascending ventral noradrenergic pathway, which arises from cell groups in the medulla oblongata and pons of the hindbrain. The evidence is therefore quite confusing, insofar as Grossman's findings do not support a commonly held view that noradrenaline suppresses feeding, although as Green (1987) points out: 'Leibowitz's ideas on this probably deserve more attention'.

It was mentioned in Chapter 1 that individuals may have a 'set point' weight which is regulated by the hypothalamus. It appears that both the VMH and LH play a part in this regulation, and it has already been mentioned that the search for such a mechanism has led to investigations into the role played by noradrenaline. Two further approaches to the 'set point' theory will be examined here, namely the glucostatic and lipostatic theories.

Lipostatic Theory

The amount of fatty acids in the fat storage cells (**adipocytes**) could hold the answer to the question of how our weight keeps within quite narrow limits. Nisbett (1972) suggested that the VMH is responsible for the regulation of feeding according to whether there is a low level of fatty acids (resulting in feeding behaviour) or a high level (leading to inhibition of feeding).

The quantity of fat storage cells in the body is determined by several factors, not least of all genetically, but also by early dietary habits (Brownell, 1986). The number of cells remains fixed in later life.

It has been found that by lesioning the VMH, weight increases, whilst lesioning of the LH causes weight loss. This is not merely a temporary phenomenon, but rather a permanent adjustment of the 'set point'. In other words, following hypothalmic damage, feeding behaviour is aimed at meeting the new set point (Keesey and Powley, 1975). To say, however, that this is a conclusive explanation would be to ignore an important fact. It appears perfectly reasonable to assume that in order to meet a higher set point, then more eating would take place, and this does seem to be true. However, an interesting thing happens if normal feeding behaviour is imposed, and that is that the weight still increases, indicating that metabolic changes also occur.

Glucostatic Theory

Lowered blood glucose (and hence lower brain tissue utilisation of glucose) is a powerful stimulus for the individual to eat. Mayer (1953) showed that low levels of glucose were most definitely correlated with initiating feeding, although the reverse situation, namely high blood glucose, is not as reliable in the cessation of feeding (Thompson, 1975). It is possible that the level of glucose is detected by glucoreceptors in the hypothalamus.

Lateral Hypothalamus

If the VMH is considered as being responsible for the long-term control of dietary intake, then questions need to be asked as to the function of the **lateral hypothalamus**. Perhaps the most relevant point to start with is the fact that if bilateral lesioning of the lateral hypothalamus (LH) is carried out, then the animal will starve to death. Teitelbaum and Epstein (1962), however, found that if the animal is then subsequently 'tube-fed' it will recover, but such a recovery follows a certain pattern, which provides us with a very clear picture of this LH syndrome. A brief summary of the recovery is given below.

Stage 1. **Aphagia** and **adipsia**.
Stage 2. Will eat wet palatable food, but no fluids.
Stage 3. Secondary dehydration due to not drinking.
Stage 4. Recovery. (Beginning to determine dietary intake, but drinking is never again normal, and will only drink if food is presented. This is known as prandial drinking).

Even in recovery, these animals (rats) are very sensitive to the palatability of food, and do not respond to deficits in glucose, such as that produced by injecting insulin.

The fact that any form of recovery is achieved at all, suggests that other systems must be compensating, and since the evidence regarding the mechanisms which underlie the functioning of the VMH are also in doubt, we have to assume that feeding behaviour is dependent upon multiple controls.

Insulin

Insulin, which is a hormone produced in the pancreas and regulated by the hypothalamus, stimulates the synthesis and deposition of triglycerides in adipose tissue, as well as inhibiting the release of fatty acids. Eating increases the amount of insulin which is secreted, and indeed the greater the obesity, the higher the level of insulin (hyperinsulinaemia). This can be conditioned so that merely thinking about food can produce hunger.

Cholecystokinin

Cholecystokinin (CCK) is a hormone produced in the upper part of the small intestine, and has been found to be a powerful appetite suppressant in humans and other animals (Pi-Sunyer *et al.*, 1982). Its exact action is unknown, but it is released in response to fatty acids in the bloodstream.

SLEEPING

The exact reasons why we sleep are still a matter of some uncertainty, although investigations have been carried out to determine the nature of sleep and suggestions have been made as to its possible functions. Oswald (1966), for instance, has suggested that it could serve the purpose of facilitating restoration of the body and brain, although Meddis (1979) suggests that sleep is necessary to keep the animal immobilised for a long period of time, and hence at less risk of being hunted.

Two approaches will be considered. Firstly, we will consider sleep from an observational point of view, using various investigations such as electroencephalograph (EEG) examination. Following this, sleep deprivation studies will be examined.

THE PATTERN OF SLEEP

Sleep progresses through a certain sequence of stages characterised by different brain activity. These stages have been described by Meddis (1979) as being light quiet sleep (LQS), deep quiet sleep (DQS), and active sleep (AS) which is often associated with rapid eye movements (REM), which in turn are indicative of dreaming. This distinction between 'quiet' and 'waking' phases is reflected in the EEG configurations recorded at different times of the individual's sleep. The pattern of sleep thus described would progress like this:

$$LQS \rightarrow DQS \rightarrow LQS \rightarrow AS$$

This sequence would take somewhere in the region of about an hour, and is then repeated. Meddis' terminology are not the only way of describing sleep, and the reader will find several alternative names for the stages mentioned. For instance, AS is often referred to as REM sleep (for obvious reasons), desynchronised sleep (describing the activity detected on the EEG which, despite the fact that the subject is deeply asleep, gives the appearance of wakefulness), and paradoxical sleep (because of the reasons just given). Dream sleep is the other name frequently given to AS. Other authors (e.g. Steptoe, 1992) have utilised the terms REM and non-REM sleep. Certainly there is not complete agreement as to how many stages are involved, but usually four or five are agreed, and the distinction is not particularly important to our discussion.

Probably, what is meant by these different stages could be best explained by taking a closer look at the variations in brain activity that occur at each stage. In the earliest part of the sleep pattern, as the individual falls asleep, there are peaks of activity recorded. As the sleep progresses, lower frequency waves predominate with bursts of activity (sleep spindles) occurring. The initial stage of sleep is therefore desynchronised, but as the individual passes into a deep sleep, the waves observed are slower and synchronised, and this is called by some researchers slow wave sleep (SWS) as a result. The AS is characterised, as already mentioned, by desynchronised waves that closely resemble wakefulness, although in fact the subject is more difficult to rouse during this stage. If the subject is woken during this stage, they are more likely to report that they have been dreaming than if woken at other times. In the second half of the period of sleep, we spend more time in the LQS and hence AS stages, and therefore dreaming is often recalled on waking.

PHYSIOLOGICAL MECHANISMS AND SLEEP

This section began by making a rather strange statement, namely that the function of sleep is still unknown. It is easy to assume that sleep is a passive process that occurs as a general consequence of the body requiring rest, and this to a large extent is true. This is made all the more confusing by the fact that sleep is an active process in terms of neurological activity.

It is now becoming apparent that the process of sleep and arousal is not the product of any one structure in the central nervous system, but rather is a result of the integration of the actions of several structures and mechanisms. The answer to our earlier dilemma appears to be that sleep is both an active process, inasmuch as it is the result of specific sleep mechanisms, and passive insofar as it will occur when sensory stimuli decrease.

Although the exact relationship between these mechanisms continues to be investigated, it has been suggested (Bremer, 1977) that the activity of the brain stem, more specifically the **reticular activating system** (RAS) which is a collection of grey matter ascending into the posterior part of the forebrain (the **diencephalon**), has an important role in creating and maintaining behavioural alertness by stimulating the cortex.

The RAS also has an inhibitory effect on certain mechanisms, namely the hypnogenic mechanisms in the forebrain, which are responsible for sleep. In considering the structures contained within the diencephalon (**hypothalamus**, thalamus, metathalamus and epithalamus) it should be mentioned that various studies have revealed associations with sleeping and arousal. For instance, lesions of the posterior hypothalamus result in a sleep-like state, and lesions of the thalamus can lead to synchrony or desynchrony (Hunter and Jaspers, 1949).

As Green (1987) points out, it seems likely that, from a neurochemical point of view, particularly in terms of explaining SWS and **REM**, a complex series of interactions between many neurotransmitters would be involved, although it is known that both serotonin mechanisms in the brain stem and cholinergic mechanisms in the forebrain are implicated in the process.

SLEEP DEPRIVATION STUDIES

Arguably one of the most obvious ways to find out just what sleep does is to find out what happens if someone is prevented from sleeping.

In a now famous study on sleep deprivation, Dement (1960) deprived subjects of REM sleep (as distinct from non-REM sleep) over a period of 5 days. The results were interesting, although procedural variations on this and other such studies have cast doubt on their total reliability. The subjects were found to be irritable, nervous, unable to concentrate, and in some cases began to hallucinate. When they were allowed to sleep normally, more REM sleep occurred (up to 60% more) than would do normally. This pattern continued for several nights afterwards (REM rebound). It is interesting to note that they did not sleep for a vast amount of time; indeed, after the first period of sleep following the experiment, the amount of sleep was near enough normal.

Naturally, in order to understand this effect, we need to have some understanding of the function of REM sleep in the first place. It might be suggested that REM sleep enables us to sort through the data that we have had to deal with (and may still be continuing to deal with) during our waking life. If this is the case, then it could be suggested that Dement's results could indicate an 'overloading' of the 'circuits' was occurring due to the backlog of unprocessed information, but this is mere conjecture.

DISCUSSION: IMPLICATIONS IN CLINICAL PRACTICE

Sleeping is an important part of our lives, and it is an area of experience that we all have. In relation to some disorders such as depression, it is automatic to ask the individual whether they are able to sleep and to describe the nature and pattern of that sleep. Respiratory disorders such as asthma will usually attract the same attention, to such a degree that we may associate excessive waking during the night as being indicative of poor medical control over the disorder.

A few points could be considered by the reader in light of the discussion on sleep. Firstly, and perhaps most obviously: what constitutes a good night's sleep? Naturally, in terms of time there is a lot of variation, with some individuals requiring only 4 or 5 hours sleep whilst others require 8 or 9 hours. The total amount of time that the individual has spent in sleeping, as we have seen, is certainly irrelevant if that person has, for one reason or another, been deprived of REM sleep. The reasons for this could be due to noise, or even pain, but it is much more likely to be due to procedures that are carried out on them during their sleeping time, such as neurological observations, blood pressure recording etc. Although such procedures are undoubtedly necessary, it should be remembered that excessive disruption of REM sleep may lead to irritability and even confusion. Perhaps more pertinently, the individual must make up this sleep on subsequent nights (or days), and should be allowed to do so in order to aid their recovery.

We often make judgements concerning the quality of the sleep that the patient has had. It may sound obvious but it is impossible to judge the quality of sleep either by the apparent duration of sleep or by the amount of snoring that has taken place! The individual may have woken up many times during their period of sleep due to discomfort of one sort or another and hence may wake up in the morning still feeling tired. It is important that the individual should be consulted as to what sort of night's sleep they have had, rather than relying solely on our periodic observations of them.

MEMORY AND LEARNING

The notion that there existed a chemical memory trace has been investigated for many years, as has the search for a neurophysiological basis for learning. As with our discussion on sleep earlier in the chapter, learning and memory cannot be confined to one structure in the brain.

The hippocampus which is situated in the forebrain has been linked with memory and learning, and along with the neurotransmitter, **glutamate**, is seen as an important centre for learning (Gustaffson and Wigstrom, 1988), although it seems much more likely that it is only part of the system. Thompson (1978) has suggested that the frontal cortex, the posterior **thalamus**, and the **amygdala** are all responsible for fear-initiated responses, whilst the occipital cortex, **hippocampus** and mammilary bodies are important for cognitive mapping. The **basal ganglia** are responsible for sensorimotor integration, and the cerebellum, parietal cortex and anterior thalamus are concerned with somatosensory function.

From a functional viewpoint, it has been suggested that learning involves the formation of new circuits within the brain (Ungar, 1974), and others have suggested that changes in RNA could be the key to the physiological basis of learning. The true picture is immensely complicated, and at times the evidence points us in several different directions, although it is highly likely that given time, a complex interrelated system will be discovered.

STRESS AND EMOTION

It is about a hundred years since William James and Carl Lange, working independently, first formulated what was to become known as the **James–Lange theory**, which attempted to explain the relationship between physiological events and emotional feelings. As Gray (1987) states: 'According to the James–Lange Theory, as it is known, emotional feelings consist of the perception of the physiological changes initiated by the emotional stimulus'.

The theory is at best difficult to completely substantiate, but it has nevertheless stimulated a tremendous amount of interest in the relationship between stress and its physiological correlates.

We have all been in situations where we have had to take action quickly to avoid danger. Most obviously, we can relate to avoiding accidents. We may also perceive less blatant events as a threat. Very often, such events require spontaneous responses, and may leave us shaking, sweating and distraught. Sometimes we may not even believe that we have, say in the case of avoiding another vehicle, taken the evasive action that we have. It is clear that in such 'emergencies' where we have acted 'automatically', and where we feel the effects of the shock so clearly, that some mechanism outside our conscious control is at work. Not all stress comes under this classification, and some stress persists far longer than just a split second.

GENERAL ADAPTATION SYNDROME

Perhaps the most famous of all twentieth century researchers in the field of **stress** has been Hans Selye. According to Selye (1956), the body's response can be seen in three separate stages.

Stage 1: Alarm Reaction
In this initial reaction, **ACTH (adrenocorticotrophic hormone)** is secreted by the anterior pituitary gland and stimulates the adrenal cortex, and hence additional hormones (**glucocorticoids** and **mineralocorticoids**) are

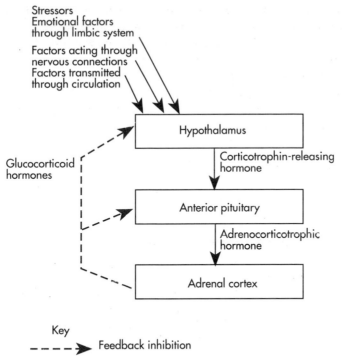

Fig. 3.2 Hormonal stress responses (Reproduced with permission from Hinchliff, S. and Montague, S., *Physiology for Nursing Practice*, Baillière Tindall, 1988).

released. These hormones will cause fluid retention, increase plasma renin activity, suppress inflammatory responses, and will facilitate the production of free fatty acids.

Essentially though, the emergency reaction (as in our example with the narrowly averted accident) is due to the effects of adrenaline and noradrenaline which are secreted by the adrenal medulla. Heart rate and strength of heart beat are increased, bronchioles are dilated, respiration increases, and more red blood cells are released from contraction of the spleen in order to increase the amount of oxygen reaching the tissues. Stored sugar is released in order to provide energy. In other words, the body is prepared to take high energy, evasive action, or to meet the problem if necessary.

Stage 2: Resistance

The reactions described in stage 1, with the actions of adrenaline and noradrenaline, are more or less instant. In the second stage it is the actions of the **glucocorticoids** that dominate. The release of glucocorticoids is under the control of **ACTH**. The hormones included in the glucocorticoids are hydrocortisone, corticosterone and cortisol, and their major function in this case is to turn non-sugars into sugars in order to provide the body with resources of energy.

There is also an increase in the enzymes responsible for **catecholamine** synthesis in the adrenal medulla. It can be seen therefore that under prolonged **stress**, mechanisms which favour action (or at least the readiness for such action) to deal with stress are maximised at the cost of mechanisms which are directed towards reproduction, growth and even combatting existing infection. It would appear that the same reaction takes place regardless of the situation, whether it be psychological, environmental or physiological.

Stage 3: Exhaustion

There appears to come a time when the individual can no longer respond to stress, even as far as the alarm reaction is concerned. The secretion of hormones which is so much a part of both the alarm reaction and resistance appears to cease, meaning that the individual can no longer respond to **stress**. At this point, as with an extreme case in the alarm reaction, the individual may actually die.

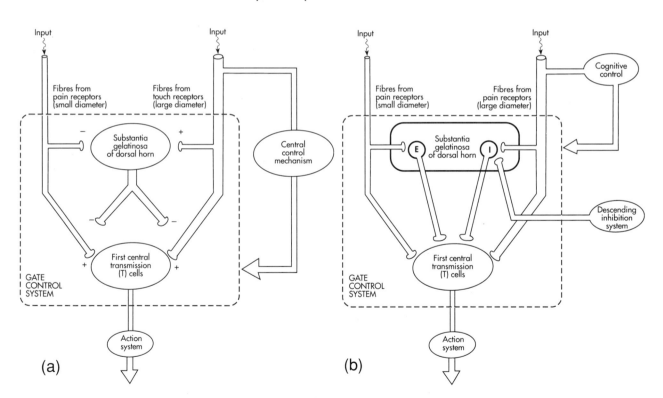

Fig. 3.3 The gate control theory of pain proposed by Melzack and Wall. (a) In the original formulation of the theory (1965), the inhibitory effect of the substantia gelatinosa (SG) on the T cells is enhanced by pain fibres. (b) In the updated model, excitatory links (E) from the SG to the T cells, and descending inhibitory control from the brain-stem is included although the actual situation appears to be more complex. The round knot at the end of the inhibitory (I) link indicates that its action may be pre- or postsynoptic, or both.

PAIN

Although some theories of pain are purely physiological in nature, one theory embraces both psychological and physiological aspects, and this is known as the **gate control theory**.

GATE CONTROL THEORY

Melzack and Wall (1965) proposed this theory of pain perception that takes into account the possible psychological modifying factors that may affect the way we perceive pain. In other words, they proposed that a 'gate' mechanism is located in the spinal cord, in the substratia gelatinosa of the dorsal horns (part of the grey matter), which is capable of 'closing', and hence preventing pain messages from reaching the brain. The pain signals enter the spinal cord via pain fibres which pass through the gate mechanism, when open to transmission cells, which in their turn transmit the message to the brain. Naturally, the greater the output from the transmission cells, the greater the pain that is perceived, and this is directly related to the amount of activity in the pain fibres in the first place. The pain fibres, however, are not the only fibres to enter the spinal cord, and the peripheral fibres that detect touch and mild irritations are of major importance here. Counterstimulation, for instance such as rubbing a sore muscle, can actually ease the pain because the stimulation entering the spinal cord from the peripheral fibres closes the gate, and hence prevents the transmission of 'pain' messages to the brain.

It was stated at the beginning of this short account of gate control theory that the theory incorporates psychological factors, and these take on an

important role when considering the messages descending from the brain stem and the cortex. Emotional conditions such as anxiety can serve to open or close the gate, as can depression or excitement. Certainly, most of us are aware that by engaging in an exciting activity, or when we are placed in a stressful situation, we may well forget the toothache that has perhaps been a constant companion for days! Naturally, one of the most obvious ways of 'closing the gate' is by taking analgesia, and research has shown that morphine is effective because it activates the brain stem to transmit impulses down the spinal cord (Melzack and Wall, 1982).

Other theories of pain perception have centred around physiological mechanisms. For instance, specificity theory maintains that the mechanism for dealing with pain, from its detection through special receptors to its own unique pathways, to its own area of the brain, is an entirely separate system. Pattern theory, on the other hand, suggests that any stimulation, as long as it is intense enough, will be interpreted as pain, as soft stimuli and excessive stimuli produce different patterns of neural activity.

PHYSIOLOGICAL ASPECTS OF MENTAL ILLNESS

Sigmund Freud was convinced that it would only be a matter of time before physiological mechanisms were uncovered that would provide the explanation for many of the psychological phenomena that he was investigating. His beliefs are now beginning to show considerable substance, with many advances being made in this area.

ENDOGENOUS DEPRESSION

From a biochemical viewpoint, 'theories [of depression] rest on the proposal that the illness is a consequence of a reduction in one or more neurotransmitters' (Weller, 1992). The picture does in fact point to more than one neurotransmitter being reduced.

A reduction in **monoamines** has been associated with endogenous depression. Investigations have centred around the metabolites of various transmitters, and the inference is clearly that if the metabolite is raised or lowered, then so must the original neurotransmitter. The metabolites of **serotonin** (Asberg *et al.*, 1984), for instance, have been found to be lower in depressed subjects, as has the metabolite of noradrenaline, whilst others show a diminished amount of **dopamine**, or even a reduced amount of CSF adrenaline. The situation is not particularly clear at the moment, but it does appear apparent that some form of neurotransmitter disturbance is involved.

Hormonal influences, such as those seen in Cushing's syndrome, and electrolyte changes, namely an increase in intracellular sodium, have both been associated with depression, as has vitamin B12 deficiency.

SCHIZOPHRENIA

Schizophrenia has also been associated with neurotransmitter changes. As with the work concerning neurotransmission and depression, the various theories are difficult to consistently substantiate, although there is some evidence that dopamine is implicated, and it has been suggested that the abnormally high arousal response of schizophrenic subjects may be due to the effects of cortical **dopamine**.

Other neurotransmitters could also be implicated, such as **glutamate**, noradrenaline and serotonin, but as Mackay and Iverson (1992) point out, the eventual identification of a responsible gene will probably be the quickest way to identify the neurotransmitter responsible.

DEMENTIA

Alzheimer's disease has long been known to have very definite physiological correlates, and examination of the brain during post-mortem has found multiple changes compared to normal brains. Perhaps most blatantly, the diseased brain is in fact significantly smaller, with enlarged ventricles, and a significant reduction of neurones and cholinergic cells in certain areas. Up to 60% of large pyramidal cells are lost from the cortex.

Genetically, familial Alzheimer's disease accounts for about 15–20% of all sufferers, and is an autosomal dominant condition, probably associated with the same chromosome responsible for Down's syndrome (chromosome 21).

CONCLUSIONS

Physiological correlates of behaviour are being researched vigorously, and this branch of psychology is yielding vast amounts of data. The consequences of such research are difficult to anticipate, but certainly the eventual treatment of some psychiatric disorders may well be more successfully accomplished. Physiological data, for instance with regard to sleeping and eating, should be used in conjunction with our behavioural observations when planning care.

SUMMARY

Lesioning of the **VMH** has been found to produce hypophasia (overeating) leading to gross obesity over a period of time.

Leibowitz (1970) suggested that two different types of noradrenaline receptors exist in the **hypothalamus**, one with excitatory effects (causing feeding) and the other with inhibitory effects (inhibiting feeding).

It appears that both the **VMH** and **LH** play a part in the regulation of a set point weight.

Nisbett (1972) suggested that the VMH is responsible for the regulation of feeding according to whether there is a low level of fatty acids (resulting in feeding behaviour) or a high level (leading to inhibition of feeding).

The quantity of fat storage cells in the body is determined by several factors, not least of all genetically, but also by early dietary habits (Brownell, 1986). The number of cells remains fixed in later life.

Lowered blood glucose (and hence lower brain tissue utilisation of glucose) is a powerful stimulus for the individual to eat.

We have to assume that feeding behaviour is dependent upon multiple controls.

Eating increases the amount of insulin which is secreted, and indeed, the greater the obesity, the higher the level of insulin (hyperinsulinaemia). This can be conditioned so that merely thinking about food can produce hunger.

Cholecystokinin (CCK) is a hormone produced in the upper part of the small intestine, and has been found to be a powerful appetite suppressant in humans and other animals.

Leibowitz (1970) suggested that two different types of noradrenaline receptors exist in the **hypothalamus**, one with excitatory effects (causing feeding) and the other with inhibitory effects (inhibiting feeding).

Sleep progresses through a certain sequence of stages characterised by different brain activity. It is now becoming apparent that the process of sleep and arousal is not the product of any one structure in the central nervous system, but rather a combination.

Excessive disruption of REM sleep may lead to irritability and even confusion.

According to Selye (1956), the body's response is in three separate stages: alarm reaction, resistance and exhaustion.

A reduction in **monoamines** has been associated with endogenous **depression**.

REFERENCES

* indicates a classic or standard text

Asberg, M., Bertilsson, L., Marlensson, B., Scalia-Tomba, G.P., Thorn, P. and Traskman-Bendy, L. (1984) CSF monoamine metabolites in melancholia. *Acta Psychiat. Scanda* **69**, 201–209. (Reprinted in Weller, M.P.I. and Eysenck, M.W. (eds) (1992) *The Scientific Basic of Psychiatry*. W.B. Saunders, London.

Bremer, F. (1977) Cerebral hypnogenic centers. *Annals of Neurology* **2**, 1–6.

Brownell, K.D. (1986) Social and behavioural aspects of obesity in children. In: Krasnegor, N.A., Arasteh, J.D. and Cataldo, M.F. (eds) *Child Health Behaviour: A Behavioural Pediatrics Perspective*. Wiley, New York.

Dement, W.C. (1960) The effect of dream deprivation. *Science* **131**, 1705–1707.

Gold, R.M. (1973) Hypothalamic obesity: the myth of the ventromedial nucleus. *Science* **182**, 488–490.

Gray, J.A. (1987) *The Psychology of Fear and Stress*, 2nd edn. Cambridge University Press, Cambridge.*

Green, S. (1987) *Physiological Psychology: An Introduction*. Routledge & Kegan Paul, London.

Grossman, S.P. (1960) Eating or drinking elicited by direct adrenergic or cholinergic stimulation of the hypothalamus. *Science* **132**, 301, 202.

Gustaffson, B. and Wigstrom, H. (1988) Physiological mechanisms underlying long term potentiation. *Trends in Neuroscience* **11**, 156–162.

Hetherington, A.W. and Ranson, S.W. (1942) The relation of various hypothalamic lesions to adiposity in the rat. *Journal of Comparative Neurology* **76**, 475 (in: Green, S., ed. (1987) *Physiological Psychology: An Introduction*. Routledge & Kegan Paul, London.

Hunter, J. and Jaspers, H. (1949) Effect of thalamic stimulation in unanaesthetized animals. *Electroencephalography and Clinical Neurophysiology* **1**, 304–324 (in: Green, S., ed. (1987) *Physiological Psychology: An Introduction*. Routledge & Kegan Paul, London.

Keesey, R.E. and Powley, T.L. (1975) Hypothalamic regulation of body weight. *American Scientist* **63**, 558–565.

Leibowitz, S.F. (1970) Hypothalamic -adrenergic 'satiety' system antagonizes an -adrenergic 'hunger' system in the rat. *Nature* **226**, 963–964.

Mackay, A.V.P. and Iverson, L.L. (1992) Neurotransmitters and schizophrenia. In: Weller, M.P.I. and Eysenck, M.W. (eds), *The Scientific Basis of Psychiatry*. W.B. Saunders, London.

Mayer, J. (1953) Genetic, traumatic, and environmental factors in the etiology of obesity. *Physiological Review* **33**, 472–508.

Meddis, R. (1979) The evolution and function of sleep. In: D.A. Oakley and H.C. Plotkin (eds), *Brain, Behaviour and Evolution*. Methuen, London.

Melzack, R. and Wall, P.D. (1965) Pain mechanisms: a new theory. *Science* **150**, 971–979.

Melzack, R. and Wall, P.D. (1982) *The Challenge of Pain*. Penguin, Harmondsworth.*

Nisbett, R.E. (1972) Hunger, obesity and the ventromedial hypothalamus. *Psychological Review* **79**, 433–453.

Oswald, I. (1966) *Sleep*. Penguin, Harmondsworth.*

Pi-Sunyer, X., Kissileff, H.R., Thornton, J. and Smith, G.P. (1982) C-terminal octapeptide of cholecystokinin decreases food intake in obese men. *Physiology and Behaviour* **29**, 627–630.

Sachs, O. (1986) *The Man who Mistook his Wife for a Hat*. Picador, London.

Selye, H. (1956) *The Stress of Life*. McGraw-Hill, New York.*

Skinner, B.F. (1938) *The Behaviour of Organisms*. Appleton-Century-Crofts, New York.

Steptoe, A. (1992) Sleep activation. In: Weller, M.P.I. and Eysenck, M.W. (eds), *The Scientific Basis of Psychiatry*. W.B. Saunders, London.

Teitelbaum, P. and Epstein, A.N. (1962) The lateral hypothalamic syndrome. *Psychological Review* **69**, 74–90.

Thompson, R.F. (1975) *Introduction to Physiological Psychology*. Harper and Row, New York.*

Thompson, R.F. (1978) Localisation of a 'passive avoidance memory system' in the white rat. *Physiological Psychology* **4**, 311–324.

Ungar, G. (1974) Molecular coding of memory. *Life Sciences* **14**, 595–604.

Weller, M.P.I. (1992) Depressive illness and anti-depressant drugs. In: Weller, M.P.I. and Eysenck, M.W. (eds), *The Scientific Basis of Psychiatry*. W.B. Saunders, London.

SUGGESTED READING

Gray, J.A. (1987) *The Psychology of Fear and Stress*, 2nd edn. Cambridge University Press, Cambridge. (Chapter 5 gives an in depth account of the physiology of fear and stress, although rather extensive.)

Green, S. (1987) *Physiological Psychology: An Introduction*. Routledge & Kegan Paul, London. (A good general text on the subject.)

Mackay, A.V.P. and Iverson, L.L. (1992) Neurotransmitters and schizophrenia. In: Weller, M.P.I. and Eysenck, M.W. (eds), *The Scientific Basis of Psychiatry*. W.B. Saunders, London. (Chapter 31 gives the reader an up-to-date account of recent research.)

Melzack, R. and Wall, P.D. (1982) *The Challenge of Pain*. Penguin, Harmondsworth. (Provides the reader with a complete account of gate control theory.)

Selye, H. (1956) *The Stress of Life*. McGraw-Hill, New York. (This classic text deserves consideration virtually in its entirety.)

CHAPTER 4

MOTIVATION

'So little done, so much to do'

CECIL JOHN RHODES (1853–1902)

INTRODUCTION

The question that many of us ask when considering a person's behaviour is: Why did they do that? It is an obvious question which occupies an important place in the study of behaviour. We may ask ourselves why people do the job they do, why a person chooses the marriage partner that they do, or, perhaps more relevant to this discussion, what made this particular individual seek medical advice where other individuals did not. The permutations to these questions are almost infinite, but lead to an all-embracing question of motivation.

A significant part of this chapter has been devoted to motivation and work, for several reasons. Firstly, work is a major activity of our daily lives, and the stresses placed upon us within the workplace have an unquestionable effect on our families, but more especially on our health, particularly in relation to stress-related illnesses. Secondly, as health professionals, we are called upon to fulfil managerial roles soon after we qualify, such as acting as a 'mentor' to students, or taking charge of a group of patients (and hence other members of the health team), albeit in a very short-term capacity. Thirdly, we need to have some knowledge as to why we sometimes feel discontented with our jobs, but perhaps more importantly, we need to have some objective insight into our reasons for doing the job in the first place. Quite naturally, the answers to some of these points will emerge elsewhere in the text, but some approaches will be covered here which will hopefully provide 'food for thought'.

It will be seen during the following discussion that the question of what motivates the individual is far from straightforward. Several schools of thought have contributed to an understanding of the subject, and it is possible that our answers lie within a combination of several approaches. Initially at least, an overview of some of the more well-established approaches will be given.

INSTINCT

The study of instinct as a motivator is one which can be traced back many years, and is still the subject of considerable argument. Those actions that are part of an animal's innate neural mechanisms (or indeed a human's), have been investigated by both biologists and psychologists, and are usually termed '**ethology**'. Many of the studies have been carried out using animals, and the work of Lorenz, McDougall and others is well documented elsewhere. The work of McDougall in particular, at the turn of the century, pointed towards instincts as the source of energy for all behaviour.

Once again though, the effects of the environment cannot be ignored, and therefore the sphere of research into this area is generally confined to those behaviours which appear consistent and fixed across the broad spectrum of humanity. Even with such an apparently precise brief, the area is far from clear cut because of the environmental effects which will in many instances become apparent early in life.

Despite any objections that may exist towards the ethological approach, it would be most foolish to ignore the existence of instincts as motivators, although the strength, number and direction of such instincts remains a matter of debate, and the manifestations of such instincts in everyday life (such as the sexual instinct) may be modified by the environment to such an extent as to make it unrecognisable.

PSYCHOANALYSIS AND MOTIVATION

Certainly the concept of behaviour having its origins within instinctual drives has been extensively debated, and Freud in particular was instrumental in the formulating of influential theories in this field. The existence of two major drives, **thanatos** (death seeking) and **eros** (life seeking), was a relatively late addition to his theory, particularly in the case of the death instinct.

Briefly, thanatos endeavours to return the individual to the ultimate state of peace, namely death. Attempts are made by the individual to pull against thanatos, and as a result, destructive behaviour is directed towards others. Eros on the other hand directs the individual towards the engaging in pleasurable activities.

The thanatos aspect of the theory was relatively incomplete but was later developed by others, principally Melanie Klein, who maintained that we have an inborn aggression which reflects the death instinct and is expressed mentally as unconscious fantasies which are expressed as primitive emotions such as envy, in the form of fears of persecution and fear of ego annihilation. All unpleasurable experiences are projected onto persecutory objects, thus preserving a purified pleasure principle.

FUNCTIONAL AUTONOMY

Allport (1961), although rejecting many of the cornerstones of psychoanalysis, nevertheless accepted the existence of instinctual drives, although he sees a more optimistic future for the individual insofar as he maintains that, although they completely dominate the infant, the motives that we have as adults consist of cognitive processes which are relatively independent of the instinctual drives. These cognitive process are, for the most part, unique to the individual, and are largely 'functionally autonomous' of their earlier childhood origins.

COGNITIVE DISSONANCE AND MOTIVATION

There are times when we are confronted with conflicts in the form of differing cognitions. For instance, we may like to smoke and yet we know that smoking causes lung cancer. Festinger (1957) suggests that when the implications of our cognitions regarding a situation or behaviour are mutually exclusive (as with the above example), then a state of dissonance will exist. The conflict that this produces for the individual is a most uncomfortable one, and therefore there must be some attempt at resolving the dissonance by bringing the cognitions into a more consonant relationship. In order to achieve this, one of several things may happen with the above example:

(1) We may give up smoking.
(2) We may choose not to believe the evidence (usually supporting our case with several anecdotes about friends and relatives who have lived to ripe old ages after a lifetime of heavy smoking.
(3) We may form affiliations with others who smoke in order to justify our behaviour.
(4) We may underestimate the amount we smoke.
(5) We may invent a positive case for smoking ('it helps me to relax', 'I can't concentrate without them' etc.).

Needless to say, smoking is not the only behaviour in which this could occur, and the theory of **cognitive dissonance** could well explain the persistence of some possibly life-threatening behaviours in the face of medical advice.

The need to minimise dissonance is therefore a motivator, which is capable of changing our behaviour. The subject of cognitive dissonance will be discussed further in Chapter 8.

LOCUS OF CONTROL

The work originally carried out by Rotter (1966) suggested that we either believe that we have control over our lives, or that external forces will rule our destiny. If we predominantly believe in the first statement then we are said to have an internal **locus of control**, whereas if we predominantly believe the second statement we are said to have an external locus of control (more commonly called 'internals' and 'externals').

If we belong to the group of 'internals', we will tend to believe that we can shape our future by our own actions, and will grow to believe that such actions will bring about reinforcements that we value most. Alternatively 'externals' would tend to believe that fate will lend a significant helping hand, for better or worse. The implications for motivation are immediately apparent with this theory, with our beliefs towards the shaping of our futures directing our behaviour.

Like many other aspects of our psychological make-up, parental influence plays a large part in the development of the locus of control (Levenson, 1973), and as far as health behaviour is concerned, it seems possible that it could be related to the direction of the locus of control (internal or external). Research into many different aspects of health behaviour has been carried out, and some examples of the results obtained may serve to illustrate the point.

As far as our everyday behaviour, in relation to health, is concerned, it has been found that individuals with an internal locus of control tend to be nearer to a 'normal' weight (Manno and Marston, 1972), are more likely to use contraceptives (Phares, 1976), and to be non-smokers (James *et al.*, 1965). As far as 'illness'-related behaviour is concerned, differences have again been noted. For instance, one piece of research with patients with epilepsy showed that internals tend to exhibit a lesser degree of compliance with medical advice (DeVellis *et al.*, 1980). Internals given the chance of participating in their care, and externals who were offered little participation, fared better in their treatment for myocardial infarction than those patients who were offered the option contrary to their inherent preferences (Cromwell *et al.*, 1977).

It would seem, upon a very superficial scan of some of the evidence, that we may have happened upon a major contribution to the decisions we all need to make regarding the mode and progression of treatment to our patients/clients, and that we could utilise this information in just about every sphere of practice, from the G.P.s' prescribing practices to the nurses' selection of a model of care. To do so, however, could lead us astray, because once again other factors may, and in many cases do, modify the behaviours that we may have predicted. Amongst the most obvious of these factors is the degree of difficulty involved in the task, and the individual's belief in the possibility of achieving a particular goal (**self-efficacy**) may be of immense importance when embarking upon a specific course of action (Bandura,

1986). Probably the most common example of this factor having an influence is when someone wishes to give up smoking: the more difficult it is perceived to be, the less likely it is to happen. The same is usually true of dieting in order to lose weight.

One factor that should be mentioned more specifically, possibly in relation to self-efficacy, is the lifestyle of usually less privileged and less well-educated groups within the community. Pill and Stott (1985) found that women living in a community in Wales could identify the relevance of certain lifestyles to health, but did not believe that their actions could affect the outcomes. In other words, they saw themselves as being constrained by their lifestyle. It could well prove the case that self-efficacy is the key to answering such cases, with the haul away from certain lifestyles and all that entails being simply a task which is too daunting.

Other more general factors, such as attitudes, personality, past experience and numerous others, will all have their effect.

COGNITIVE-ATTRIBUTION THEORY

In considering this theory, a few words are required to explain what is meant by the term '**attribution**'. In looking at attribution, we are attempting to find out the causes to which people attribute their own and other people's behaviour. These attributions are perceptions, and may or may not be an accurate reflection of reality. The reasons someone will give for succeeding or failing have been seen by Weiner (1972) as being dependent on two factors: locus of control and stability. Locus of control has been discussed earlier, but it can now be viewed as an attribution (did I succeed because of something that I did, or was it outside my control?). Stability refers to whether the success or failure was due to fixed or variable causes. If it was due to fixed causes, then it is likely to have the same outcome the next time the task is undertaken. If it is variable, then the outcome will be unpredictable. It will come as little surprise that subjects who persistently fail a task, and attribute it to the fixed causes, ability and task difficulty, will persevere less than those who attribute their failure to the variable causes of effort and luck (Weiner *et al.*, 1972).

NEED THEORY

Probably one of the most well known of all the theories of motivation is the hierarchy of human needs described by Abraham Maslow (1970). For some reason, this theory appears to have received greater popularity in the health professions than most others, probably because it is seen as most readily adaptable to health needs.

Maslow's theory typifies the **humanistic** approach to psychology which places considerable emphasis on studying the individual from a health rather than from a disordered basis (in contrast to the psychoanalytic approach), and places the subjective views that the individual has regarding their world at the forefront of research.

Maslow describes two types of motives which direct our behaviour. The first type are '**D-motives**' (deficiency motives), which are concerned with the reduction of drives such as hunger and thirst, obtaining love and esteem from others, and of course safety. D-motives are largely dependent upon external individuals and objects to fulfil needs; the most obvious example is utilisation of an external object (food) to fulfil a need. The preservation of the individual is one of the principal objectives of D-motives, and by implication, is instrumental in the preservation of health.

The second type of motive are the so called '**B-motives**' (being motives), and are concerned with growth. They are relatively independent of external factors, as they are concerned with the increase in pleasure drives such as curiosity. It can therefore be seen that B-motives come from within, and are unique to the individual.

In identifying human needs, Maslow has postulated that some will remain relatively unimportant until certain other needs have been satisfied, hence the hierarchical nature of the model..

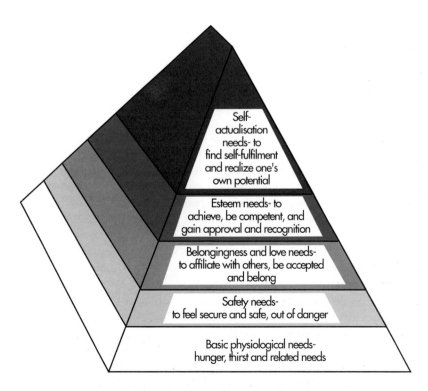

Fig. 4.1   Maslow's hierarchy of needs.

PHYSIOLOGICAL NEEDS

The physiological mechanisms which underlie certain behaviours are covered in Chapter 3, but some mention of some other aspects involved in what appears to be physiological phenomena will be given here.

The first point to note is that although some of the physiological needs can be deficiency based (such as hunger), others, such as sexual arousal, are not. Further, as will be seen, even with those behaviours which appear to be fulfilling a deficiency-based need (e.g. eating as a response to hunger), other factors need to be considered which may change our view of what we perceive as a need. Maslow pointed out the difficulties in explaining a person's motives, due to their complicated interrelations. Some needs, such as the need for oxygen, are quite naturally uncomplicated.

To state that being hungry motivates us to eat, and being thirsty motivates us to drink, would not be of particular help to this discussion, and to further state that the mechanisms are purely physiological would be misleading. The simple rule that an organism attempts to maintain a state of homeostasis does not take into account the peculiarities of anorexia, bulimia or obesity, nor does it explain the social aspects so readily observed in everyday life.

The behaviours which we engage in can be broadly divided into two categories, namely those behaviours that contribute to the satisfaction of a physiological need, and eating (and drinking) behaviours which are motivated by factors other than physiological ones. This second category involves not only the social motivation to eat, but also cultural aspects, psychological factors (see also Chapter 2), and childhood influences (see Chapter 1).

In considering the first category, both hunger and thirst will, if extreme, threaten the very existence of the organism and the whole pattern of behaviour will be towards survival. In any case, non-life-threatening hunger and thirst will still modify other behaviours, for instance contributing to a loss of concentration and hence a possible reduction of learning within an educational environment in the session immediately preceding lunch!

As far as the social motivations to eat are concerned, these can be immense and range from the well-ingrained habits of eating at certain times of the day (whether we are hungry or not) to the partaking of meals in pursuit of a business deal (similarly, whether we are hungry or not). Certainly, other people may contribute to the amount we eat, usually in a misguided attempt at being polite, and culturally we may have yet another motivation to (or not to) eat and drink certain things.

As far as sleeping is concerned, little can be said about its function except that it fulfils the need to rest and consequently to lower the activity of the organism, particularly during illness.

The need to eliminate waste products from the body is not a deficiency need, and is once again influenced by factors other than physiological ones. Psychological traumas may for instance lead to enuresis or encopresis, and on the 'everyday' level, social pressures may lead us to elimination patterns and practices which could be construed as lying outside normality (e.g. the overusage of laxatives, particularly when even the recommended usage is unwarranted). It comes as no surprise that stressful toilet training has (amongst other things) been put forward as a possible explanation for abnormal elimination patterns.

It looks, therefore, as though a physiological need is rather more than it would seem on first inspection, and as the carer is assessing needs of the patient/client, they would do well to take into account the social, cultural and childhood influences which may have led to apparently clear-cut physiologically based behaviours.

SAFETY AND SECURITY

It is only when the physiological needs are met that the individual begins to be motivated by safety needs. The scope of safety needs is enormous by virtue of the individual's unique perspectives. If we define safety as a stable, stress-free environment, it can be seen that in some instances it can prevent growth, if such growth involves risks. Indeed, Maslow maintains that if there is a choice between safety and growth, then safety will usually take precedence.

It is not difficult to observe this sort of motivator in everyday life; it may take the form of an unwillingness to embark upon a course of action which has an uncertain outcome (such as starting a small business), to over-insuring ourselves against all eventualities.

One aspect of this motivator that health professionals may like to ponder is this: what constitutes safety when considering seeking medical advice? The question is a fascinating one on at least two counts. Firstly, we have to consider whether the individual considers that the seeking of medical advice will enhance his safety in the long term. This must certainly be the case with many of us who take the view that the sooner the ailment is treated, the sooner we will be able to return to a more stable lifetime. Here, though, we may like to consider the second aspect, namely how the individual may attempt to maintain his psychological safety within the context of seeking medical advice. Certainly, upon receiving a verdict that we find worrying, we may evoke a whole range of defence mechanisms (see Chapter 10). Alternatively, the individual may attempt to preserve their psychological safety by not seeking medical advice in case they are told something that they may find difficult to cope with (for instance, when finding a breast lump, a woman may not seek medical advice in case she is told that she has cancer).

LOVE AND BELONGING NEEDS

We are all familiar with the old saying that suggests that we all need to be loved; for Maslow this rather selfish motivator (which he calls **D-love**) can have an unpleasant side, as the individual resorts to somewhat devious strategies to achieve the tenderness and frequently the sexual satisfaction that is craved. The other side of the coin is a more 'giving' type of love (**B-love**), which involves a more generous interchange of emotions, and is generally thought of as more rewarding in the long term than D-love, although the satisfaction of the deficiency need is required in order for growth to take place.

SELF-ESTEEM NEEDS

Once again, the emergence of **self-esteem** as a motivator will only take on significance if the three preceeding needs have been satisfied. The achievement of self-esteem will be the result of being recognised and appreciated by others for the mastery that we have achieved in one direction or another. The implications for the patient or relative who are not made an integral part of the care that is being given, and hence may feel inferior, may involve difficulty in coping following discharge and more dependent behaviour on subsequent admissions.

The student who is required to move from one experience to another may also suffer from a lack of self-esteem because of an inability to master such a diversity of skills, quite apart from the difficulties of never having enough time to feel as though they belong in a particular place.

SELF-ACTUALISATION

Maslow sees the highest form of need as quite distinctly different from the lower needs, and sees its achievement as a relative rarity. Highlighting this difference, Maslow identified '**metaneeds**', which are in fact growth ('B') values, which are usually only of importance to the older individual who has at least partially fulfilled the lower needs.

Metaneeds are concerned with more nebulous needs such as 'goodness' and 'truth' and contribute to what Maslow terms as 'full humanness'.

Maslow attributes certain characteristics to the **self-actualising** individual:

(1) They perceive reality efficiently.
(2) They can tolerate uncertainty.
(3) They can accept themselves and others with more tolerance.
(4) Because of their greater self-knowledge, they are more spontaneous in thought and actions.
(5) They tend to be more problem-centred than self-centred.
(6) They have a greater need for privacy.
(7) They tend to be more independent, as they are more concerned with fulfilling their inner potential than with seeking approval or rewards.
(8) They are more creative and innovative.
(9) They have a concern for mankind which is typified by their abhorrence of cruelty and injustice.
(10) They tend to have deep meaningful relationships with a few people.
(11) They tend to have a sense of humour which excludes the mockery of individuals.
(12) They are capable of a deep appreciation of life.

Rogers (1951) sees the individual as having one basic tendency, namely the motivation to **self-actualise**, and agrees with Maslow's assumption that such a motivation is innate.

Maslow's theory goes at least some way in helping us to prioritise care (Wallingham-Smith, 1986), or at least activities of living (Roper *et al.*, 1980), and gives us some direction to go when the physiological needs have been met. Its apparent willingness to be used as a model around which we can plan care is to a great extent offset by the complexities of each individual's unique set of experiences and circumstances, which will dictate if and how he will meet his needs. Maslow pointed out that there are great cultural differences in, for instance, how the individual meets their esteem needs, and further that there are occasions where the higher order needs emerge when lower needs have been frustrated (such as in the case of the individual who is incapable of meeting their physical needs due to illness or disability).

ACHIEVEMENT MOTIVATION

The motivation to achieve can be likened to Maslow's **self-esteem** needs which places emphasis on mastery. Achievement motivation has its most direct applications in occupational psychology and has been most extensively researched in this connection.

The individual's need to achieve (nAch) has been measured in a variety of ways by different researchers. McClelland *et al.* (1953) used pictures and asked subjects to make up stories about them (**thematic apperception test**-'TAT') and then calculated the amount of achievement themes that emerged. French and Thomas (1958) presented subjects with unsolvable anagrams and timed how long the subjects persisted with them, whereas Atkinson and Litwin (1960), in asking subjects to recall tasks on a test, noticed that by virtue of those tasks remembered that were left uncompleted, a motivation to avoid failure was evident. This fear of failure appears to make certain individuals avoid certain tasks.

The need to achieve is not constant with every task that we embark upon, and Atkinson and Litwin went on to postulate that the strength of a tendency to approach a situation with a view to success is dependent on both our need to achieve and our objective analysis of the possibility of the chances of success. This has become known as the expectancy valence theory. The implications of such a theory could account for the subjects we choose to study, and even our decisions to leave a job or course of study.

INTRINSIC AND EXTRINSIC MOTIVATION

It remains a fact that humans can confound even the best of motivation theories by, for instance, overcoming fear of failure, or even doing things which are completely out of character. There is however a very close link between achievement need and intrinsic motivation. It is therefore appropriate at this stage to briefly discuss **intrinsic** and **extrinsic motivators**.

Intrinsic motivators are the stronger and more enduring of the two, and can be described as a drive from within. Curiosity and interest are the major intrinsic motivators, and this is seen perhaps within ourselves when we are learning.

Extrinsic motivators involve the use of incentives which can be either positive or negative, and both are at best an artificial means of directing behaviour. The positive incentives revolve around such rewards as money, conditions of work, praise, encouragement etc. Negative incentives include punishment, fear of failure and **anxiety**.

Quite naturally, the directing of behaviour by extrinsic incentives is far from ideal, and if possible, they should be discontinued (gradually) if they are being used to help patients/clients to acquire, for instance, life skills, and the goal has been achieved. The overall aim of any such programme should be to foster intrinsic motivation if at all possible, even if extrinsic incentives were necessary for the initial activation of a behaviour.

EQUITY THEORY

The question of why we do the jobs we do, and the degree of satisfaction or otherwise that we experience whilst we do them, must be one of our most important considerations, both from a personal and a managerial viewpoint.

One theory which attempts to explain our motivation at work is the **equity theory** (Adams, 1963; Berkowitz and Walster, 1976), which suggests that an individual's motivation is largely influenced by how the individual feels she is being treated by those around her. The degree of equity is defined in terms of a ratio of an individual's input into a job to the outcomes from it, as compared to another person's.

In order to give an idea of how the individual forms judgements regarding input and outcomes, some examples of what we may regard as inputs and outcomes are listed. The list is by no means exhaustive, and most of us can (and indeed as an exercise, should) add to the list.

Inputs
Education (Pym, 1969)
Intelligence
Experience (Pym, 1969)
Training
Skill (Pym, 1969)
Age (Pym, 1969)
Gender
Ethnic background

Social status
Job effort
Outcomes
(Positive)
Pay (Homans, 1961; Pym, 1969)
Satisfaction intrinsic to the job (Herzberg, 1966)
Satisfactory supervision (Katz *et al.*, 1950)
Seniority benefits
Fringe benefits (Herzberg *et al.*, 1959)
Job status and status symbols (Brown, 1978)
(Negative)
Monotony
Poor working conditions
Fate uncertainty (Herzberg *et al.*, 1959)

The theory therefore places great emphasis on group influences and the individual's perception of others. The point regarding perceptions is a vital one, for it appears that in forming a judgement about our inputs and outcomes, we are highly subjective, and react on our individual perceptions rather than an objective analysis. These perceptions are frequently inaccurate, particularly when estimating the salaries of others (Lawler, 1971).

Achieving equity can be an uphill and often impossible task, either because an inbalance does genuinely exist, or the individual's perceptions are distorted. Whatever the reasons, we now need to consider what could happen if equity does not exist. We do not have to search very far to find a ready answer, in fact towards a set of very ready solutions.

Firstly, the individual can alter their 'inputs' (for instance, if they consider that they are underpaid, they may do less work in order to compensate). Alternatively, they may decide to alter the outcomes by claiming for large amounts of overtime which previously they had not bothered with. It may well be the case that the imbalance is too great to adjust, in which case the individual may leave the job.

Many of us feel, at times, that our workload is too heavy, nobody (least of all our managers) understands our burden, and just about everyone is better off than we are. These are of course normal reactions in the short term, but manifesting over a lengthy period of time they can often lead to disastrous results. Some of the implications for managers (or perhaps more especially, potential managers) will therefore require some discussion.

SOME IMPLICATIONS FOR MANAGERS

It would seem logical that if the individual's stability, performance and happiness at work is dependent upon the equity between the input and the outcomes, then an effective manager must be in a position to alter at least some of the factors, should the need arise. This is not always possible, and

the more complex the management structure is, the less likely it becomes. Conversely, a simpler structure with all employees responsible to one or two individuals who have 'executive' powers would make the possibility of maintaining equity more likely. Certainly, if the correct appraisal system is used for staff, and individual needs are assessed on a regular basis (and acted upon), then many difficulties and misconceptions can be resolved before they become unmanageable.

Possibly the easiest 'reward' to manipulate is 'satisfactory supervision' which refers to the quality of supervision that we receive from managers, the relationships that this entails, the guidance we receive, and by implication, the style of leadership which is employed.

CONCLUSIONS

The approaches to the study of motivation are many and varied, and there is no real dividing line between what makes us the people we are, and what directs our behaviour. Indeed one will influence the other throughout our lives, and although we may be able to identify factors that will motivate a person to do certain things, to assume that any human being will react in the same way as another human being would be taking assumption too far. This is not to say that certain aspects of certain behaviours under certain conditions cannot be directed at all, given the correct motivators.

SUMMARY

Several approaches have been discussed, and the direction of the discussion focused on two main areas, namely health behaviour and work.

The study of **ethology** provides us with an interesting question, namely what is instinctual behaviour, and what is learned. The fact that instincts exist must not be ignored, but their strength and direction continue to be the subject of much debate.

Psychoanalytic theory also refers to instincts and drives, and the death (**thanatos**) and life (**eros**) instincts form an important part of this school of thought, accounting for many of our adult behaviours.

The **dissonance** which emerges as a result of having mutually exclusive cognitions towards a behaviour can also create a motivation inasmuch as we will strive to reduce the amount of dissonance, and hence a change of behaviour may result (e.g. smoking).

The perceptions that we have about the events happening to ourselves and others can, according to some researchers, be seen as dividing us into those who see their actions as having a significant influence over their lives (internal **locus of control**), and those who see outside influences as having the major impact (external locus of control). The direction of our locus of control has been seen as one of the determinates of health behaviour, although it may be modified by other factors such as the difficulty of the task (self-efficacy). The cognitive attribution model suggests that the stability of perceived causes may affect our behaviour.

Maslow's hierarchy of needs puts forward the suggestion that human needs are hierarchical, with the physiological needs being the most basic, and the individual striving for **self-actualisation**. Broadly, Maslow identifies deficiency and growth needs, although self-actualising individuals are attempting to fulfil a different type of need (metaneeds).

The individual's need to achieve has been investigated, and has its most direct application to occupational psychology. The individual's fear of failure has been highlighted as one of the major indicators for future success.

We may be motivated by rewards, either positive or negative, although such **extrinsic motivators** are not as strong or as long lasting as **intrinsic motivators** such as curiosity or interest.

The individual, according to equity theory, perceives their inputs into a job, and the outcomes that they receive in terms of the inputs and outcomes of others. Input should be equal to outcomes if the individual is to maximise his potential.

REFERENCES

* indicates a standard text or article

Adams, J.S. (1963) Towards an understanding of inequity. *Journal of Abnormal and Social Psychology* **67**, 422–436.*

Allport, G.W. (1981) *Pattern Growth in Personality*. Holt Rinehart Winston, New York.

Atkinson, J.W. and Litwin, G.H. (1960) Achievement motive and test anxiety conceived as a motive to approach success and avoid failure. *Journal of Abnormal and Social Psychology* **60**, 52–63.*

Berkowitz, L. and Walster, E., eds (1976) *Equity Theory: Towards a General Theory of Social Interaction. Advances in Experimental Social Psychology*, Vol. 9. Academic Press, London.

Bandura, A. (1986) *Social Foundations of Thought and Action: A Social Cognitive Theory*. Prentice-Hall, Englewood Cliffs, NJ.

Brown, R. (1978) Divided we fall: an analysis of relations between sections of a workforce. In: H. Tajfel (ed.), *Studies in Intergroup Behaviour*. Academic Press, London.

Cromwell, R.I., Butterfield, E.C., Brayfield, F.M. and Curry, J.J. (1977) *Acute Myocardial Infarction: Reaction and Recovery*. C.V. Mosby, St. Louis. (Quoted in Fitzpatrick, R., Hinton, J., Scrambler, G. and Thompson, J. (1984) *The Experience of Illness*. Tavistock, London.

DeVellis, R.F., DeVellis, B.M., Wallston, B.S. and Wallston, K.A. (1980) Epilepsy and learned helplessness. *Basic and Applied Social Psychology* **1**, 241–253.

Festinger, L. (1957) *A Theory of Cognitive Dissonance*. Stanford University Press, Stanford.*

French, E.G. and Thomas, F. (1958) The relation of achievement motivation to problem-solving effectiveness. *Journal of Abnormal and Social Psychology* **56**, 45–48.

Herzberg, F. (1966) *Work and the Nature of Man*. World, Cleveland.

Herzberg, F., Mausner, B. and Synderman, B. (1959) *The Motivation to Work*. Wiley, Chichester.

Homans, G.C. (1961) *Social Behaviour: Its Elementary Forms*. Routledge & Kegan Paul, London.

James, W.H., Woodruff, A.B. and Werner, W. (1965) Effects of internal and external control upon changes in smoking behaviour. *Journal of Consulting Psychology* **29**, 184–186.

Katz, D., Maccoby, N. and Morse, N. (1950) *Productivity, Supervision and Morale in an Office Situation*. University of Michigan, Institute for Social Research, Ann Arbor. (Quoted in: Vroom, V.H. (1964) *Work and Motivation*. Wiley, New York.)

Lawler, E.E. (1971) *Pay and Organisational Effectiveness*. McGraw-Hill, New York.

Levenson, H. (1973) Multidimensional locus of control in psychiatric patients. *Journal of Consulting and Clinical Psychology* **41**, 397–404.

Manno, B. and Marston, A.R. (1972) Weight reduction as a function of negative covert reinforcement (sensitisation) versus positive covert reinforcement. *Behaviour Research and Therapy* **10**, 201–207.

Maslow, A.H. (1954) *Motivation and Personality*. Harper, New York.*

McClelland, D.C., Atkinson, J.W., Clark, R.W. and Lowell, E.L. (1953) *The Achievement Motive*. Appleton-Century-Crofts, New York.

Phares, E.J. (1976) *Locus of control in personality*. General Learning Press, New York.

Pill, R. and Stott, N.C.H. (1985) Concepts of illness causation and responsibility: some preliminary data from a sample of working class mothers. *Social Science and Medicine* **16**, 43–62. (Quoted in Wilkinson, S.R. (1988) *The Child's World of Illness*. Cambridge University Press, Cambridge.)

Pym, D. (1969) Education and the employment opportunities of engineers. *British Journal of Industrial Relations* **7**, 42–51.

Rogers, C.R. (1951) *Client-Centered Therapy*. Houghton Mifflin, Boston.

Roper, N., Logan, W.W. and Tierney, A.J. (1980) *The Elements of Nursing*. Churchill Livingstone, Edinburgh.

Rotter, J.B. (1966) Generalised expectancies for internal versus external locus control of reinforcement. *Psychological Monographs* **80**, 1–28.*

Wallingham Smith, S.A. (1986) Care of the multi-injured patient. *Care of the Critically Ill* **2**(1).

Weiner, B. *et al.* (1972) *Theories of Motivation: From Mechanism to Cognition*. Markham, Chicago.

SUGGESTED READING

Evans, P. (1989) *Motivation and Emotion*. Routledge, London. (Chapter 9 gives an interesting account of arousal and motivation.)

Ewen, R.B. (1980) *An Introduction to Theories of Personality*. Academic Press, New York. (Chapter 9 gives a very readable account of the work of Carl Rogers and Abraham Maslow.)

CHAPTER 5

COMMUNICATION

'All life therefore comes back to the question of our speech, the medium through which we communicate with each other; for all life comes back to the question of our relations with one another'.

HENRY JAMES

INTRODUCTION

Communication is a subject which appears regularly (or should do) on most curricula for health professionals. Its prominence, and indeed its very inclusion, indicates that this most basic of interactive skills is either something which, for all the communicating we do, is still not done effectively, or its application to novel situations (as in clinical practice, teaching etc.) requires us to learn new skills. In fact both are correct, although it is the former which is probably the more disconcerting, and possibly something that we might choose to ignore.

The subject of communication covers a wide range of topics, and this chapter attempts to give an overview of some of the more important ones. The communication process, and the manner in which we impart messages will be examined, as will the topic of **transactional analysis** which attempts to explain our patterns of communication in terms of '**ego states**'. Communication as a subject is not only confined to this chapter, and numerous references to communication in connection with health care, teaching etc. will be found in other chapters.

In experiencing an angry response from student nurses during a tutorial on communication, Barnes (1983) speculated that, particularly in the early part of training, nurses experience great anxiety because of a general lack of proficiency in their work, and 'feel the one area they can safely ignore is that of relating to patients'.

We all probably like to think that communication is as simple and straightforward as the equation below, involving two people (X and Y), illustrates:

X communicates message → Y hears and acts upon message.

The factors involved in X communicating and Y perceiving the message accurately are numerous, but before these are examined, a brief overview of how such interactions develop would serve as a useful basis for later discussions.

THE EMERGENCE OF SOCIAL INTERACTION

Bruner (1974) maintains that a child should have a multitude of skills in place before they can communicate effectively using language. Visual and auditory perception and the motor abilities associated with mouth and tongue movement are probably the more obvious skills, but alongside these are the social aspects required to initiate and maintain an interaction.

Crying is the first communication initiated by the baby in the first weeks of life, and is quite simply a way to convey to his caretakers that he has a need for something. Unfortunately, many parents are initially at a loss to interpret the need so hence the communication is rather ineffective. The baby does, however, get fed, changed and cuddled, not so much as a result of interpreting the cry, but more because (usually) the mother has interpreted the context of the cry (Swanwick, 1984). For instance, if the baby wakes up and cries, the mother may assume that, since the previous feed was 4 hours earlier, the baby is hungry.

The first two-way communication appears to be eye contact and mutual looking. The prolonged/mutual looking engaged in by a mother and her baby becomes a form of communication in itself (Stern, 1977)

In looking at mothers feeding their infants, Kaye (1977) noted that the infants do not feed continuously, but rather in 'bursts', which diminish as the child becomes satiated. When sucking ceases the mother will tend to encourage the infant to take more feed by talking to them. One conclusion that can be drawn from this 'on/off' sucking behaviour is that it allows for social interaction, which may form the basis of learning the rules of holding a conversation.

Throughout the first year especially, the mother and child develop the patterns of looking in a more sophisticated way. For example, the mother usually attempts to give the child who is looking at something a reason for looking, e.g. 'Are you looking for your Dad?', whilst at the same time providing gaps in the conversation in order for a response to be given by the child. In other words the mother will behave as though the baby is capable of giving a coherent response to her comments or questions. This 'turn taking' (or 'the dance' as Stern calls it) is thought to be an important component in the development of social interaction.

Further research has indicated the existence of an 'active listening phase' in the first 6 months (Berger and Cunningham, 1983) which progresses to more speech discrimination in the second 6-month period. Furthermore it was found that infants with Down's syndrome were more likely to vocalise whilst their mothers were talking to them than were normally developing infants.

The interactions engaged in by the mother and her child in these early weeks and months may be disrupted by factors on both their parts. On the part of the child, early illness and hospitalisation may interfere with the process of early exchanges by virtue of the difficulties that they have in responding to the mother (e.g. due to artificial ventilation). On the part of the mother, such factors as depression (as mentioned in Chapter 1) can seriously disrupt the communication process.

COMMUNICATION NOISE

It may now be an appropriate juncture to return to our equation mentioned at the beginning of the chapter. We have looked at numerous developmental aspects which affect our communication, but given that X is still communicating (regardless of his developmental background), factors which will interfere with Y hearing and acting upon the message need to be examined. For this reason we will now introduce a new factor into the equation:

X communicates message $\rightarrow$ NOISE $\rightarrow$ Y hears and acts upon message.

Noise in terms of communication does not necessarily only refer to the audible sort of noise, such as other people talking, that we would expect. Instead it refers generally to anything that will interfere with communication channels and will prevent X's message reaching Y in its entirety, and Y perceiving it correctly. Put like this of course, the list appears to be endless but includes psychological factors such as attitudes, fear, cognitive factors (maybe the person does not have the knowledge to comprehend our message), as well as the more familiar factors such as physical interference from fatigue, physical discomfort, etc.

We cannot altogether rule out that Y does not particularly feel inclined to receive the message from X for a variety of reasons:

(1) Y does not like X.
(2) Y does not think X's message relevant.
(3) Y thinks he has something better to say than X.
(4) Y is not motivated to listen.
(5) Y is trying to anticipate what X will say.
(6) Y has something else on his mind.
(7) Y is prejudiced against the subject X is talking about.

Verbal communication therefore has its definite drawbacks not least of all from a language and audibility point of view. If you need further convincing try the following exercise and see what happens. At the end of this exercise it may be a good idea to discuss amongst yourselves some more serious implications for our communications with patients.

CHINESE WHISPERS

(1) Get together in a group of about eight people.
(2) Select a reader who will start the message off.
(3) With only the reader and the first person to take the message in the room, the reader should give the following message:

'Please prepare a bed for Mr Stanley Adams, who is 67 years old, suffering from congestive cardiac failure, and will be transferred from Newbert Ward. His daughter can be contacted after 13.15 h at her business address in Canterbury.'

(4) Repeat the message once more.
(5) The recipient gives the message to the next person, and so on.
(6) Be careful not to allow anyone else to listen.
(7) See what you end up with!

NON-VERBAL COMMUNICATION

Naturally verbal communication alone is just a part of the overall process; serious consideration needs to be given to the role played by non-verbal communication.

During any encounter we emit a variety of verbal and non-verbal signals, which may or may not be intentional. These signals enable the other party to understand our message. Verbally, we use tone and pitch of voice (as well as our choice of words) to indicate the severity or humour of the message, and indeed our mood at the time.

Having established how a message can be manipulated verbally, a situation familiar to most of us may illustrate how it can go wrong when divorced from non-verbal communication. Consider for a moment how often, following a telephone conversation, we are left with a sense of confusion because we were not certain whether the communicator was being serious, or joking, or being sarcastic. The uncertainty that we are left with is frequently a result of not being able to see the person who was giving the message.

Sometimes, though, we actually experience confusion when we both see and hear the communicator. Once again a familiar scenario could serve to

illustrate the point. How often do we not believe what someone is telling us, even when we have no evidence to the contrary? The discussion involved in both of these scenarios centres around our use of verbal communication in conjunction with non-verbal communication.

PHYSICAL APPEARANCE

We very often form opinions about people on our first meeting, frequently before a word is spoken. We often categorise people as 'hard' or 'motherly' or 'miserly' just by looking at them. We naturally take notice of how a person dresses, whether they are fat or thin, tall or short, and how they wear their hair. Later we will simultaneously observe many different non-verbal cues in order that we may collect data about the person, and in time, combined usually with verbal cues, more concrete opinions are formed. Frequently it takes a considerable amount of such data before a first impression is either confirmed or altered.

One theory which attempts to explain why instant impressions are formed is concerned with an individual's facial features and the impressions they may create. The schematic faces all have quantitative differences in relation to: (1) the distance between the eyes; (2) height of the eyebrows; (3) position of the nose; (4) length of the nose; (5) position of the mouth. Individuals are asked to rate each face according to mood, age, intelligence, and energy (Brunswick and Reiter, 1937). The experiment reveals how we judge schematic faces, but their application to how we judge real faces is relatively difficult to assess. However, a search which would not be too exhaustive will find someone (perhaps ourselves) who never trusts a person whose eyes are too close together, or who will attribute 'miserly' behaviour to someone with a small mouth.

Allport (1961) attributes many of our perceptions to a variety of associations of ideas, particularly when judgements are about age and temperament. For instance, we may look at an elderly couple and associate 'kindly' grandparent qualities with them. We may, of course, be stereotyping on a more personal basis, namely: 'he looks like Mr Smith, I don't like Mr Smith, therefore I don't like him either'. We may even inherit our rules of judgement from our parents or others that are trusted. If you wish to see just how comprehensive first impressions can be, you may wish to try this exercise:

(1) Choose some photographs of people known to you.

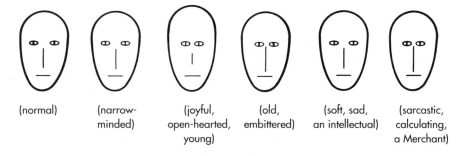

| (normal) | (narrow-minded) | (joyful, open-hearted, young) | (old, embittered) | (soft, sad, an intellectual) | (sarcastic, calculating, a Merchant) |

Fig. 5.1 Brunswick Reiter Schematic Faces. Various features, separately and in combination, appear to affect our judgements at least of schematic faces. But is it so reliable in real life?

(2) Making sure that they do not know anyone in the photographs, show them to your group.

(3) Ask them to comment on each photograph in terms of the subject's temperament, intelligence and occupation.

(4) Compare what you know about the subjects with what members of your group say about them.

(5) Discuss amongst yourselves how reliable the first impressions were.

The results of the above exercise frequently yield comparatively large amounts of emphatic judgements (which incidently are usually wrong!). The implications for health professionals cannot be overstated, especially if we act upon our first impressions.

It does not usually take long, however, for more 'mobile' aspects of non-verbal communication to emerge in order to enable us to make more reliable judgements.

FACIAL EXPRESSIONS

Our facial expression, often combined in context with the subject in hand (whether giving or receiving the message), can give us immediate feedback about the other person's reaction to a situation or message. Additionally, important information may be gleaned to supplement the verbal message.

It would appear that one of the prime functions of facial expressions is to communicate emotion (Argyle, 1983), principally happiness, surprise, fear, sadness, anger, disgust/contempt and interest (Ekman, 1972), with the mouth and eyebrows carrying significant amounts of information, with movements such as frowning, smiling, raising eyebrows and pouting.

While facial expression is in the main easy enough to interpret, it is also easy to fake. For instance, we can attribute happiness to smiling, and sadness to frowning, surprise and disbelief to raising eyebrows and sulking to pouting. We really need to ask ourselves how often we smile when conversing with a person whom we do not like, or who is saying something we are not particularly happy to hear. Some people will feign puzzlement when told something with which they disagree.

It is precisely the ability to manipulate facial expressions (as well as other non-verbal signs) which enables us to give someone the impression that we are interested in what they are saying, whereas in reality, only a small part of the dialogue (if any at all) is of interest to us. Combined with other signs such as hand movements, head movements (nodding, shaking etc.), eye contact, we can enhance both the message we are giving as well as projecting the impression to the communicator that we are interested in what they are saying.

The perception of facial expression is something that most of us would regard as one of the easiest indicators of how an interaction is progressing. Recent research however, is beginning to identify groups of people who experience difficulty in this area. In research which investigated discrimination of facial expression of emotion (Cooley and Norwicki, 1989) it was

found that depressed patients were slower in discriminating facial expression of emotions than were non-depressed subjects, thus providing us with a possible explanation, at least in part, of the poor interpersonal skills of this particular group.

Difficulties in processing information of facial expressions have also been found in schizophrenic subjects (Grosser *et al.*, 1990), and by comparing adolescent schizophrenics with adult schizophrenics, the likelihood of the effect being due to the duration of the disease or institutionalisation has been largely discounted. This adds credence to the view that the disease itself could be the cause of the phenomenon.

Both of the above pieces of research draw the conclusion that there is an apparent defect of some kind within the non-verbal processing system that to some extent may affect the subjects' response (or lack of it) to interpersonal contacts, in other words the abnormal perception may result in behavioural manifestations. Perceptual defects have also been suspected with autistic subjects (Hobson *et al.* 1988), who similarly displayed difficulties in recognising bodily expressions of emotion.

EYE CONTACT

If you were to ask people what was the one non-verbal cue that would lead them to suspect that someone was being less than honest, they would probably reply that avoiding eye contact was the dominant feature. When listening to a message, if we avoid eye contact the message giver would probably think that we were not listening. If on the other hand we attempt to impart a message with verbal sincerity, including using the appropriate tone and pitch of voice, but avoiding eye contact, the receiver is likely not to believe us.

Eye contact, or lack of it, can also be an indication of intimacy, hostility, submissiveness, or more commonly shyness. As will be seen later eye contact can be avoided in many other ways apart from just looking away.

PHYSICAL PROXIMITY

The distance that we keep between ourselves and the person we are talking to can vary considerably depending on the situation and circumstances. The study of personal space is known as proxemics (Hall, 1959).

We do not have to look far to see an individual's personal space dictating their actions. For example, we can observe a new passenger getting on a bus, and see where she will sit. Will she choose a seat with somebody occupying an adjacent seat if seats with spaces either side are available?

Most of us are very aware that we do not feel comfortable if distant acquaintances invade our most intimate body space voluntarily (as distinct from in a crowd). This sort of closeness normally would indicate either loving intimacy (which would require mutual consent) or hostility.

A four-point classification of body proximity with approximate distance between the parties may serve to illustrate the point (Hall, 1963):

Intimate   0–1.5 ft
Casual/personal 1.5–4 ft
Social/consultative 4–12 ft
Public 12 ft or more.

The accompanying verbal and non-verbal signs, such as tone of voice, touching, smiling, etc., will further define a situation although frequently the situation is defined by other outside factors, such as travelling on a crowded train, or being at a party, in which case the personal space has to become modified just for that particular occasion. We can nevertheless, maintain some control, for instance we may wait for an empty train, or at a party go and talk to someone in the kitchen (or indeed spend a very long time getting a drink!). We all know of these situations and how we cope with them, but now it may be appropriate to consider the patient who is immobile either in bed or in a chair and the patient's contact with carers.

Usually as time goes on the patient will redefine his personal space because of the care he needs to receive (although this does not always happen). As health professionals, we need to appreciate that the patient will feel uncomfortable, particularly if his intimate space is invaded too abruptly (although with many therapeutic procedures this is difficult to avoid). If at all possible when admitting a patient, do not assume that your definition of a 'comfortable' distance is the same as his. Instead ask him if he minds you sitting close or distant when recording details on your first contact. In other words, if circumstances permit, treat their personal space as their property, which you need their permission to invade.

The whole situation is further complicated when we consider that different cultures have different definitions of intimate body space, for instance the intimate limit for a Western European is about 3 ft, whereas for some Mediterranean races it could be half this distance (Morris, 1977). The differences are of little consequence if we never mix with individuals of different cultures, but problems may arise when we do. In brief, if our personal space values are far larger than the person we are talking to then we may be viewed as 'standoffish', and if our values are significantly less we may be viewed as threatening.

There are other factors which may influence our personal space. In order to feel comfortable, some groups of people need to have larger spaces between themselves and others. One such group are those people with schizophrenia (Horowitz, 1968), and another is those demonstrating paranoid behaviour, with a history of violence (Hildreth et al., 1971). Both of these groups are likely to feel threatened by someone invading their space if there is no means for them to escape, and this space needs to be carefully assessed in order to prevent a potentially explosive situation.

POSTURE

The posture that we adopt can tell others a great deal about not only us but also the situation we are engaged in, although once again it should not be considered in isolation.

It would be ridiculous to consider merely the postures of sitting and standing as indicators of a situation on their own, although the manner in which they are done and the pattern they follow may yield considerable information. Whether we are relaxed in our movements or tense can for instance indicate how nervous we are at an interview. The way a person stands when engaged in conversation can possibly tell us whether the person is bored or tired (possibly by slouching) or whether the person is ready for action.

One of the most interesting phenomena of posture is that of 'mirroring', which can give a clue as to the intimacy between the two people. Mirroring (or postural echo) is when during the course of an encounter two or more people adopt similar postures, such as leaning forward or crossing legs etc. Mirroring is very much an unconscious action in which the parties attempt to identify with each other in an affiliation process. Hence we are saying 'I am like you/I understand you'.

As a simple exercise, watch people around you, possibly in a rest room or in a canteen, who are engaged in conversation. If possible, try to choose people whom you know are friends, and watch how similar the posture is for each party.

Like most other forms of non-verbal communication mirroring can be manipulated, for example in the counselling situation. The client may adopt a posture of sitting on the edge of the chair and leaning forward. The counsellor is more likely to encourage the client to express themselves more clearly if they adopt a similar position. Many offices of senior personnel now have easy chairs and coffee tables in which customers/clients/employees may feel they can talk on a more informal basis, and more mirroring can be facilitated if both parties have equal 'props' (as distinct from one party sitting behind a desk).

BODILY CONTACT

Actual bodily contact with another person is something to which most people would give a ready interpretation. The variety of contacts is enormous, and can range from intimate contacts such as stroking and kissing, to the aggressive contacts such as hitting. Once again though, manipulation of this aspect of communication is common, and indeed socially is considered desirable on occasions. The handshake, for instance, is a friendly gesture and could be construed as an intimate gesture if other forms of communication are employed (both verbally and other touching behaviours). The interesting point about this behaviour is that it is usually performed by people who have no wish to be intimate, but who only do it because etiquette demands it.

The person who does not necessarily desire the relationship to advance, whether through shyness or dislike of the other party, will usually keep verbal communication to a minimum, and probably bend forward to shake hands so that subsequently returning to an erect standing position will re-establish the space between them without the person having to take a step backwards.

Ritualistic contact and the more spontaneous intimate contacts are frequently combined to give the other party an impression of wanting closeness or wanting to be seen to be close. The prolonged handshake is often combined with prolonged eye contact and touching/holding of the clasped hand or arm with the free hand. Observing politicians (especially if they have never met) is an interesting exercise if you wish to study this phenomenon further! Certainly as Morris (1977) points out, such rituals combined with more intimate contact is normally confined to friends.

As well as intimacy, body contact can also indicate nurturance, companionship and affinity. Consider for example the bereaved relative. Why do we frequently touch them? The answer seems obvious, namely that we wish to comfort them. In fact, the answer could be a little more involved. Parkes (1972) writes, 'Help derives therefore, from the quiet communication of affectionate understanding and this can be conveyed as well by a squeeze of the hand as by speech'. So the first part to our answer could be that we wish to convey an affectionate understanding. Secondly, we may affiliate with the relatives in sharing, to a lesser extent, the sense of loss, particularly when children die (Tiety and Powars, 1975), and may demonstrate this by holding/contact behaviours. Thirdly, and most obviously, the relative may be so upset that we just feel as though we want to comfort them and sympathise.

'Guiding' is a behaviour which can have, once again, many interpretations. It can naturally have some of the same meanings as holding behaviour, if the situation and circumstances are appropriate. It is indeed a good way to open up 'touching channels' which may need to be advanced later (for instance when the results of investigations yield bad news), but conversely could lead to an interpretation of superiority or even (if they are being more than gently guided somewhere they may not want to go—such as the door) as a way of concluding an interaction in an unsatisfactory manner.

It is possible, to return to our earlier comments regarding first impressions, that we interpret the non-verbal cues and combine them with other observations on tone of voice, content of message and circumstances, and then we proceed to form a judgement. There are indeed commonalities in non-verbal behaviour, but consistency in interpretation intellectually is a difficult task because of the apparent lack of pattern to so many of our behaviours. With this as a basis we can examine some of the more common interpretations, firstly of how we can identify possible tension, and secondly how we can sometimes look a little deeper into a message other than merely listening to the words.

INDICATING TENSION

Morris (1977) identifies activities (**displacement activities**) which indicate tension in a person. The most obvious is smoking, although as with most non-verbal activities, it is necessarily the act which should lead to an interpretation rather than the deviation from the person's normal behaviour. Observe someone making a speech at a wedding, or a teacher in front of a class for the first time, and watch how their hands in particular demonstrate how nervous they feel. Behaviours such as fiddling with or rearranging notes on the desk and jangling loose change in their pockets are familiar to many of us who have watched new teachers struggle through their first sessions.

The activities a person can indulge in to reduce tension are many and varied, ranging from hand wringing or lip biting of the anxious patient, to the unnecessary adjusting of a perfect hairstyle before an encounter.

Non-verbal communication therefore is an enormous arena for investigation and interpretation and, as in most arenas, there are winners and losers, with the losers frequently being people who attempt to interpret things which, at the end of the day, just have no underlying message.

If we return to our original equation with X and Y, and our search for why Y does not always get the message as it was sent, we can add to the difficulties the fact that words alone are only a small part of communication, and in normal everyday life are supplemented heavily by non-verbal communication, without which (as in the example with the telephone conversation) messages are often misunderstood. This relates particularly to facial expression and posture (Pudovkin, 1954).

INDICATING LISTENING

Communicating has been identified as one of the essential 'activities of daily living' (Roper *et al.*, 1980), and any health professional will tell you how essential it is to gain the patient's trust and co-operation in order for treatment to succeed.

The reasons why we may not feel inclined to listen while someone is talking to us have in part been explored. Admitting several patients in succession, being too tired to be interested in the conversation or even predicting what the patient will say next (and hence miss what he actually does say) can all lead to non-verbal behaviours which may convey disinterest to the patient or client. This in turn may lead to less information being given.

It is unlikely, for many reasons however, that the communication process is as effective as it could be in such situations. Certainly the high incidence of iatrogenic illness (more specifically iatrogenic disease arising out of lack of understanding over ongoing treatment) would suggest that all is not well.

Many aspects of routine questioning may be seen by the patient/client as highly invasive, and considerable effort may need to be exerted in order to convey interest, empathy and even to disguise our emotions. It is vital therefore to give the impression that we are listening by virtue of our verbal and non-verbal behaviours.

ENCODING AND DECODING

Perhaps an appropriate place to start looking at the health care communicating problem would be to examine the processes of **encoding** and **decoding**. Encoding refers to the process of converting an idea into symbols (words). Conversely, decoding is the process by which we translate words back into ideas. In order for a communication to be effective between two or more people, the conventions for encoding and decoding need to correspond (Lantz and Stefflre, 1964).

The logical sequel to our brief explanation of encoding and decoding is to consider the extent to which conventions are shared by different groups of people, and the effect this may have on communication. Certainly, some occupational groups practically adopt their own language (Elkin, 1945) and this would have marked effects on how doctors, for instance, communicate with their patients. For example, a tumour is something that a patient may only talk about if he is talking about cancer, while a doctor would use the term to describe a swelling or overgrowth of tissue. If both the patient and the doctor were following the same conventions, the process would be uncomplicated:

Doctor
Concept: Abnormal swelling *Encoded message sent*: Tumour

Patient
Encoded message received: Tumour *Concept*: Abnormal swelling.

In other words, the patient could translate the message accurately from its encoded form, the word 'tumour', into the concept, 'abnormal swelling'. If, however, the conventions underlying the encoding and decoding are different, that is the patient has a different/restricted concept of the word 'tumour', then a different outcome will result:

Doctor
Concept: Abnormal swelling *Encoded message sent*: Tumour

Patient
Encoded message received: Tumour *Concept*: Cancer.

The conclusions that can be drawn from the above example relate to altering the conventions in a way that the message which we encode is decoded correctly. The most effective way of achieving this is by giving full explanations to the patient, or more obviously, using language which is within the patient's scope of experience. Research would appear to confirm the theory of encoding inasmuch as the patient apparently is able to recall more information given by doctors if the patient has some medical knowledge (Cassata, cited in DiMatteo and DiNicola, 1982).

ELABORATE AND RESTRICTED CODES

It would appear that there are times when we give the patient sufficient information but he interprets the message wrongly. There are other times, however, when we simply do not give enough information. For example, a patient could be told, upon discharge from his stay in hospital, to keep to a certain regime; he is most certainly more likely to comply if he has had an explanation and been given reasons for the regime. The essential difference in the two messages is that one gives only a statement or command (**restricted code**) and the other gives far more detail behind the proposed action (**elaborated code**).

The phenomenon is perhaps best observed in children, who may be given the instruction 'Do not touch' (restricted code), or 'Do not touch, because if you do, this' (whatever it is) 'will happen' (elaborated code). The work of Bernstein (1961) indicated that the restricted code was the predominant code used by lower socio-economic groups, with both codes being used by the 'middle classes'.

An apparent dominance of 'restricted code' usage would result in relatively little information being given, with minimal unprompted expansion of the message. The 'Black Report' (1980) indicates that patients from the lower social classes spend less time with their G.P. during consultations than do middle class patients, and certainly a patient only giving information within a framework of a restricted code is going to derive less satisfactory treatment than one who has virtually spontaneously described her condition or problem with appropriate elaboration.

TRANSACTIONAL ANALYSIS (BERNE)

The problem of talking with different code conventions may in many ways help us to identify where some of our communications break down. When considering our everyday instructions, it would help to obtain a more complete picture if we considered next how our feelings in relation to our behaviour patterns (**ego states**) were manifested in our interactions with others. Berne identifies only three ego states:

Parent – ego state: **exteriopsychic**.
Adult – ego state: **neopsychic**.
Child – ego state: **archaeopsychic**.
i.e., parent, adult and child.

These ego states are psychological realities during our interactions, but are changeable, depending on the circumstances, emotions, feelings, etc. Briefly, the parent ego state is one in which the individual will 'parent'-type approach. The adult ego state is characterised by an autonomous objective approach of reality. The child ego state refers to those ego states from early childhood which are still active.

In any of these 'states' we are capable of either stimulating a response or responding to a stimulus. These transactions may be either 'crossed' or 'complementary'.

COMPLEMENTARY TRANSACTIONS

If we now return to our original equation:

$$X \text{ communicates message} \rightarrow Y \text{ hears, understands and acts upon message}$$

and modify it to

$$X \text{ stimulates} \rightarrow Y \text{ responds}$$

the participants X and Y can now be represented in their possible ego states:

For the purposes of this exercise, X is assumed to be the patient, whilst 'Y' is the carer.

X - 'I'm far from happy about my admission through Casualty the other night.'

Y - 'I know exactly what you mean. They really should get their act together.'

With this exchange, both X and Y are manifesting parent ego states.

Alternatively:

X - 'I was waiting rather a long time in Casualty, but their workload makes that inevitable.'

Y - 'That's very understanding. They are a very busy department.'
or finally:

X - 'I thought I'd never get to the ward. I haven't had a drink for ages.'

Y - 'Never mind Mr Jones, I'll make you a nice cup of tea.'

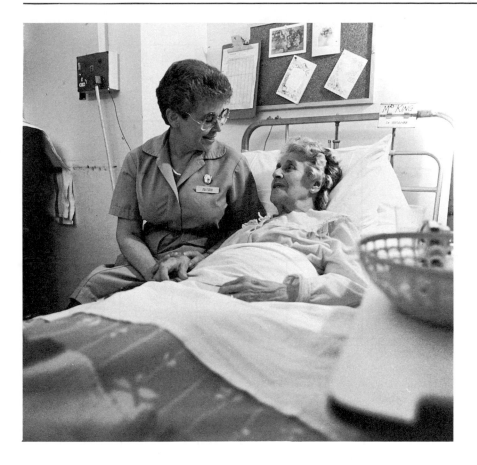

Fig. 5.2 Sometimes touch can say more than words.

As long as the transactions are complementary (any of the above), the communication will continue. It should always be remembered that often the 'response' can act as a stimulus to the other person to continue the interaction. Not all transactions are this straightforward, and the problem of interacting with someone in an incompatible (to our own) ego state needs to be considered.

CROSSED TRANSACTIONS

When a crossed transaction occurs, then the communication between the two parties will either cease or undergo disturbance in some way. Thus:

X - 'I don't have any drugs to take home.'

Y - 'So why didn't you remind me before·instead of waiting until I'm due to go off duty.'

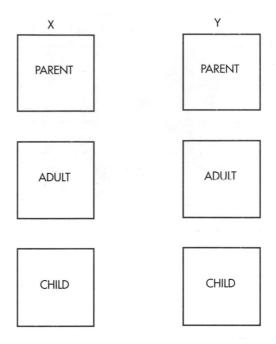

Fig. 5.3 The Ego-States.

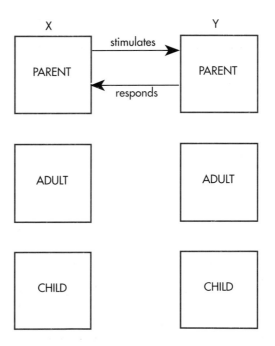

Figures 4, 5, and 6 Complementary Transactions.

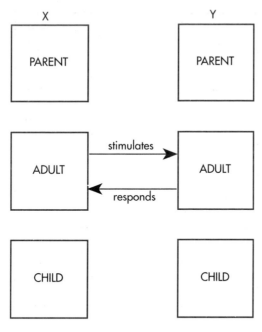

Fig. 5.5

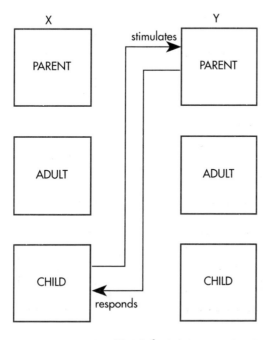

Fig. 5.6

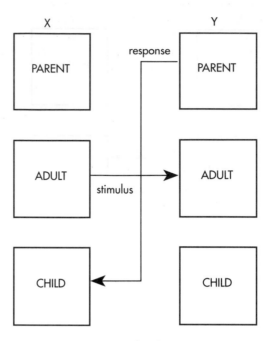

Fig. 5.7

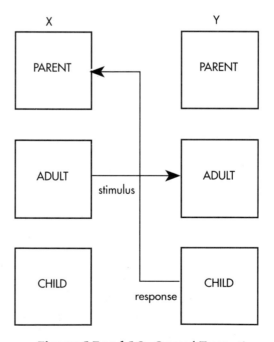

Figures 5.7 and 5.8 Crossed Transactions.

In this interaction, X has made a reasoned statement concerning his discharge and the drugs he needs (adult). The health care worker has responded in a mode other than adult (parent). Conflict will therefore occur until a 're-alignment' to a complementary pattern takes place (if it ever does).

Alternatively, Y could react to the same question in a child ego state, for instance:

'It's not my fault you haven't got them, why can't someone else sort it out for a change?'

Care must be taken to interpret both the message and the 'ego state' so that conflict does not occur, by giving a response incompatible with the stimulus. It may happen that the message has a hidden meaning (ulterior transaction). For instance:

'It's probably just me, but I don't see how this can be achieved' (adult) could really mean:

'That's a ridiculous idea!' (parent)

Conflict may therefore arise if the reply consists of a 'parent'-type explanation, with the result that the questioner may feel that he is being 'talked down to'. A more satisfactory reply could have been to ask the questioner exactly where he sees the problem, hence making him reveal his true 'ego state'.

THE PATIENT/CLIENT-CENTRED DIAGNOSIS AND COMMUNICATION

Long before any help is sought from health care professionals, the patient/client has often made a diagnosis for themselves. This diagnosis is sometimes a guess as to its medical name (e.g. angina). It is more common, however, for the diagnosis to be a combination of 'life activities' and symptoms. For instance, the patient may complain of 'feeling a tight band around my chest when I walk down the High Street'. Alternatively, the patient may make statements which can be readily translated into terminology, e.g. 'I feel sick' can be translated into nausea.

It is always a danger that the patient's actual problems may become lost within a more blanket diagnosis and a plethora of valuable information will be lost. The difficulty is essentially one of coding, as different codes are being used by the patient and, for instance, the physician. This situation is further complicated by a series of patient-centred problems being reduced, often to a single word or phrase, hence:

PATIENT	PRACTITIONER
'I'm frightened to go out'	
'I can't breathe properly'	Angina pectoris
'My arm aches'	
'I get a tight band around my chest'	

When recording the patient's history, care needs to be taken to ensure that:

(1) The patient has had an explanation (if one exists) for each of his problems.
(2) Problems are identified, if possible using the patient's own words.
(3) Explanations of treatment are given in relation to problems identified by the patient as well as those discovered by the practitioner.
(4) The resolution (or otherwise) of problems are evaluated, and the patient involved in this process if possible.

CONCLUSIONS

Effective communication is one of the crucial foundations that underlie patient assessment, treatment and the evaluation of care. In order that effective communication can take place, attention needs to be paid to the terminology used, and the type of approach to the individual. It has become apparent that without an effective communication between the health care professional and the patient, compliance with treatment, and indeed accurate identification of patient problems, becomes unlikely.

CHAPTER SUMMARY

Effective communication relies on the interaction of verbal and non-verbal communication by the sender of the message, and the correct interpretation by the recipient. The possible factors involved are summarised below.

Aspects of the communication process	Message received	Message not received
Message context	Agreed	Not agreed
Message content	Heard	Not heard
Tone of voice, appearance, facial expression, posture, proximity, eye contact, body contact, gestures	Non-verbal communication is interpreted correctly	Not interpreted correctly due to previous experience, attitude towards speaker or message, 'noise', physical blocks to non-verbal cues, e.g. telephone
Encoding convention **Elaborate/restricted codes**	Convention matches Codes match or difference agreed by participants	Different convention Mixed codes (unidentified by participants)
Ego state	Complementary transaction	Crossed transaction

REFERENCES

* indicates a standard text or article

Allport, G.W. (1961) *Pattern and Growth in Personality*. Holt, Rinehart and Winston, New York.

Argyle, M. (1983) *The Psychology of Interpersonal Behaviour*, 4th edn. Penguin, London.*

Barnes, D.M. (1983) Teaching communication skills to student nurses – an experience. *Nurse Education Today* **32**, 45–48.

Berger, J. and Cunningham, C.C. (1983) Development of early vocal behaviours and interactions in Down's Syndrome and nonhandicapped infant mother pairs. *Developmental Psychology* **19**, 322–331.

Berne, E. (1964) *Games People Play*. Penguin, New York.*

Bernstein, B. (1961) Social class and linguistic development: a theory of social learning. In: Halsey, A.H. *et al.* (eds), *Education, Economy, and Society*. Free Press, New York.

Bruner, J.S. (1974) From communication to language: a psychological perspective. *Cognition* **5(3)**, 255–287.

Brunswick, E. and Reiter, L. (1937) Quoted in Allport (1961).

Cooley, E.L. and Norwicki, S., Jr (1989) Discrimination of facial expression of emotion by depressed subjects. *Genetic, Social, and Genetic Psychology Monograph* **115(4)**, 449–465.

DiMatteo, M.R. and DiNicola, D.D. (1982) *Achieving Patient Compliance*.

The Psychology of the Medical Practitioners Role. Pergamon, New York. (Quoted in Sarafino, E.P. (1990) *Health Psychology Biopsychosocial Interactions.* Wiley, New York.)

Ekman, P. (1972) Universals and cultural differences in facial expressions of emotion. Nebraska Symposium on Motivation. University of Nebraska Press. (Quoted in Argyle (1983).)

Elkin, F. (1945) The Soldiers Language. *American Journal of Sociology* **51**, 414–422.*

Grusser, O.J., Kirchhoff, N. and Naumann, A. (1990) Brain mechanisms for recognition of faces, facial expressions and gestures: Neuropsychological and electroencephalographic studies in normal, brain lesioned and schizophrenic. Research Publication – Association of Research into Nervous and Mental Disorder, Vol. 67, pp. 165–193.

Hall, E.J. (1963) A system for notation of proxemic behaviour. *Amer. Anthropol.* **65**, 1003–26.

Hall, E.T. (1959) *The Silent Language.* Doubleday, New York.*

Hildreth, A.M., Derogatis, L. and McCusker, K. (1971) Body buffer zone and violence: a reassessment and confirmation. *American Journal of Psychiatry* **127**, 77–81.

HMSO (1980) *Inequalities in Health – Report of Research Working Group ('The Black Report').* HMSO, London.

Hobson, R.P., Ouston, J. and Lee, A. (1988) Emotion recognition in autism; Co-ordinating faces and voices. *Psychological Medicine* **18(4)**, 911–923.

Horowitz, M.J. (1968) Spatial behaviour and psychopathology. *The Journal of Nervous and Mental Disease* **146**, 24–35.

Kaye, K. (1977) Towards the origin of dialogue. In: Schaeffer, H.R. (ed.), *Studies in Mother/Infant Interaction.* Academic Press, New York.

Lantz, D. and Stefflre, V. (1964) Language and cognition revisited. *Journal of Abnormal and Social Psychology* **69**, 471–481.

Morris, D. (1977) *Manwatching – A Field Guide to Human Behaviour.* Jonathan Cape, London.*

Parkes, C.M. (1972) *Bereavement – Studies of Grief in Adult Life.* Tavistock, London.

Pudovkin, V.I. (1954) *Film Technique and Film Acting.* Vision, London. (Quoted in McDavid, J.W. and Harari, H. (1974) *Psychology and Social Behaviour.* Harper & Row, New York.)

Roper, N., Logan, W.W. and Tierney, A.J. (1980) *Elements of Nursing.* Churchill Livingstone, London.

Swanwick, M. (1984) Early language development. *Nursing* **2(22)**, 645–647.

Stern, D.N. (1977) *The First Relationship: Infant and Mother.* Fontana/Open Books, London.*

Tiety, W. and Powers, D. (1975) The paediatrician and the dying child. *Clinical Paediatrics* **14**, 585–591.

SUGGESTED READING

Argyle, M. (1983) *The Psychology of Interpersonal Behaviour*, 4th edn. Penguin, London.* (See Chapter 2 for an account of verbal and non-verbal communication.)

Berne, E. (1964) *Games People Play.* Penguin, New York.* (A very readable text on transactional analysis by its originator.)

Morris, D. (1977) *Manwatching – A Field Guide to Human Behaviour.* Jonathan Cape, London.* (An excellent book which covers the subject of non-verbal communication. See in particular the sections dealing with non-verbal leakage and displacement activities.)

Scherer, K.R. and Ekman, P. (eds) (1982) *Handbook of Methods of Non-verbal Behaviour Research.* Cambridge University Press, Cambridge. (See Chapter 1 for an excellent introduction to investigating non-verbal behaviour.)

CHAPTER 6

COGNITION AND LEARNING

'The vine that has been made to bear fruit in the spring, withers and dies before autumn.'

ROUSSEAU (1762)

Whenever we attempt to educate colleagues, patients, relatives or the general public at large, an understanding of the processes involved in the acquisition of knowledge as well as the best ways to impart information is desirable. Cognition refers to an individual's ideas, knowledge and thoughts. In examining such a vast subject we not only have to consider how an individual gains knowledge (learning), but also those factors which affect such an acquisition and indeed how a cognitive structure is formed.

Perhaps the most appropriate place to begin such a study would be to examine one such theory of cognitive development.

JEAN PIAGET AND COGNITIVE DEVELOPMENT

The work of Jean Piaget has led to a descriptive analysis of development. Piaget was a biologist completing his studies at Neuchatel in Switzerland. He had always been fascinated by how a structure evolved to its current state and on completion of his studies began to consider how mental structures had evolved. It was during his work with Binet and Simeon standardising Burt's I.Q. test in Paris, that Piaget became interested in investigating how the child had arrived at the answer he had. In other words he became increasingly interested in the processes by which the child achieved answers, especially the incorrect answers. On the basis of his research, he was offered a job as Director of Studies at the Institut J.J. Rousseau in Geneva and it was here from 1921 onwards that Piaget was to carry out most of his investigations.

In essence Piaget's theory is (1) genetic in origin (Piaget, 1950); (2) maturational; (3) hierarchical in that each stage forms the basis of the following stage (Piaget, 1952). Intellectual growth is dependent upon two major principles, namely organisation and adaptation.

Fig. 6.1 Jean Piaget.

ORGANISATION

An important feature of Piaget's work is the concept of **schemas**, namely the child's ability to organise new experiences in such a way as to classify them, not in the light of an individual experience occurring at a certain stage of development, but rather as a contribution to a stage-free cognitive structure which refers to a class of similar action sequences (Flavell, 1962). It is these sequences which give rise to their labels, hence Piaget describes the schema of sight, the schema of sucking, etc. (Piaget, 1952).

ADAPTATION

Adaptation is dependent upon two processes, namely assimilation and accommodation, which can only occur once a **schema** is in place.

Assimilation and Accommodation
Assimilation refers to the perception and interpretation of new information. Quite how new information is dealt with is dependent upon existing knowledge which may be very limited. For instance, a child will classify objects in terms of properties of that object which he has observed, hence he may have ascribed the properties of an aeroplane with something that flies and in the absence of existing information may describe a helicopter as an aeroplane.

Another process must therefore complete this system of adaptation otherwise intellectual development simply would not occur. In other words if new information is introduced, the mental structure needs to change in order that understanding takes place. This process is called **accommodation** and works in conjunction with assimilation. When both accommodation and assimilation are in balance a state of equilibrium exists. Therefore the child will see the helicopter, compare it with existing schemas and will integrate new information about the helicopter to form new mental structures.

PERIODS OF INTELLECTUAL DEVELOPMENT

In Piaget's theory there are three major periods with subperiods and stages within them.

(1) The **sensory motor period** – birth to 2 years.
(2) **Concrete operational period** – 2 years to 11 years.
(3) **Formal operational period** – 11 years onwards.

The ages which Piaget gives are only intended as averages and cannot be taken as arbitrary. The speed at which a child will progress from one stage to another is dependent upon the stage before it, and the transition from one stage to another indicates that the organisation of thought has taken place. Progression through the stages indicates a child's adaptation to a wider environment.

Sensory Motor Development (0–2 Years)

Sensory motor development is so called simply because the child is attempting to discover use and co-ordinate her motor abilities as well as perceptually exploring her environment. This period is divided into six stages.

Stage 1: *Reflex activities* (0-1 month). The baby, if healthy, arrives in this world with a complete set of innate reflexes the nature of which will change as time progresses. Piaget, in observing his own son, Laurent (Piaget, 1952), noticed that the sucking reflex underwent subtle yet significant changes in as little as 3 days following the birth. The response to environmental stimuli became more selective, insofar as he began to distinguish and localise the nipple as opposed to the surrounding skin area. In other words, accommodation was taking place. The neonate soon learns which objects can be sucked and which objects cannot, although this does not mean that the child will not continue to explore his environment, using amongst other things his mouth.

Stage 2: *Primary circular reactions* (1-4 months). Activities are centred around and focused upon the infant's own body and when a new activity is discovered it is repeated continually. It is during this stage that some co-ordination is achieved, principally hand to mouth, eye co-ordination, and eye/ear co-ordination. Towards the latter part of the stage vocalisation occurs.

Stage 3: *Secondary circular reactions* (4-8 months). Unlike the previous stage which is essentially centred around the child's body, this stage begins by the infant interacting with her environment. The infant will return to play if interrupted and will look for objects that may have been dropped. Although the concept of permanency of objects has not been fully achieved the child will nevertheless recognise and attempt to retrieve an object that has been partly covered. Random movements frequently initiate new behaviour patterns and show the beginnings of goal orientation of intentionality.

Stage 4: *Coordination of secondary schema* (9-12 months). Having learned various skills in relation to certain problems the infant can now attempt to apply them to new problems. The child's activities are now definitely intentional in nature. She will now search for objects that have been totally hidden from view. However, if the object is hidden from one location to another in view of the infant, she will still attempt to find it in the original location.

Stage 5: *Tertiary circular reactions (12-18 months).* The child is now attempting to discover cause and effect (i.e. what results certain actions will bring), and will engage in trial and error activities. She will now comprehend movements of objects from one location to another as long as she can see where the object has been placed.

Stage 6: *Beginnings of thought* (18-24 months). Mental representation begins to develop along with occasional flashes of insight. True object permanence has been achieved. Conceptual thought has begun.

The Development of the Concept of Time
It is difficult to identify the appropriate juncture at which to discuss the development of the time concept, as it permeates more than one period of development. It would appear that it develops in stages, although precise experimental verification is lacking in Piaget's theory.

The early stages in infancy are probably only concerned with a sensation of duration, although in the latter part of the first year the infant develops (through his actions) a sense of 'before and after'. At around one year of age, the child is beginning to retain a sequence of events, as demonstrated by the searching for an object which has been hidden. This capacity appears to increase quite rapidly as the child's ability to seriate events helps him to solve more complex problems, such as looking for objects which have been displaced more than once. Before the age of two, the child is beginning to recall events further in the past.

Concrete Operational Period
Before any discussion takes place about the nature of this period it may be as well to describe what Piaget means by the term '**operations**'.

In the sensory motor period, the infant is engaged in activities such as sucking, searching and moving. In other words, their actions are both observable and externalised. As the child gets older, however, these actions become more complex and tightly integrated and develop into systems of actions which become internalised. Any given operation can only gain meaning from the larger structure of which it is a part and cannot therefore exist in isolation. Put another way, 'operations' are such acts as combining, subtracting and adding within existing structures.

When the child is able to represent an object in his mind the beginning of the **concrete operational period** has been reached. The early part of this period is known as the **pre-operational stage**.

Pre-Operational Stage. *Pre-Conceptual Thought.* Piaget noticed that children during the early part of the pre-operational period begin to classify objects and events in a very elementary way that lacks adult logic. This stage lasts from about 2 years of age to about 4 years of age.

Although limited, pre-operational thought is a definite advance over the previous stage. The further development of the concept of cause and effect is seen at this phase, but obviously still within a very limited framework. Accidents which to most adults would appear as spontaneous may be observed by the child as a punishment for some misdemeanour on the part of the victim (**immanent justice**). Particular care must therefore be taken with children of this age group who are involved in accidents, especially if they are admitted to hospital, because of their facility for seeing such events as punishments.

The child is able to represent his environment in a symbolic form and distinguish between himself and objects around him. This stage is characterised by **egocentrism,** which is typified by the perception of the world from their own point of view only. Observing a child at this stage conversing with one of his peers will often reveal a very different exchange to that seen in most older children and adults, inasmuch they may appear to be expressing their thoughts out loud rather than engaging in an exchange which takes the other's point of view into consideration (**collective monologue**). When telling something to the mother (or anyone else), the child does not set the scene, but assumes it is known to the listener already, and certainly does not appear to appreciate other points of view.

The egocentricity which is such an important characteristic of this stage of development can at times lead to difficulties, particularly in its early stages of formation, i.e. around the 2–3-year-old age group. Playing together for such toddlers is not always an easy task and indeed may at times lead to some amount of discord. It is only as the child progresses through this stage and begins to integrate the wishes and demands of others, that more co-operative play begins to take place. The child in the pre-operational stage of development frequently will play in such a way so as to develop the concept of **conservation** (see below).

It is during the phase of pre-conceptual thought that the child attributes many feelings, emotions and other qualities usually associated with humans and other animals, to inanimate objects (**animism**). The family car for instance, is having a 'drink' when being filled with petrol, and a train in a

Fig. 6.2   Learning about mass, volume, area and of course movement are all part of normal play.

railway shed may be viewed as sleeping. Many popular children's stories actually foster this concept with trains talking to each other, and cars enjoying quite meaningful discussions with their owners! The concept of **animism** is also applied to many of the child's toys, particularly a favourite cuddly toy or doll who may emerge as the child's constant companion particularly at bedtime or in times of stress.

Intuitive Thought. In the latter part of the period, children become more capable of classifying than quantifying events and objects, and apply and integrate them into their developing mental operations. As a result problem solving becomes more prevalent at this stage (4–7 years) but the child does not appear capable of explaining how he has solved the problems. It is for this reason that Piaget termed this the intuitive stage of the pre-operational period.

The child is limited to handling one aspect of a stimulus at a time, usually only the most obvious physical attributes. The concept that certain properties do not alter whilst undergoing certain transformations (**conservation**) will become apparent to the child much later. In order to observe how this is manifested, try the two following simple exercises with pre-school children.

Exercise 1:
(a) Take a piece of Plasticine and form it into two equal sized balls.
(b) Ask the child if the Plasticine balls are equal in size.
(c) If the child agrees that they are equal, roll out one ball into a 'sausage' shape, allowing the child to observe what you are doing.
(d) Ask the child which of the two shapes contains the most Plasticine.

Exercise 2:
(a) Pour some water into a tumbler.
(b) With the child watching, pour the water from the tumbler into a long thin container.
(c) Ask the child whether the tumbler or the thin receptacle contains the most water.

With the first exercise it is the 'sausage' shape which is credited with having the most Plasticine, and in the second exercise the thin container with having the most water. This inability of the child to concentrate on more than one feature of a situation is called centering. Hence in Exercise 2, he is only taking account of the height of the water column. Moreover reversibility has not yet been achieved thus preventing the child from, in many instances, exploring the phenomenon further by returning the objects to their original state, e.g. the sausage-shaped Plasticine to a ball. The child finds it difficult to go back to an earlier stage of an **operation** and this is strongly connected to the fact that children at this stage pay more attention to states than transformations. In other words the child will remember the starting point of an action and also the result but will not be able, in many instances, to describe the intervening process. A simple illustration of this phenomenon is provided in the following exercise.

Exercise 3
(a) Using a pencil, stand it on its end whilst holding it perpendicular to and in contact with the surface.

(b) Move the pencil down to the surface in three stages by keeping the end of the pencil in contact with the surface and leaning it towards the surface, stopping the process three times during its transition, until it is flat against the surface.

(c) Ask the child to replicate your actions.

Commonly, the child will miss out all the intervening processes, and will merely replicate your starting and finishing points.

Piaget states that: 'It is difficult to agree as to the earliest examples of reasoning' (Piaget and Inhelder, 1951). Whilst observing his own children, he noted the emergence of a type of reasoning that, for the child, links various preconcepts, but is not as a result of true deduction or induction. Flavell (1962) describes it as: 'Centering on one salient element of an event, the child proceeds irreversibly to draw as conclusion from it some other, perceptually compelling happening'. This form of reasoning is described as **transductive**, and although the conclusion that may be reached through this form of reasoning may be correct, the mechanism by which it is reached may not have been altogether logical. The child who observes the father wearing a suit to go to work may reason that firstly he cannot go to work unless he wears a suit, and secondly, if he wears a suit he is going to work (in contrast to attending a social event or receiving guests). In attempting to explain events the child is once again using the 'cause and effect' framework developed in the **sensory motor period** in order to accommodate information that is being assimilated from the surrounding world, and this does not allow for variables such as chance (Piaget and Inhelder, 1951).

As the child interacts with the surrounding environment, the relationship between accommodation and assimilation is in a constant state of instability due to the re-aligning of observable features and events, with an ever-increasing list of possible implications and possibilities, which their rigid cognitive structure has difficulty in dealing with. The pre-operational stage is a preparation for a time when equilibrium between assimilation and accommodation can be reached by a flexible framework in which centering and non-reversibility cease to play a part.

Concrete Operations. The difference between an intuitive and a concrete operational thinker is that the latter has at their command a more coherent and integrated cognitive system, in which logic and reasoning play a key role. Greater equilibrium is present, particularly with regard to the properties of groups, a degree of cognitive stability is attained, and thinking is deductive rather than inductive. Additionally, concrete operational thought is less egocentric than the previous stage.

Centering decreases during this stage, and the concept of **reversibility** evolves, both of which lead to an ability to analyse transformations of states rather than just an incomplete comparison between states (see Exercises 1, 2 and 3). Hence the child is now aware that when a piece of Plasticine is rolled out into a sausage shape, the mass is the same as when it was a ball. Later in this period he no longer centres his attention solely on the height of a water column in a glass, but recognises other dimensions and recognises that the water in each container may be of the same volume. The child is therefore developing conservation.

Conservation does not occur suddenly, nor does it occur in all areas simultaneously. Conservation occurs in stages, at approximately the following ages:

Conservation of numbers   5–7 years
Conservation of length   7–8 years
Conservation of matter   8–10 years
Conservation of area   8–9 years
Conservation of weight   10–12 years
Conservation of volume   12–14 years.

Probably the most effective way of illustrating these different aspects of conservation is to examine some of the investigations carried out.

Conservation of Numbers. The conservation of numbers appears to develop in two stages that can be illustrated using the following exercise:

(1) Make a row of objects (buttons or coins etc.).
(2) Ask the child to take the same number from a pile near at hand and reproduce the original row.

In the first stage the child is content to make a rough figural approximation to the original row (i.e. different density but same length). In the second stage the child will match each object one by one to reproduce the original row in both length and number.

Conservation of Length.

(1) Place two sticks of exactly the same length side by side so that all extremities are in line.
(2) Ask the child if she believes that they are of equal length, to which she should reply that they are.
(3) Keeping the sticks parallel slide one of them so that its leading end is to the right of the leading end of the other stick.
(4) Ask the child which stick is the longest.

If the child has not attained conservation of length, she will normally reply that the stick which has been moved is the longest, seemingly ignoring the fact that the amount of distance that it has been advanced is equal to the space vacated.

Conservation of Matter. A typical exercise has been described earlier (using the Plasticine ball and 'sausage').

Conservation of Area.

(1) Produce two large square pieces of card to represent two meadows.
(2) Produce two smaller squares to represent two 'potato plots'.

(3) Place one 'potato plot' in each 'meadow'.
(4) Divide up one of the 'potato plots' and distribute it around one of the 'meadows'.
(5) Ask the child: 'Is there still as much room for potatoes?' 'Is there still as much room for the cows to graze?'

Once again, this form of conservation appears to emerge in stages, with the intermediate stage producing strong affirmation for the first (conservation of areas), but denial for the second (conservation of complementary areas).

Conservation of Weight. The exercise referred to earlier (conservation of matter) can be further refined by using a pair of weighing scales to show the child that each ball of clay is equal in weight, and subsequently asking the child to predict the relative weights of each following the transformation of one into the 'sausage' shape.

Conservation of Volume. A typical exercise has been described earlier using different sizes of tumbler and water.

Formal Operations (12 Years and Onwards)
The emergence of the **formal operational period** is a landmark which signals the onset of mature thought, or as Flavell (1962) describes it: '. . . the crowning achievement of intellectual development, the final equilibrium state towards which intellectual evolution has been moving since childhood.'

One of the most striking characteristics of this period is the adolescent's ability to problem solve using logical analysis and experimentation which involves possibilities rather than just reality. The adolescent is therefore departing from the previous developmental periods, as realities which would once have formed the basis of the cognitive structures are now just a part of the overall process. This period, like all the others, is dependent on the previous periods, and therefore such an evolution cannot be viewed in isolation.

The adolescent continues to classify events and objects as he did in the **concrete operational period**, but now considers the results of such operations as propositions and hence will proceed to operate further on them by attempting to make logical connections between them.

In departing from the realities as the sole determinant, the adolescent is engaging in **hypothetico-deductive reasoning**. In order to achieve a solution to the problem, an attempt will be made to identify all the possible variants involved as well as any possible combinations, and to form hypotheses which can then be tested.

Piaget's theory has not been without its critics, not least of all those who questioned his methods. However, the inclusion of the theory in this text reflects the effects that Piaget and his associates have had on much of our thinking on the developing intellect of the individual, and moreover, the possible implications for the carer who may be responsible for the child's environment.

The processes of **accommodation** and **assimilation**, as will be seen later in the text, could provide at least the beginnings of an insight as to the child's understanding of the predicament being experienced, be it illness, hospitalisation, or both. The amount of fear that a child may endure because of how new information is dealt with in relation to the child's existing knowledge can only be guessed at. We do not need to look any further than ourselves to see how frequent a child's misconceptions may be, by remembering some of our own childhood beliefs which were so real to us at the time. These misconceptions may have been relatively benign, or they may have caused us much concern, but in either case, the key to overcoming them lay in our intellect's ability to continually integrate new information and to modify our ideas accordingly. The sick child, it can be assumed, it not immune to these mental processes, and requires not only appropriate explanations, but more importantly a patient assessment of their beliefs and fears which may not be possible from discussions with the parents.

Piaget's theory can also lead us to some thoughts as to the child's development through play, and may provide us with some basic guidelines for appropriate toys and play materials. Any list which is produced for any age group would be incomplete, so the reader is advised to re-examine the stages in terms of what the child is achieving at that time, and match the activity or toy accordingly, e.g. the infant who is striving towards the achievement of object permanence will enjoy hiding games, peek-a-boo etc., as well as those toys which will enable them to explore their senses (rattles, brightly coloured objects, etc.).

OVERVIEW OF LEARNING THEORIES

Having considered how a cognitive framework is developed it is now appropriate to consider how the individual will actually learn material and as a consequence how information may be most effectively put across.

CLASSICAL CONDITIONING

The work of Pavlov is relatively well known, although its implications for human learning need to be stressed here. Pavlov's work initially involved the use of dogs, although primates were used in his later years. Briefly, the theory is concerned with reflexes, and attributes all learning to conditioning. Alternatively it can be described as responses to specific stimuli.

The reflexes that Pavlov described were of two types: unconditioned and conditioned. **Unconditioned reflexes** (UCR) are innate, and include such basic functions as salivation. **Conditioned reflexes** (CR) are formed as a result of experience. The UCR is the normal response to an **unconditioned stimulus** (UCS) such as food. A **conditioned stimulus** (CS) is a previously neutral item which, through 'pairing' with a UCS, produces a new response. An example which might clarify the picture can be seen in a nurse's response to a cardiac arrest. Before training, the nurse's response to an individual who has collapsed (UCS) could be a sudden release of adrenalin with all of its effects (UCR). Through training, the nurse can be taught to examine the patient's pulse, and if absent, may elicit behaviours such as lying the patient flat, inserting an artificial airway, etc. It may be the case that the nurse has gleaned that asystole being recorded on the cardiac monitor is a sign of cardiac arrest, and if this is paired with a collapsed patient, may also act as a CS, and instigate the appropriate responses, if paired on several occasions. If, however, the nurse is confronted with an asystole trace due to the monitor being disconnected, eventually the CR will be 'extinguished'. The reflex can be regained by finding a new CS, in this case the one that should have been used in the first place, namely the pulse. This is known as '**disinhibition**'. As the training progresses, the nurse will begin to 'generalise' the CR to a variety of situations, rather than just a patient on a coronary care unit.

OPERANT CONDITIONING

From numerous well-documented experiments in operant conditioning, in both animals and humans, B.F. Skinner suggests that the following factors should be present before learning can take place (Skinner, 1938).

(1) Each step of the learning process must be short and should grow out of previous learned behaviour.
(2) In the early stages learning should be regularly rewarded and at all

stages be carefully controlled by a schedule of continuous or intermittent reinforcement. This reinforcement is a feature of **discovery learning** inasmuch as reinforcement for students is a discovery of a concept by its own efforts. For instance, if a student is given anti-A and anti-B antigen solutions she may work out for herself which blood group she belongs to.

(3) Reward should follow quickly when a correct response appears.

This is referred to as feedback and is based on the principle that motivation is enhanced when we are informed of our progress. Laboratory experiments provide such a feedback. With careful explanation and supervision, the student will usually be able to achieve a predicted outcome.

(4) The learner should be given an opportunity to discover stimulus discrimination for the most likely path to success.

From these principles Skinner devised a scheme known as 'programmed learning', now extensively employed using computer-assisted learning techniques, so that each student may progress at their own pace. Like discovery learning however, the method is a relatively slow one, particularly in terms of preparation time for the teacher or instructor. It is of particular value with students of mixed ability and/or when a subject area is particularly difficult. In practical terms programmed learning can be presented as follows.

TYPES OF LEARNING

Gagne' (1974) identified eight types of learning which he arranged into an hierarchy from simple responses to complex problem-solving activities.

Type 1 - Signal Learning
This is equivalent to Pavlov's conditioned response.

Type 2 - Stimulus Response Learning
This is equivalent to Skinner's discriminated operant conditioning.

Type 3 - Chaining
A chain of two or more stimulus response connections.

Type 4 - Verbal Association
Learning verbal chains.

Type 5 - Multiple Discrimination
Learning to discriminate between stimuli which resemble each other.

Type 6 - Concept Learning
See Bruner (1960), Ausubel (1968) and below.

Type 7 - Principle Learning
A chain of two or more concepts.

Type 8 - Problem Solving
Solving problems by the use of principles.

Gagne' postulates that these stages must occur in sequence for respective learning to occur. If the hierarchy is analysed it may be said that the simplest forms of learning occur using **concrete operational thought** and only with the last three components is **formal operational thought** possibly required. In order to see how we may further optimise learning it is necessary to examine two principal approaches: (1) **discovery learning** (Bruner, 1960); (2) **reception learning** (Ausubel, 1968).

DISCOVERY LEARNING

Discovery learning places emphasis on learner-centred approaches, valued first-hand experience, experimentation and the development of critical abilities. The process of learning by discovery involves (a) **induction** (taking particular instances and using them to devise a general case) with a minimum of instruction and (b) **errorful learning**, employing trial and error strategies in which there is a high probability of errors and mistakes before an acceptable generalisation is possible.

The main use of discovery learning is with regard to concept acquisition. Bruner (1960) advocates the importance of revisiting concepts continually and reinforcing them. For instance, the first step in learning about intrinsic brain failure may be for the student to talk to a patient with a condition and perhaps note the patient's response to the questions put to them. A useful session may then be developed following this exercise which is built upon students' experiences and generalisations, built up by observation and analysis, and also their attempts at classifying them. Later in the students' period of experience the theme can be returned to in a more in-depth observation and analysis which may include patterns of behaviour, responses to loved ones, orientation in time and place, etc.

Following several such experiences the student may eventually learn to distinguish between an intrinsic brain failure disorder such as **Alzheimer's disease** and extrinsic brain failure disorders by virtue of their observations and the continual refinement of their generalisations about the conditions. Because the follow-up sessions are essentially built around the students' perceptions and indeed the errors and mistakes that they are making in coming to their conclusions, it is more likely that the formal instruction will be of more value and more readily learnt.

If we again refer to Gagne's hierarchy of learning it can be seen that the ultimate type of learning is 'problem solving'. It is these problem-solving skills that discovery learning attempts to achieve. In theory at least, motivation may be increased and therefore learning made more efficient. It is hoped that by encouraging the student to discover by induction or by errorful learning that the student may become self-resourceful and self-sufficient.

RECEPTION LEARNING (ASSIMILATION THEORY)

In this theory Ausubel (1968) discusses four dimensions of learning.

With this theory Ausubel attempts to resolve problems facing Bruner's discovery learning, namely subject matter organisation. Ausubel presents two main principles necessary for subject matter organisation:

(1) **Progressive differentiation**: general ideas are presented first (advanced organisers) followed by gradual increase in details and specifity.

(2) **Integrative reconciliation**: new ideas must be consciously related to previously learned material (**subsumers**).

By '**advanced organiser**' is meant that introductory material is presented ahead of the learning task and at a higher level of abstraction and inclusiveness than the learning task itself.

Three conditions are necessary for the attainment of meaningful learning which is essential for problem solving; they are:

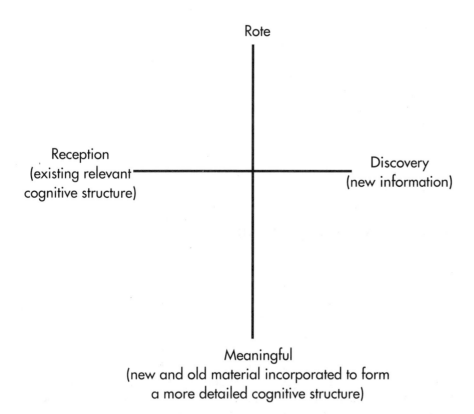

Fig. 6.3 Ausubel's four dimensions of learning.

(1) The learner must adopt a 'set' to learn the task in a meaningful manner.
(2) The task must have logical meaning.
(3) The learner's cognitive structures must contain specifically relevant ideas with which new material can interact.

Discovery teaching alone does not necessarily guarantee meaningful learning (Novak, 1969). Reception learning, on the other hand, is a highly functional conceptual framework for students.

Subsumers, which are such an essential part of the theory, enable us to integrate existing concepts with newly acquired ones. This in itself appears fairly straightforward, however Ausubel goes on to postulate as to the existence of something that he terms '**obliterative subsumption**'. In this he maintained that although much material has been forgotten, residual concepts nevertheless remain and hence can be built upon. The inference of this theory, as Ausubel himself points out, is that the student is the central focus of the learning process inasmuch as the material to be learnt must be related to what the student already knows and that once this is established, learning will progress at a faster and more reliable rate. The implication of this is that the person who is providing the instruction or experience to the student must know their student's past experiences and an honest relationship must be built up between them in order for learning to be effective. Not only this, but teaching students in large groups is seen to have many drawbacks.

Ausubel accepts that not all meaningful learning involves new instances or modifications of previously learned concepts but may bear a superordinate relationship to a previous acquired concept. For example, superordinate learning occurs when we learn that humans, cats and dogs are all mammals. As superalternate learning occurs so does **integrative reconciliation**, as existing concepts are rearranged into new order higher concept meanings. For example, the student recognises that different labels describe the same concept, e.g. alimentary tract/digestive tract.

FACTORS AFFECTING LEARNING

Many factors exist which can alter the outcome of any learning situation. Our individual differences such as personality, intelligence and past experience will inevitably play their part in virtually any learning situation whether we are facilitating the learning of a student or providing education for a patient or client. It should not be forgotten that fear of a particular situation may also affect how we learn.

The following account of some of the factors involved may give the reader some indication as to some of the considerations which may be taken into account when imparting information. The topics 'personality' and 'motivation' are covered under separate chapter headings.

INTELLIGENCE

Precisely what is meant by the term 'intelligence' is a matter of considerable debate, even today. In many ways, intelligence refers to an individual's capacity for learning rather than the amount of learning that has taken place, hence an 'educated' person is not necessarily intelligent and vice versa. Naturally, such a generalised statement is of little use to us in such a raw form, and is open to arguments regarding the nature of learning itself. Some of the more prominent theories of intelligence, therefore, need to be briefly examined.

Several schools of thought have contributed to our current understanding of intelligence, and theorists within these domains continue to add to an already massive body of research. Much of the research into intelligence centres around the testing procedures which can produce a single numerical score, such as the various **intelligence quotient** (I.Q.) tests. I.Q. is based on the ratio between the mental (test score) and chronological age, and calculated thus:

$$\text{I.Q.} = \frac{\text{mental age}}{\text{chronological age}} \times 100$$

The work of Binet has already been briefly mentioned in connection with Piaget. His work was originally commissioned in France to aid the process of classifying mentally handicapped children for the purpose of dividing them out in the education system. The resulting tests and various modifications were used for several decades afterwards. Binet stressed the higher mental processes and through several refinements attempted to eliminate those items in his testing procedures which either wholly or partially tested knowledge. Binet's work has been substantially built upon and modified by Burt in the U.K. and Stanford in the U.S.A. (Stanford–Binet tests).

Charles Spearman (1904), who was incidentally the inventor of **factor analysis** (see Chapter 2), concluded that intelligence was essentially the ability to identify relationships. He further identified two major factors: the 'g' factor and the 's' factor. The 'g' factor refers to general intelligence and is an inherited phenomenon which is unaffected by extrinsic factors such as education. The 's' factor refers to those specific abilities which have evolved as a result of extrinsic factors. Relating these factors to intelligence tests, Spearman believed that the 'g' factor was evident across the range of test items, whereas the 's' factor was specific items only.

Cattell (1963) suggested that intelligence was made up of two factors. The first of these factors, 'crystallised' intelligence, has emerged through learning and is of limited use in novel situations. The second factor, 'fluid' intelligence, is utilised when new situations requiring a new set of responses are encountered. Cattell does, however, stress the importance of the individual's personality, and the difficulties in considering intelligence in isolation.

Thurstone and Thurstone (1963) suggested the existence of seven 'primary mental abilities':

(1) Spatial ability.
(2) Perceptual ability.
(3) Numerical ability—ability to perform numerical calculations.
(4) Verbal meaning—understanding the meaning of words.
(5) Memory—recall of verbal stimuli.
(6) Verbal fluency.
(7) Inductive reasoning—formation of general rules.

Thurstone and Thurstone's factor analysis lends some support to Spearman's theory of the 'g' factor.

Guilford (1967) considers that three major dimensions, operations, products and contents, must be taken into account when attempting to analyse the structure of intelligence. The total number of ability factors which can be gleaned from these dimensions is 120, although there is considerable variation in this total from other researchers.

One of the more recent theories of intelligence has come from Sternberg (1982), and uses information processing as its basis. This is known as the componential model of intelligence. The elementary process which translates sensory inputs into mental conceptual representations is termed by Sternberg as a '**component**', of which there are five major types operating at different levels:

(1) Metacomponents, responsible for higher order reasoning and problem solving.
(2) Performance components, also associated with problem solving in relation to planning a course of action.
(3) Acquisition components, associated with new learning.
(4) Retention components, associated with remembering.
(5) Transfer components, associated with generalisations.

Sternberg maintains that these components can be measured from items on intelligence tests by virtue of the frequency of particular responses and duration of different tasks.

Some researchers, principally Furneaux (1960) and latterly Eysenck, have emphasised that the speed of mental functioning, the error checking mechanism (accuracy) and persistence are the three major components of intelligence.

NATURE VS NURTURE—WHERE DOES INTELLIGENCE COME FROM?

Intelligence, as well as many other psychological phenomena, has been and still is the subject of much discussion. The dividing line between inherited factors and environmental influences is in itself a less than obvious one, but we will for the purposes of this discussion assume that following fertilisation all influences are environmental. The implications of this definition are immediately apparent, namely that many of the disorders that we may observe at birth have occurred following fertilisation and must therefore be classed as 'environmentally caused'.

The contribution of heredity and environment to the development of intelligence, in percentage terms, has been found to be (in several studies) about 80% inherited and 20% environmental (Eysenck, 1976). More recent commentators have suggested that the variation in I.Q. test results which can be attributed to hereditary factors is approximately 50% (Rust and Golombok, 1989).

An immensely complex picture emerges when we consider that we all interact in a multitude of different ways with our environment. Such interactions are as unique as our genetic make up, and include home life styles, education provision and the individual's level of perseverence (Freeman, 1979, 1981). Other factors, such as race, have been investigated, but most of the results point towards the environment rather than racial differences as the cause for I.Q. differences detected (Mackenzie, 1984; Scarr and Weinberg, 1976).

The environmental factors involved are difficult to quantify. It is impossible to avoid cultural and environmental factors in I.Q. testing (Clarke and Clarke, 1976), and it could be argued that the best we can glean is that hereditary and environmental influences are interactive. Despite the complexities, studies have been carried out into environmental factors involved in intelligence, particularly where children have been reared in highly monitored and sometimes regimented conditions such as institutions (e.g. Lawrence, 1931). Generally, these studies would appear to substantiate the 80%/20% figures given earlier, with children from institutions having a similar variance in I.Q. to children with a more 'normal' and diverse home life.

Freeman (1981), when investigating higher ability children, concluded that '. . . I.Q. scores were found to be heavily loaded with environmental influences, which gained in strength progressively up the I.Q. scale'. Conversely, deprivation can be associated with a cumulative decrease in I.Q. score (Jensen, 1987), thus lending considerable support for the case against racial superiority.

Naturally if either genetic or environmental factors could be found to be identical between two or more individuals, the influence of each factor could be examined. It would clearly be impossible to find two individuals whose environmental influences were identical, although children reared in the same environment tend to have quite similar I.Q.'s as do those with a close biological relationship (McAskie and Clarke, 1976). Studies of **monozygotic twins** have provided us with data which suggest a higher correlation between those reared together than those reared apart (Bouchard and McGue, 1981), therefore once again indicating the importance of environmental factors.

SOME OBSERVATIONS ON THEORIES OF INTELLIGENCE

Some debates appear to reach no satisfactory conclusion, and to the observer of psychological controversies, this seems to be one such case.

The originators of intelligence theories give us a vast and at times contradictory catalogue of plausible explanations, that range from those who do not identify intelligence as a quantifiable attribute which can be extracted from personality, to those, such as Burt, who have made a lifetime study based on the assumption that intelligence can be measured. Theorists such as Guilford have postulated an extreme multi-factor approach, although as with most factoral-based theories, the path to the verification of many of the findings is a difficult and controversial one, although many theorists, such as Piaget, have gone to great lengths to stress the biological viewpoint.

One fact does appear, however, to emerge from the discussion, and that is intelligence, whatever it is, is a quality which is at best difficult, and at worst dangerous to quantify. A patient's misunderstanding or apparent lack of comprehension is just as likely to be caused by poor communication, previous misconceptions or anxiety as inadequate cognitive functioning.

MEMORY

Without memory learning would be impossible. One can go even further by saying that memory is an essential faculty, without which an individual's life would be very seriously impaired to the point of making survival doubtful unless continuous care was given. In order to understand how memory works it is probably a good starting point to examine the three processes involved, namely **encoding**, **storage** and **retrieval**. These processes have the following functions:

(1) *Encoding*: the transformation of physical information into memory codes via visual coding (transformation of the material into an image), acoustic coding (transformation of the material into the sound of the word) and semantic coding (transformation of the material into its meaning).
(2) *Storage*: the retention of encoded information.
(3) *Retrieval*: the recovery of stored information.

SHORT-TERM AND LONG-TERM MEMORY

It would appear that two different types of memory are required for remembering information for a very short period of time and for remembering information for a long period of time.

The capacities for the short-term memory and the long-term memory are rather different. The short-term memory appears to be able to only hold between five and nine pieces of information (Miller, 1956) for a very short period of time (about 30 seconds) whereas the capacity of the long-term memory is virtually unlimited as far as we can tell. The processes involved with both types of memory are the same however, namely those of encoding, storage and retrieval.

Encoding in the Short-term and Long-term Memory:
In the short-term memory, **acoustic coding** appears to play a vital role. Conrad (1964) noted that there were significant characteristics about the errors that subjects made when recalling letters from the short-term memory; they tended to substitute letters which sounded similar to those letters which were actually presented (M for N and B for T). This phenomenon even occurred if the letters were presented visually rather than verbally, implying that the letters were held in the short-term memory in terms of their acoustic rather than visual properties. The acoustic coding dominance in short-term memory appears to be further supported when words are presented (Baddeley, 1966); the results again reflected an acoustic rather than a visual or semantic coding system.

In the equivalent long-term memory study (Baddeley, 1966) it was found that semantically similar words were remembered poorly suggesting that in long-term memory words were remembered in terms of their meanings. This lead to the conclusion that semantic similarity affects the long-term memory (Baddeley and Dale, 1966). Therefore the long-term memory has a preferred code, i.e. semantic, the preferred code for short-term memory is acoustic, but other codes may be used, although to a much lesser extent.

STORAGE AND ATTENTION

The manner in which information is stored is a matter of some controversy, and is in many ways linked to how we attend to information. Two models will be discussed here.

Multi-store Model
Possibly the best known of the two models is that proposed by Atkinson and Shiffrin (1968), which describes a multi-store comprising sensory registers, a short-term store and a long-term store. Information is initially received and stored for as little as a fraction of a second in the 'sensory memory' or register. From here, information may either be lost, or attended to and transferred to a 'short-term store' (STS). Once again the information may be lost after about 20–30 seconds, this time by a process of displacement. There is a way, however, to prevent its loss from the STS, by 'rehearsal', which will increase the possibility of transfer to the 'long-term store' (LTS). Once in the LTS, information may be stored permanently, and retrieved when needed. Alternatively, the information may decay or may become confused with other similar memory traces.

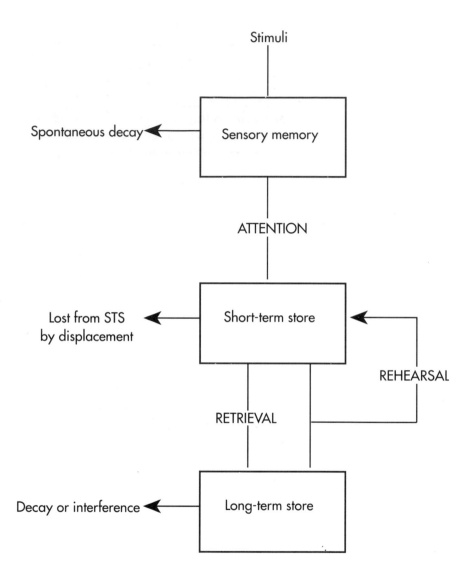

Fig. 6.4   A multi-store memory model (Adapted from Atkinson and Shiffrin

Working Memory Model

An alternative to the 'multi-store' model described by Atkinson and Shiffrin has been proposed. The working memory model proposes four separate components to replace the short-term store.

The **central executive** has, to a large extent, control over the other components, although the primary acoustic store is to an extent dependent upon

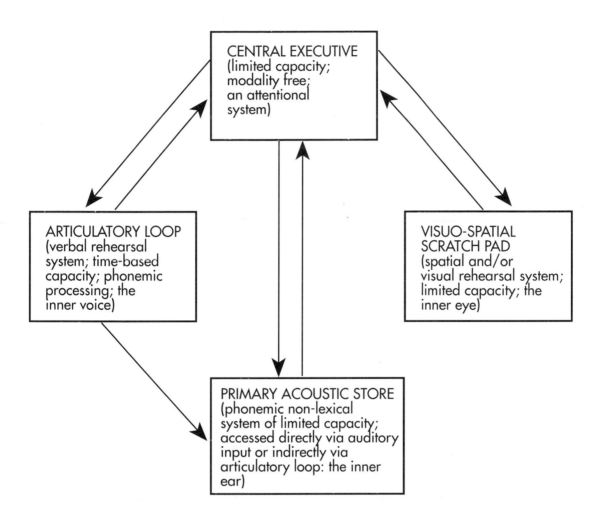

Fig. 6.5 A working memory model (reproduced with permission from *Memory: A Cognitive Approach* by G. Cohen, M.W. Eysenck and M.E. LeVoi, Open University Press, (1986).

An alternative to the 'multi-store' model described by Atkinson and Shiffrin has been proposed. The working memory model proposes four separate components to replace the short-term store.

The **central executive** has, to a large extent, control over the other components, although the primary acoustic store is to an extent dependent upon certain actions of the articulatory loop. The central executive can store information for short periods of time, can process information from sensory inputs in a variety of ways and is involved in tasks such as reading, writing,

It therefore deals with the articulation of verbal material and is considered as an 'inner voice'.

The **visual–spatial scratch pad** is responsible for dealing with visual and spatial information. It has a limited capacity, and utilises rehearsal. It can be regarded as the 'inner eye'.

The **primary acoustic store** is dependent upon the articulatory loop for the translation of visual information in an acoustic code, but deals with auditory information directly. This store can be used when reading and the printed matter can be 'heard' as we read. This store can be referred to as the 'inner ear'.

Memory Traces

The description of organisation of various stores still leaves us unclear as to how information is actually stored within them. The term 'memory trace' is not a new one, but one which still, through many refinements and interpretations, remains a popular one, and provides us with an intriguing link between the theoretical frameworks we have examined, and physical manifestations so often observed in conditions such as Alzheimer's disease.

Thorndike (1932) first put forward the theory that information which is retained leaves a trace which in time will decay due to normal metabolic processes. The nature of such traces has already been discussed in Chapter 2, and it may be remembered that much of current thinking centres around the possible physiological changes involved in learning, and that both RNA and protein mechanisms have been considered as the basis of the memory trace.

RETRIEVAL

The retrieval of information and the nature of forgetting can be considered together for the purposes of this discussion. Retrieval from the short-term memory is a very fast process, but at the same time it is not 'instant', being dependent upon the amount of items stored there. In other words, a search needs to be carried out (Sternberg, 1966). Information is lost from the STM by a process of displacement when the storage capacity is exceeded.

As far as the long-term memory is concerned, analogies can be made which may serve to explain some of the processes involved. For instance, imagine a large room full of filing cabinets which in their turn are full of files, and further imagine that we are asked to locate a particular file. Our chances of finding the file will become considerably more remote if there are no labels on the filing cabinets to indicate their contents, and if the files themselves have been placed in the cabinets in a random fashion, failure will be almost inevitable. The same result can be expected when using a word processor when someone has just labelled the files as '1', '2', '3' etc., with no clue as to their contents. Accurate naming of files in both instances will increase our chances of finding the file, and also arranging the contents are in a logical manner (e.g. if the file is labelled 'mortgage' we might expect to find not only the contract from the Bank, but also the surveyor's report, legal documents and details such as mortgage account statements).

Similarly, retrieval from the long-term memory can be said to be, at least in part, dependent on how it was organised in the first place (Bower *et al.*, 1969). Categorising the material that we encode has been found to aid recall, and this is seen perhaps most clearly when attempting to learn material, such as that relating to intestinal obstruction, which will encompass many different conditions.

This organisation of material has also been investigated by Tulving (1968), who suggested that we may group information in terms of their relationships (**primary organisation**), and that we may further remember information by categorical or associative means (**secondary organisation**). The categorical organisation has already been mentioned, but the associative aspect is concerned with the associations that we may form between different pieces of information, such as opposites. In considering the organisation of material, it can be deduced that the responsibilities of teaching both patients and junior staff lie not only in the accuracy of information, but also in the manner and order in which it is presented.

The manner in which we encode can also have a bearing on how information is forgotten. A poorly delivered lecture which makes no attempt at linking in with the recipients' past experience is less likely to be remembered. The information should be made relevant to the individual, because there is a tendency for the memory trace to decay over time as new information causes interference, unless the previously learned material is being used either in a practical sense or as a foundation for further learning. A good example of this is when we are taught a subject such as psychology or physiology in complete isolation from our main area of study, and before much time has elapsed, the learning of our more specialist subject has caused interference with previously learned material. This could have been avoided if sufficient account had been taken of the relationships between each subject when taught.

The question still remains as to how the information is brought into our conscious thought. The process involved appears to revolve around the presentation of cues which were present at the time of learning. These are most commonly words or phrases, and could be likened to looking for and finding a file in our filing cabinet with a title, and then finding the information that we require inside.

Many of us, when referring to material learned many years previously, have expressed the sentiment that 'it soon comes back', particularly when referring to a 'work' situation, and in this instance, a return to the contextual surroundings (such as a hospital ward) may act as a cue. In other words, if we return to the area where certain information was encoded then we are more likely to remember it (Estes, 1972).

Wiseman and Tulving (1976) have further developed this type of theory by suggesting that the relationship between **storage** and **retrieval** can be likened to a lock and key, with the lock representing the information stored in the memory trace, and the key representing the information available at the time of retrieval. This theory emphasises the need for there to be a match between the stored information and the retrieval information by the 'to be remembered' item being encoded '. . . with respect to the context in which it is studied, producing a unique trace which incorporates information from both target and context. For the "to be remembered" item to be retrieved, the cue information must appropriately match the trace of the item in context'. This 'encoding specificity principle' implies that during learning there should be a degree of matching to the anticipated retrieval code. For example, teaching a patient to use a syringe by merely showing him drawings of the syringe is likely to lead to some confusion because the encoded information from the drawings is likely to be an inappropriate retrieval cue.

EMOTIONAL FACTORS IN FORGETTING

The manner in which emotion makes us forget information can in part be explained by the encoding specificity principle discussed earlier, with information being remembered if the subject is in a similar mood to when the information was originally encoded, although this is by no means the only possible explanation.

The psychoanalytic explanation for forgetting could, in some instances, be that the experience was so unpleasant that the individual represses it in order to protect themselves. This form of defence mechanism is particularly prevalent in childhood.

Possibly the most obvious explanation would be that retrieval is made difficult because a strong emotion (not necessarily a bad one) is causing interference with the retrieval mechanism.

ORGANISING A 'TEACHING' SESSION

PREPARATION

There are many occasions where adequate preparation is just not feasible, for instance, when an impromptu teaching session evolves from the admitting of a new patient. However, by utilising Gestalt psychology which is concerned with organised forms and patterns in human perception, thinking and learning (Curzon, 1990), we will aid the student's learning process. Briefly, it can be applied as follows:

(1) Symmetry—in other words the session should be divided into an introduction, development and conclusion. This stage, as with some others, is highly dependent on the student's previous knowledge.
(2) **Contiguity**—ensure that any reinforcement, such as relevant observations on the patient, pieces of equipment, etc., are shown either at the time of the session or as soon as possible.

(3) Similarity—try not to 'jump' from subject to subject within the same session. If this is not possible, at least ensure that similarity is created by referring subjects back to a focal point. For instance, if the care of a patient is being discussed, and a diversion is needed to talk about the actions of certain drugs, then this should be individualised to the patient.

(4) **Closure**—try to plan the session in such a way as to allow the students to complete some parts for themselves. This can be done in at least two ways. Firstly, it can be achieved by the use of questions, e.g. 'so, if Mr Jones is retaining large amounts of sodium, what would you look for?' Naturally, care should be taken not to demotivate the student by making them feel threatened. Secondly, the student can be given something to observe or further research, but if this is done then time needs to be put aside later to discuss their findings so that it can be integrated into the overall subject.

PREVIOUS KNOWLEDGE

We discussed earlier the theory of reception learning (Ausubel, 1968), and central to this theory is a factor that Ausubel himself considered of vital importance, namely establish what the student already knows. This does sound rather obvious, but many people when teaching a subject are too rigid because they do not take account of this fact.

One of the more common ways in which previous knowledge can be applied is to build the session (at least in the initial stages) around the students' experiences. For instance, it is not uncommon for nurses to have worked with the elderly before they commenced nurse training, and their experiences are frequently a good starting point for the session on, for example, dementia.

INFORMATION GIVING

Probably the most common problem in teaching anyone is the difficulty in preventing 'information overload', so the student leaves you so confused that the session has been of little use. This can be overcome very easily by ensuring that changes of activity/breaks occur about every 15–20 minutes, and that the student is assessed continually on a verbal and non-verbal basis as to whether they are managing to firstly learn at the rate you are teaching, and secondly, not only to learn facts, but also effecting '**closure**'. The use of anecdotes frequently will help to illustrate a point.

The earlier discussion on memory gives us some indication as to the amount of information that can be imparted over a given period. Information which is given at the beginning of the session may be lost to the individual in favour of the most recent information given in the session (**recency effect**). This 'retroactive' interference will naturally be worse if the session has proceeded at a pace which is too fast for the individual, and also (as already mentioned) if there is too much information in the session. It is also

likely that such a phenomenon would occur if the session was not based on the individual's previous knowledge.

Conversely there is also some evidence to suggest that the information which is imparted first will be remembered more than other material (**primacy effect**), and this has been demonstrated, amongst other groups, with patients receiving medical information (see for instance Ley, 1972); however the recency effect still cannot be ignored (Ley, 1982).

Ley (1988) suggests the following measures that may improve recall by patients:

(1) Simplification
(2) Explicit categorisation
(3) Repetition
(4) Use of specific rather than general statements
(5) Mixtures of the above.

USE OF AUDIO-VISUAL AIDS

Anything which will reinforce information which has been given will be a great help to the individual. Visual stimuli provided by slides, overhead projectors, posters etc., are always valuable. Perhaps the best audio-visual aid are the patients themselves, although many of us tend to miss the opportunity to learn afforded to us by our patients because of a lack of guidance as to what to look for, and a lack of back-up to discuss what we have observed.

The use of discovery learning is particularly useful in this context, and can be adapted readily to the clinical situation, by asking the individual to make a pre-determined amount of observations (as well as her or his own) on the patient. The results are discussed later and the desired topic is built around these observations and the questions that have arisen.

LOCATION

Disruptions to the communications process are discussed elsewhere in the text (see Chapter 5) and it will be remembered how attention can be disturbed by external factors. If possible, therefore, a quiet area should be chosen, not only from the point of view of maximising attention, but also to allow the students to ask questions which they may deem silly if asked in front of others.

MOTIVATION

Certain fundamental questions need to be asked when assessing the motivation of the student, principally, do they want to learn out of interest (intrinsic motivation) or do they want to learn because they are in some way pressured to do so (extrinsic motivation)? It is always advisable for the student to be intrinsically motivated, and as such, the teacher is largely responsible for facilitating this by the approach to both the student and the subject. In short, the student should be made to feel not only that they have something to contribute on a personal level, but also that their experience and questions are relevant and important.

CONCLUSION

To understand how an individual learns is to form the basis for developing a strategy for education. To understand how the child learns about the world they live in is to gain some insight into how they may view their bodies, illness, treatment and even hospitalisation. The learning theories that have been discussed give us some insight into how we may facilitate the learning of others, although the factors affecting learning, such as motivation, upbringing, personality, perception and memory, must be considered.

SUMMARY

Piaget formulated a theory of cognitive development which identified three major periods, **sensorimotor**, **concrete operational thought**, and **formal operational thought**, and which is hierarchical in nature, is maturational, and is genetic in origin.

Experiences are integrated into schemas by the processes of **assimilation** and **accommodation**, and hence the intellect is constantly adapting to new experiences.

The sensorimotor stage (0–2 years) is concerned with the exploration of the immediate environment through the senses and also the motor capabilities. The development of object permanence is seen during this period.

The concrete operational period is divided into two stages: **pre-operational** and **concrete operational**. Pre-operational thought is typified by egocentrism and **intuitive thought**. The child is capable of symbolic representation. During the concrete operational stage, logical thought and reasoning become more fully developed. Conservation will substantially develop during this stage.

Formal operational thought is seen as the pinnacle of intellectual development, with the adolescent who has developed to this point being capable of problem solving through hypothesising possible outcomes which are not based solely on past experience.

The process of learning has been attributed by some researchers (such as Pavlov and Skinner) to conditioned responses to stimuli, although Gagne' describes learning in terms of a hierarchy, with stimulus–response learning being described as one of the more basic types of learning, and problem solving the highest. Reception learning (Ausubel) has practical implications for teaching by virtue of its description of subject matter organisation, while **learning by discovery** (Bruner) emphasises the importance of being able to learn through experience and the finding of solutions by experimenting.

Several factors affect learning, such as memory, intelligence, personality, motivation and the manner in which information is presented. The influences on the individual's intelligence of heredity and environmental factors has been estimated at approximately 20% environmental and 80% genetic.

In addition to the factors which affect learning, perceptual considerations such as symmetry, contiguity, similarity and closure need to be integrated into the planning of teaching sessions, both to patients/clients and health professionals.

REFERENCES

* indicates standard texts or articles

Atkinson, R.C. and Shiffrin, R.M. (1968) Human Memory: A Proposed System and it's Control Processes. In: Spence, K.W. and Spence, J.T. (eds), *The Psychology of Learning and Motivation*, Vol. 2. Academic Press, London.*

Ausubel, D.P. (1968) *Educational Psychology—A Cognitive View*. Holt Rinehart and Winston, New York.*

Baddeley, A.D. (1966a) Short term memory for word sequences as a function of acoustic, semantic and formal similarity. *Quarterly Journal of Experimental Psychology* **20**, 249–264.*

Baddeley, A.D. (1966b) The influence of acoustic and semantic similarity on long term memory for word sequences. *Quarterly Journal of Experimental Psychology* **18**, 362–365.*

Baddeley, A.D. and Dale, H.C.A. (1966) The effect of semantic similarity on retroactive interference in long and short term memory. *Journal of Verbal Learning and Verbal Behaviour* **5**, 417–420.*

Bouchard, T.J. and McGue, M. (1981) Familial studies of intelligence: a review. *Science* **212**, 1055–1059.

Bower, G.H., Clark, M.C., Winzenz, D. and Lesgold, D. (1969) Hierarchical retrieval schemes in recall of catagorised word lists. *Journal of Verbal Learning and Verbal Behaviour* **8**, 323–343.

Bruner, J. (1960) *The Process of Education.* Harvard University Press (Discovery Learning), Cambridge, Mass.*

Cattell, R.B. (1963) Theory of fluid and crystallised intelligence—a critical experiment. *Journal of Educational Psychology* **54**, 1–22.*

Clarke, A.M. and Clarke, A.D.B. (1976) *Early Experience: Myth and Evidence.* Open Books, London.

Cohen, G., Eysenck, M.W. and LeVoi, M.E. (1986) *Memory —A Cognitive Approach.* Open University Press, Milton Keynes.

Conrad, R. (1964) Acoustic confusion in immediate memory. *British Journal of Psychology* **55**, 75–84.

Curzon, L.B. (1990) *Teaching in Further Education.* Cassell, London.

Estes, W.K. (1972) An associative basis for coding and organisation in memory. In: Meltron, A.W. and Martin, E. (eds), *Coding Processes in Human Memory.* Winston, Washington DC.

Eysenck, H.J. (1976) *The Measurement of Intelligence.* MTP, Lancaster.*

Flavell, J.H. (1962) *The Developmental Psychology of Jean Piaget.* D. Van Nostrand, New York.*

Freeman, J. (1979) *Gifted Children: Their Identification in a Social Context.* MTP, Lancaster.

Freeman, J. (1981) The intellectually gifted. In: Abroms, K.I. and Bennett, J.W. (eds), *Primer in Genetics and Exceptional Children.* Jossey-Bass, San Francisco.

Furneaux, W.D. (1990) Intellectual ability and problem solving activities. In Eysenck, H.J., *Handbook of Abnormal Psychology*, Pittman, London.

Gagne', R. (1974) Learning hierarchies. In: Clarizo, H. (ed.), *Contemporary Issues in Educational Psychology.* Allya & Bacon,*

Guilford, J.P. (1967) *The Nature of Human Intelligence.* McGraw Hill, New York.*

Jenson, A.R. (1977) Cumulative deficit in IQ of blacks in the rural South. *Developmental Psychology* **13**, 184–189. (Quoted by J. Freeman in Weller, M. (ed.) (1983) *The Scientific Basis of Psychiatry.* Baillière Tindall, London.

Lawrence, E.M. (1931) An investigation into the relation between intelligence and inheritance. *British Journal of Psychology Monograph* **16**, 5.

Ley, P. (1972) Primacy, rated importance and the recall of information. *Journal of Health and Social Behaviour* **13**, 311–317.

Ley, P. (1982) Giving information to patients. In Eiser, J.R. (ed.) *Social Psychology and Behavioural Medicine.* Wiley, New York.

Ley, P. (1988) *Communicating with Patients.* Chapman and Hall, London.

McAskie, M. and Clarke, A.M. (1976) Parent–offspring resemblence in intelligence; theories and evidence. *British Journal of Psychology* **67**, 243–273.

Mackenzie, B. (1984) Explaining race differences in I.Q.: the logic, the methodology, and the evidence. *American Psychologist* **39**, 1214–1233. (Cited in: Atkinson, R.L., Atkinson, R.C., Smith, E.E. and Benn, D.J. (eds), *Introduction to Psychology.* 10th edn, 1990, HBJ, London.

Miller, G.A. (1956) The magical number seven plus or minus two: some limits on our capacity for processing information. *Psychological Review* **63**, 81–97.

Pavlov, I.P. (1927) *Conditioned Reflexes*. Oxford University Press, New York.*

Piaget, J. (1950) *Introduction à L'épistémologie Génétique*, Presses Univer. France, Paris.

Piaget, J. (1952) *The Origins of Intelligence in Children*. International University Press, New York.

Piaget, J. and Inhelder, B. (1951) *La Genese de L'idea de Hasard Chez L'enfant*. Presses Univer. France, Paris.

Rust, J. and Golombok, S. (1989) *Modern Psychometrics*. Routledge, London.

Scarr, S. and Weinberg, R.A. (1976) I.Q. test performance of black children adopted by white families. *American Psychologist* **31**, 726–739.

Skinner, B.F. (1938) *The Behaviour of Organisms*. Appleton Century Crofts, New York.

Spearman, C. (1904) General intelligence objectively determined and measured. *American Journal of Psychology* **15**, 201–293.*

Sternberg, R.J. (ed.) (1982) *Handbook of Human Intelligence*. Cambridge University Press, New York.*

Sternberg, S. (1966) High speed scanning in human memory. *Science* **153**, 652–654.

Thorndike, G.J. (1932) *The Fundamentals of Learning*. Teachers College Bureau of Publications, New York.

Thurstone, L.L. and Thurstone, T.G. (1963) *SRA Primary Abilities*. Science Research Associates, Chicago.*

Tulving, E. (1968) Theoretical issues in free recall. In: Dixon, T. and Horton, D. (eds), *Verbal Behaviour and General Behaviour Theory*. Prentice Hall, NJ.

Weller, M. (ed.) (1983) *The Scientific Basis of Psychiatry*. Baillière Tindall, London.

Wiseman, S. and Tulving, E. (1976) Encoding specificity: relation between recall superiority and recognition failure. *Journal of Experimental Psychology: Human Learning; Memory* **2**, 349–361.

SUGGESTED READING

Cohen, G., Eysenck, M.W. and LeVoi, M.E. (1986) *Memory—A Cognitive Approach*. Open University Press, Milton Keynes. (See in particular the section dealing with the 'working memory model'.)

Curzon, L.B. (1990) *Teaching in Further Education*. Cassell, London. (A good general guide to teaching.)

Flavell, J.H. (1962) *The Developmental Psychology of Jean Piaget*. D. Van Nostrand, New York.* (See particularly Chapters 1 and 2 for a lengthy overview of Piaget's theory. This text is rather advanced, but infinitely more readable than Piaget's original works!)

Ley, P. (1988) *Communicating with Patients*. Chapman and Hall, London. (See Chapter 12 for an account of how to improve patients' recall.)

Rust, J. and Golombok, S. (1989) *Modern Psychometrics*, Routledge, London. (See Chapter 1 for an account of the current trends towards intelligence testing.)

CHAPTER 7

THE SELF

'Each of us exists at the center of our own private world that can never be perfectly understood by anyone else'

CARL ROGERS (1951)

While many personality theorists have attempted to find common characteristics between individuals, an alternative approach has emerged which considers the individual as unique. In examining the topic of self, the work of two psychologists will be reviewed, namely Carl Rogers and Gordon Allport.

Our starting point though, must be to consider what is meant by the term **'self'** or **'self-concept'**, and to discuss how it emerges.

The individual's self-concept, 'or his attitude to and perception of himself, is intimately related to how he learns and behaves' (Burns, 1982), and is composed of all the individual's beliefs and evaluations about themselves. As such, the development of self is of vital importance to all of us, and the importance of relationships of those who surround the individual cannot be overemphasised.

The individual's attitudes and perceptions of themselves will naturally direct their behaviour in terms of health care. If for instance we consider the person who suffers disfiguration either through an accident or as a result of surgery, then we may see that considerable changes in the self-concept may occur. If we take this one step further, we can observe that males and females may react rather differently because they tend to view attractiveness as being related to different body parts (e.g. females: bust, waist, teeth and mouth; males: body build, shoulder width, height, etc. (Lerner *et al.*, 1976)).

THE SELF—SOME THOUGHTS ON ITS MEANING

The self is usually taken to mean those attributes that can be used to characterise 'I' or 'me'. Once again, it is those characteristics that we perceive that are relevant. The characteristics that we believe we possess can affect the way we behave, and how we perceive the world we live in..

Other prominent figures in the areas of psychology (apart from Rogers and Allport) have used the term 'self' in their work. Amongst these are Carl Jung who views the self as the ultimate goal of personality development and emphasises its uniqueness.

Sullivan (1954) sees the self (or self system) as primarily an anxiety-reducing mechanism, and as an organised perception which includes both the good and the bad.

We have already discussed in previous chapters other theorists who have contributed to an understanding of the uniqueness of the individual, most notably Erikson who described identity formation; also Freud and Piaget who went to great lengths to explain the emergence of a child as an entity distinct from the environment. Most theorists, however, have attempted, whilst acknowledging unique aspects, to find commonalities of personality which can be applied to just about everyone.

PERSPECTIVES ON THE DEVELOPMENT OF THE SELF

Jung views the development of the self as being from the process of individuation, which is the lifelong unfolding of our personality. If the individuation is successful, large amounts of **libido** formally associated with the archetypes are liberated through the increased knowledge of the collective unconscious (see Chapter 2). This libido is between the **conscious** and the **unconscious**, and forms the self.

Sullivan suggests that the self emerges as a result of childhood experiences, and our interactions with other people, and is highly resistant to change. In complete contrast to Rogers and Allport, Sullivan stresses the similarities between individuals.

If we consider the highly varied views of Freud, Jung, Sullivan, Erikson and others towards both a definition and emergence of the self in the light of the following discussion, we should then be in a position to explore the possible implications for not only health care, but also for education.

THE SELF-CONCEPT

Before a discussion of the Allportian and Rogerian theories of self can take place, some of the more well-used 'self' terminology needs to be briefly explored.

The self is often said to be composed of three elements:

(1) The **self-image**/self-picture/actual self/ego identity.
(2) The **ideal self**.
(3) **Self-esteem**.

SELF-IMAGE

The self-image is how we would describe ourselves, and includes the **body image**. It is not always a favourable description, and neither is it necessarily objective, but the way we view ourselves will dictate how we behave towards ourselves and others. It can include a considerable amount of description such as gender, name, relationships, occupation, physical attributes, personality traits.

In order to get some idea of how you see yourself, sit down quietly with some paper and write a list of 20 items that describe yourself. Usually we will use terms that describe our physical characteristics, relationships, gender, occupation and aspects of our personality and general demeanour. It may be that we describe temporary states such as illness and pain, and possibly emotional states such as happiness or sadness.

THE IDEAL SELF

The **ideal self** (or **ego ideal**) is the sort of person we would wish to be, as distinct from who we actually are (**self-image**). The characteristics of this ideal self may be in connection with our occupation, our social life or even our whole personality.

It may have been deduced by now that some people's ideal image bears little or no relationship to their self-image, and the things that they see as being ideal are just not attainable. The dissatisfaction that may result from this discrepancy is variable. It may be, however, that the self-image and ideal self are not so far apart, but certain events such as illness could serve to widen the gap. The possible implications of illness on various aspects of the self will be discussed in Part 3 of this text.

SELF-ESTEEM

Our self-esteem (or self-regard) develops from our self-image and is essentially a judgement of aspects or the totality of our self-image. It is therefore essentially an evaluation, but once again it is subjective to a greater or lesser degree, and is dependent on how much worth is put on our perceived attributes and deficiencies by the society in which we live as well as the perceived gulf between the ideal and self-image.

In everyday language, we use the term 'high self-esteem' to describe someone who thinks well of themselves, and 'low self-esteem' for someone who does not. In doing so, we are often passing value judgements which may be more subjective than the subject's own evaluation of themselves. It is a wrong assumption to assume that if someone tells us that they are hopeless at, for instance, management, that this indicates a low self-esteem, and it may be wrong for at least two reasons. Firstly, it may be the case that the individual concerned has been highly objective in their self-evaluation, and is genuinely not 'cut out' for a managerial role. Secondly, although some people will inevitably form an overall judgement of themselves, most will have a more balanced approach that looks at specific areas of their lives, and form large numbers of judgements, some favourable and some not.

FACTORS AFFECTING THE DEVELOPMENT OF THE SELF

Four factors have been identified as being instrumental in directing the development of the self (Argyle, 1983):

(1) The reaction of other people to us.
(2) Comparing ourselves with others.
(3) The past, present and future roles that we play.
(4) Identification with models.

REACTION OF OTHER PEOPLE

One aspect of other people's reactions and the possible effects that this may have upon us is discussed in relation to the work of Rogers below. The theory that we begin to see ourselves as other people do ('looking-glass self'), and that we change our behaviours according to the reactions that we get from others, is one that we can easily relate to. Particularly when we are in a strange or new situation, we are usually anxious to see how other people react to us, and adjust our behaviours accordingly.

The nurse in uniform for the first few weeks will develop a whole new set of behaviours to go with it. On the one hand, the nurse may observe that more senior nurses treat her very much as a junior who is expected to ask questions and seek guidance, and hence the behaviour may be of a hesitant, almost subservient nature. On the other hand, the patients may just perceive that here is another nurse in uniform who knows what they are doing, and will interact on that basis, leading, perhaps, to the nurse displaying more confident behaviour, and indeed possibly improving their self-esteem.

It should come as no surprise that the opinions and reactions of others have most effect when we respect their opinions and judgements, and when we feel that they are being sincere and appear to be knowledgeable. Naturally, the less developed the individual's self-image is, the more effect the opinions and reactions of others will have (Rosenberg, 1981).

COMPARING OURSELVES WITH OTHERS

If we now return to the list that you may have prepared earlier in response to the statement 'I am', we can ask the question: 'How do I reach such conclusions?' One answer is that we have compared ourselves with others with regard to at least some of the answers. 'I am short', 'I am poor'and 'I am intelligent' are all examples of opinions that have probably been based on either what other people are doing, or what other people are like.

ROLES

The social roles that we have will also have a marked effect on the shaping of the self-concept. The roles of daughter, mother, man, woman, nurse, physiotherapist and countless others besides, leads us to evaluate and modify our self-concept, with obvious changes in our self-esteem and our **ideal self** as those roles develop, change, or even disappear.

IDENTIFICATION WITH MODELS

That we all base ourselves on people that we would wish to be like is demonstrable from childhood when we may try to emulate our parents, and later teachers and possibly others as well. As Argyle puts it, 'The ego-ideal is mainly based on a fusion of these models'.

GORDON **W**. ALLPORT

Allport asserts that not only is every personality unique, but also that it grows and changes dynamically throughout life. Allport, like Maslow and Rogers (see below), investigated the individual as a unique entity, and was one of the most renowned of the theorists of **humanistic psychology**.

Although Allport's theory differs substantially from those of Freud, Jung and others, he nevertheless accepts the existence of instinctual drives such as hunger, the need for sleep, oxygen, eliminating waste, etc. All other motives are secondary to these innate drives as long as a need such as hunger exists, and indeed, in early childhood such drives are dominant (see Chapter 4), although in later life he stresses the uniqueness of our motives.

In discussing Allport's theory, we will need to turn again to the subject of personality, discussed in Chapter 2, in order to gain an overall perspective.

TRAITS

Like Cattell and Eysenck, Allport places emphasis on **traits**. Unlike the other two psychologists, however, Allport asserts that there are around 5000 separate traits which he describes as neuropsychic, thus underlining his belief in a yet to be discovered physiological basis.

Stressing the influence of the culture in which we live, Allport proposes the existence of '**common traits**', although any suggestion of a standard trait which is identical between two people is rejected, as he is emphatic about the individual's unique ways of responding to a given situation. Common traits can therefore provide only a rough comparison between individuals within a given culture. Perhaps more importantly, he also proposes the existence of a second category of traits which go to make up our true personality, namely '**personal traits**', which are entirely unique to the individual.

THE PROPRIUM

Interpretations of what is meant by the term 'self' are in abundance, as reflected in our own brief introduction to this chapter, so much so that we are left with a confusing collection of information, some differing greatly in meaning. Allport prefers to use the term '**proprium**' when describing those aspects which are private to us, and which contribute to our 'inward unity'. The proprium is composed of eight personal aspects of existence:

(1) Sense of bodily self.
(2) Sense of continuing self-identity.
(3) **Ego enhancement** (self-esteem).
(4) Extension of the self to other things and people (**ego-extension**).
(5) Self-image
(6) The self as a 'rational coper'.
(7) **Propriate striving**.
(8) The self as knower.

Sense of Bodily Self
This is the first aspect of the self to emerge, and is a result of the infant's interactions with the environment, and the sensations and frustrations that he experiences. The infant thus learns to distinguish between herself and the environment, along with the beginnings of an awareness of the scope and limitations of their bodies. Our bodily sense is heightened during physical pursuits such as exercising, but this will also happen when we are in pain, and when we are experiencing sensual pleasure. The strength and inti-

macy of this sense was illustrated by Allport in the following example which the reader may like to try:

Firstly, swallow the saliva in your mouth. Secondly, imagine spitting it out into a cup, and then imagine drinking it!

The mere thought of drinking our saliva from a cup is quite repulsive, and yet when we considered it as being 'mine', we had no such feelings, in fact we all do it many times each day.

Our sense of bodily self is the mainstay of our self-awareness throughout life. Like Piaget's sensorimotor period (Chapter 6), this process proceeds between the ages of 0 and 2 years.

Sense of **Self-Identity**

Between the ages of about 1 and 2 years of age, the child begins to develop a **self-identity**, aided by the infant's increasing ability to communicate, although it only really becomes a stable entity at about the age of 4 years. In particular, learning, hearing and responding to his own name will be important to the earliest formation of self-identity.

The self identity has four components:

(1) Uniqueness
(2) Individuality
(3) Continuity
(4) Private experience.

That there is no other person like us (uniqueness), that we are hence individuals (individuality), and that we continue to exist as such (continuity) are perceptions that we all recognise, and will readily use to describe ourselves. We all have our own personal experiences that we cannot share with other people (private experience) that further enhance our individuality and uniqueness.

Ego Enhancement

Equivalent to self-esteem, **ego enhancement** is strongly correlated to **narcissism** (self-love), which again develops in early life. Most individuals will go to great lengths to avoid humiliation and to maintain a certain amount of pride, self-respect and self-satisfaction. Certainly, we cannot necessarily regard the ego enhancement as anything other than a largely subjective process in which our perceptions could be readily challenged by others.

Ego Extension

At about 4–6 years of age, the child begins to involve important external aspects of her world, and the concept of 'mine' emerges, initially applied to parents, brothers and sisters, and pets, as well as material possessions that they grow attached to. This, in turn, will normally lead to ego extension in more abstract matters such as ideals (e.g. love of country), beliefs (e.g. religion) and values (e.g. career).

Fig. 7.1 Learning to share—a difficult lesson to learn.

Self-image

Allport considers the self-image to be not only the perceptions of ourselves at a given time, but also how we would like to be in the future (ideal image). It may serve us as a helpful appraisal of our strengths and weaknesses with appropriate goals to work towards, or alternatively unrealistic goals due to an unrealistic idealised image. Like the **ego extension**, the self-image develops at around the age of 4–6 years.

The Self as a Rational Coper

This is similar to Freud's concept of the **ego**. The individual must cope with needs and impulses in terms of the realities of the environment in which they exist. According to Allport, most of us will confront such difficulties, and will usually find a solution to most problems, although he does accept the Freudian view that there will be times when we will avoid facing such difficulties, and thereby evoke defence mechanisms (see Chapter 10). This aspect of the **proprium** develops somewhere between the ages of 6 and 12 years.

Propriate Striving

Allport sees the motivation of the individual towards long-term goals as more than just the reduction of tensions, and suggests that we form intentions and goals that will give an overall purpose in life. **Propriate striving** first emerges during adolescence.

The Self as Knower
This is the part of the proprium around which all the other aspects gather. The 'knowing self' is not only aware of its existence, but also of the other seven aspects, and all other conscious aspects of the personality.

CARL ROGERS

Rogers, like other **humanistic (phenomenological) psychologists**, rejected the Freudian ideas that human behaviour is basically destructive and as a response to unconscious forces. Instead, he saw a far more optimistic future for the individual's actions, with the striving towards **self-actualisation** as the ultimate goal. Like Maslow (see Chapter 4), Rogers believed that we have an innate actualising tendency, and as such believed that generally other needs such as the biological ones are subservient to the individual's motivation to grow and mature.

Unlike Maslow and Allport, Rogers developed his theory from the study of individuals with emotional difficulties, and only later extended it to embrace areas such as education.

THE SELF-CONCEPT

The **self-concept** is central to Rogers' theory, and hence should be explored in terms of his interpretation of it. The self is entirely conscious, and includes not only the 'I am', but also 'what I can do'. Once again, it should be stressed that these are perceptions, and may bear little or no resemblance to reality.

Naturally, the self-concept will dictate not only our further perceptions, but also our behaviour. For example, if we perceive that we are not very intelligent we may avoid situations where we are expected to formally learn something, or if we think that we are ugly, it may affect how we form relationships.

Our experiences are evaluated in relation to this self-concept, and the individual will normally strive to behave in a way which is consistent with their self-image. Most human behaviour can be explained in these terms, although such consistency is not always achieved. Such 'incongruence' may be threatening to such an extent that we may consciously deny its existence, or even distort it, although persistence of such **defence mechanisms** may lead to **anxiety** with all its implications for the individual.

These incongruences, and more especially the defence mechanisms that the individual may evoke, will prevent growth and hence **self-actualisation**, and the individual's rigid **self-image** will further detach them from reality. The converse is true for the individual whose self-image is flexible and hence with feelings and beliefs that are consistent with their behaviour.

THE IDEAL IMAGE

The second kind of incongruence that may occur is concerned with the **ideal image**. It has already been mentioned that the ideal image is concerned with the sort of person that we would like to be, and Rogers maintains that the closer this ideal image is to the self-concept, the more likely the individual will be fulfilled. If the gulf is too wide, then dissatisfaction and unhappiness will result. This subject will be examined further in Chapter 13.

ROGERIAN PERSPECTIVES ON THE DEVELOPMENT OF THE SELF-CONCEPT

Positive Regard

Rogers does not describe development in terms of stages, although he does maintain that self-concept development begins in early childhood, and is essentially in the hands of parents and others close to the child, and centres around what Rogers calls our need for '**positive regard**'. As a result of our experiences, some of us will act in a way that does not reflect our true feelings because we may feel that doing so may not bring about acceptance or even love from those who are important to us.

If the child perceives that they are valued by their parents and others, regardless of whether their behaviour and attitudes have been ideal (**unconditional positive regard**), then they are likely to behave in a way which will reflect their true feelings. If, on the other hand, their parents and significant others only value the child when their behaviour is seen as correct (**conditional positive regard**), the child's feelings and actions become less satisfying and unreal. The reactions of other people are therefore of crucial importance, as we strive towards attaining their love and acceptance.

Conditions of Worth

In the process of fulfilling our need for positive regard, we develop '**conditions of worth**', which are the standards that the individual perceives they must attain in order to receive conditional positive regard from others. If we now take the actualising tendency and look at it in the light of these conditions of worth, it can be seen that they are not compatible, principally because these are the values that we perceive that others will value in us, and as such will obstruct the path to *self-actualisation*, as we have ignored or distorted those feelings that are important to us.

Positive Self-Regard

The need for positive regard is not only confined to childhood, but rather is a lifelong need and, as has already been observed, it can be a significant obstacle to the progression of actualisation. The fact remains, however, that we do have a need to feel loved and accepted by others, and indeed to feel as though we are lovable and acceptable people. To this end, we internalise the behaviours and values that other people approve of in order that we feel good about ourselves. Rogers calls this **positive self-regard**, and it is approximately equivalent to self-esteem.

Unconditional Positive Self-Regard
We can now deduce that in order to us to feel good about ourselves, we may need to match our behaviours with our conditions of worth and hence ignore our true feelings. It is Rogers' assertion that such a process can lead to maladjustment, and he noticed that many of his clients in the therapeutic setting were experiencing the results of incongruence between the self and reality. One of the cornerstones of Rogerian therapy is to divorce conditions of worth from positive self-regard and hence to work towards the 'Utopian' unconditional positive self-regard, which is a state of total self-acceptance.

SELF-DISCLOSURE

One of the central features of all health care is the assessment of the patient, not only in a physical sense, but also from a social viewpoint. Quite simply, the more we know about someone, the more able we are to plan their care, whether in a formal or community setting.

The importance of effective communication has already been stressed in Chapter 5. It is perhaps appropriate at this point to discuss not how the patient/client communicates, but rather what he communicates and why.

If we can think back to encounters that we have had with people who have later become friends (or more!), we will probably remember the pattern of interaction that occurred. Usually we divulge small pieces of information about ourselves (probably superficial facts), and if the other party reciprocates with information of a similar nature, then we will normally follow it up with more information and another response. In the case of the friendship that we have formed, these exchanges probably became more lengthy and intimate as time went by. The more intimate the information that we give, the higher the possibility of being given intimate information in return (Jourard, 1971). It often seems like a 'bartering'situation, where one party will not reveal information unless they have some information on 'deposit'!

Certainly, the more we trust someone, the more likely we are to disclose to them information of a personal nature. The environment that we are in will also affect disclosure.

SELF-DISCLOSURE AND PATIENT CARE

Quite how much we disclose to the patient is often the personal choice of the carer involved, and sometimes is dictated by the establishment that we work in, where it may be an unwritten rule to avoid getting involved with the patients, with all the possible connotations that policy will bring with it.

We have already discussed the importance of obtaining information from the patient, and the circumstances whereby self-disclosure may occur. There are possible advantages of the health professional self-disclosing (Nelson-Jones, 1983):

(1) It may give the impression of genuineness.
(2) It may encourage the patient/client to 'model' on your self-disclosing behaviour.
(3) It may lead to a sharing of feelings.
(4) It may lead to a sharing of experiences.
(5) It may lead to a sharing of opinions.
(6) It can allow assertiveness to be used effectively, for example in the case of an aggressive patient.

Of course, this is all assuming that the self-disclosures are appropriate. The patient will not benefit at all if we just want to unburden ourselves on someone, and of course there is always the potential problem of the health professional completely 'taking over' the interaction.

THE SELF AND HEALTH CARE

A number of points have been raised that could affect the practice of a wide range of health disciplines. For example, we can return to the very start of the chapter, with Rogers' assertion that (we) '. . . can never be perfectly understood by anyone else'. If we accept this statement, and many psychologists do, we really need to ask some questions of our practice.

Perhaps the experience of Allport can give us some direction. During his first (and last) meeting with Freud, he attempted to alleviate his own anxiety by passing a comment about a little boy that he had just seen who had an apparent phobia against dirt. Freud did no more than to ask Allport: 'And was that little boy you?' This incident caused him to comment many years later: 'This experience taught me that depth psychology, for all its merits may plunge too deep' (Allport, 1968). Perhaps here is a twofold warning: to look at manifest motives first (as Allport went on to suggest), and to respect the individual's dignity! From the Rogerian standpoint, we have to consider ourselves as partners with our clients, and as such must recognise that we will only understand what they allow us to, and that a complete understanding would be impossible anyway.

The uniqueness of the individual is a recurring theme in **humanistic psychology**, and could possibly lead us to build on our first question, namely, to what extent can we generalise the care that we give? Is it enough to merely acknowledge that the patient undergoing treatment is anxious, or do we need to recognise their uniqueness in order that the problem can be identified more clearly? Rogers' assertion that we all have a need for **positive regard** may mean that our clients and patients may deny their real feelings in front of us in order to make us like them more. The patients, according to Rogers, must be accepted for what they are, without conditions.

The implications of **humanistic psychology** on patient care also extend to areas such as health education, and indeed some aspects of our own education. Do we acknowledge the individual's needs in education? Certainly, to be sat down and lectured at regardless of the individual's needs is most definitely not in the best of Rogerian traditions. The individual should be allowed and encouraged to find their own starting point and direction for many aspects of their education, in order that they may begin to fulfil their true potential. If we consider the patient who is being discharged into a community setting, where they will need to carry out self-care, then sessions based on their perceptions, fears and strengths, carried out with full unconditional acknowledgement of their worth, will perhaps increase the effectiveness of their self-care.

CONCLUSIONS

The concepts that have grown up around the term self have many implications for health care. The concept of a **body image**, for instance, has far-reaching consequences for not only the individual undergoing surgery, but also for the way in which very young patients view impending treatment and illness. Certainly the humanistic approaches to psychology emphasise a highly individualised form of patient care, based substantially on the individual's perspective. In order to achieve this individualised perspective, it is essential for effective communication to take place between the individual and the health care professionals.

SUMMARY

The term 'self' has been used by many researchers, and has many different connotations. Humanistic psychology has emphasised the importance of the uniqueness of the individual.

The self is often said to be composed of three elements:

(1) The **self-image**/self-picture/actual self/ego identity.
(2) The **ideal self**.
(3) Self-esteem.

Four factors have been identified as being instrumental in directing the development of the self (Argyle, 1983):

(1) The reactions of other people to us.
(2) Comparing ourselves with others.
(3) The past, present and future roles that we play.
(4) Identification of models.

Allport asserts that not only is every personality unique, but he also believed that it grows and changes dynamically throughout life. Allport proposes the existence of '**common traits**', although any suggestion of a standard trait which is identical between two people is rejected.

For Allport, the **proprium** (self) is composed of eight personal aspects of existence, sense of bodily self, sense of continuing self-identity, **ego enhancement** (self-esteem), extension of the self to other things and people (**ego extension**), **self-image**, the self as a 'rational coper', propriate striving and the self as knower.

For Rogers, the self is entirely conscious, and includes not only the 'I am', but also 'what I can do'.

The individual will normally strive to behave in a way which is consistent with their self-image. Consistency is not always achieved. Such 'incongruence' may be threatening to such an extent that we may consciously deny its existence, or even distort it.

Rogers maintains that the closer that the ideal image is to the self-concept, the more likely that the individual will be fulfilled, and vice versa.

The need for **positive regard** is a lifelong need, and it can be a significant obstacle to the progression of actualisation.

Rogerian therapy attempts to divorce conditions of worth from **positive self-regard** and hence to work towards unconditional positive self-regard, which is a state of total self-acceptance.

Self-disclosure is an important aspect of communication which is crucial when assessing patient/client needs.

REFERENCES

* indicates a standard text or article

Allport, G.W. (1961) *Pattern and Growth in Personality.* Holt, Rinehart and Winston, New York.*

Allport, G.W. (1968) *The Person in Psychology; Selected Essays.* Beacon Press, Boston.*

Argyle, M. (1983) *The Psychology of Interpersonal Behaviour.* Pelican, London.

Burns, R. (1982) *Self-Concept Development and Education.* Holt, Rinehart and Winston, London.

Journard, S.M. (1971) *Self-Disclosure.* Wiley, London.*

Lerner, R.M., Orlos, J. and Knapp, J. (1976) Physical attractiveness and self concept in late adolescence. *Adolescence* **11**, 317–326.

Nelson-Jones, R. (1983) *Practical Counselling Skills.* Holt, Rinehart and Winston, Eastbourne.

Rogers, C.R. (1951) *Client-centred Therapy, its Current Practices, Implications and Theory.* Houston, Boston.*

Rogers, C.R. (1959) A theory of therapy, personality and interpersonal relationships as developed in the client-centered framework. In: S. Koch (ed.), *Formulations of the Person and the Social Context*, Vol. 3. McGraw-Hill, New York.*

Rosenberg, M. (1981) The self-concept; social product and social force. In: Rosenberg, M. and Turner, R.H. (eds), *Social Psychology; Social Perspectives.* Basic Books, New York.

Sullivan, H.S. (1954) *The Psychiatric Interview.* Norton, New York (reprinted 1970).

SUGGESTED READING

Argyle, M. (1983) *The Psychology of Interpersonal Behaviour.* Pelican, London. (See particularly Chapter 9 on self-image and self-presentation.)

Rogers, C.R. (1959) A theory of therapy, personality and interpersonal relationships as developed in the client-centered framework. In: S. Koch (ed.), *Formulations of the Person and the Social Context*, Vol. 3. McGraw-Hill, New York.*

CHAPTER 8

ATTITUDES

'Man need only to divert his attention from searching for the solution to eternal questions, and pose the one true inner question of how he should lead his life, and all the external questions will be resolved in the best possible way'.

LEO TOLSTOY (1879)

The subject of **attitudes** and **prejudice** is one in which many people take an immense interest. Advertisers, politicians, teachers, and even architects have been known to give the subject more than just a fleeting examination, and rightly so, since our behaviour towards objects or people will often depend on our attitude toward them. We really do not have to look very far in order to see how we are affected by our attitudes. Take for instance buying a new car. How much of the decision is based on solid facts, and how much is based on ill-founded prejudice against certain models?

The concept of attitudes is a hypothetical construct which cannot be observed directly, but can be observed indirectly from behavioural manifestations, which in turn may be measurable.

Understanding how attitudes are formed is one of the central issues in health care, and for that matter, social psychology. Without an understanding of their formation and nature we may expect little success in key areas such as health education. It is for this reason that an understanding of the origins of attitudes is so essential.

Allport (1935) has defined an attitude as: 'A mental and neural state of readiness, organised through experience, exerting a directive or dynamic influence upon the individual's response to all objects and situations with which it is related'.

The discussion in this chapter will commence with an overview of theories which describe the 'make-up' of an attitude, and will then progress to examine how attitudes can be measured. The topics of attitude change and prejudice will also be covered. This chapter attempts to look at attitudes in a very general sense in order to give the reader an overall picture. The subject of attitudes is revisited in Chapter 13 where it is examined in the context of illness.

COMPONENTS OF AN ATTITUDE

An **attitude** can be viewed as having three components (Secord and Backman, 1964):

(1) Cognitive
(2) Affective
(3) Behavioural.

THE COGNITIVE COMPONENT

The cognitive component is the rational part of an attitude and defines what the attitude is directed towards (object or situation). Naturally, the object of the attitude may be a person or a group of people and indeed the scope is vast. The cognitive component therefore could be said to consist of our knowledge about an object, situation or person, although such knowledge may be incomplete. To give an example, we may in the past have been given an extremely hot curry, when we had not experienced any Indian cuisine, and upon eating the curry, we may feel extremely uncomfortable. It may subsequently be the case that we say that we do not like Indian food because it is always too hot, and hence the cognitive core of our attitude is incomplete, as many other Indian dishes that we have not tried do not share the characteristics of the hot curry that we have tried. The cognitive core of our attitude could therefore be described as our beliefs or ideas (McDavid and Hariri, 1974).

Like many other subjects within psychology, attitudes cannot be considered to be the sole property of a particular branch (social psychology), and particularly when looking at the cognitive core of an attitude we can readily see that the study of personality development, developmental psychology, clinical psychology, etc., will all contribute to our understanding of how this belief part of our attitude emerges.

THE AFFECTIVE COMPONENT

The affective part of an attitude is frequently the most difficult component of the attitude itself to change. It consists of the feelings that we may have towards the object or situation and is very much a matter of being positive or negative, or at least some degree towards either and as such may be very deep-rooted. To put it another way, the emotional or affective component of attitude actually refers to our liking or disliking of the attitude object (Jaspars, 1978).

THE BEHAVIOURAL COMPONENT

The behavioural (or conative) component of an attitude refers to our tendency to behave in a certain way towards the attitude object. If we have positive feelings towards a particular attitude object, then we may develop approach tendency towards it, that is, we will tend to behave in such a way as to bring us into closer contact with that object. The converse is true with negative feelings, in which we will have a tendency to behave in such a way as to distance ourselves from the object (avoidance tendencies). The association between this component of our attitudes and motivation is a strong one, as it can be seen that it will direct our behaviour.

This 'three component theory' of attitudes brings with it, for many theorists, the assumption that all three components are consistent with each other; in other words, if we have positive beliefs, it will give us positive feelings, which will lead to positive actions. In the first instance, this is probably extremely difficult to observe in real life, as it is difficult to dissect out a specific attitude which is responsible for a specific behaviour, but rather a complex matrix of attitudes is involved in a complex set of behaviours.

There is however some evidence to suggest that such a consistency does exist (Campbell, 1963) and as Jaspers (1978) points out the idea of cognitive and affective components of attitude being related leads to attempts to change people's feelings towards certain objects or situations by introducing new information about them.

THE EXPECTANCY VALUE MODEL

An alternative way of looking at the three component model is to examine it in terms of expectancy value. The expectancy value model assumes that expectations are a key feature of attitudes and that the attitude object is viewed as being useful or otherwise to the individual's goals and further to their values. The explanation of cognitive and affective components also differs with this theory, with the cognitive component being defined as a section of associations between the object of attitude and certain attributes or goals (Jasper, 1978), and the affective component as the evaluation of the associated goals or attributes.

ATTITUDE FORMATION

Attitudes are formed in a number of ways, the most obvious of which is by direct experience; indeed attitudes based on direct experience are more accurate than those based on second-hand knowledge (from other people, television or reading). Attitude formation may also be strongly correlated with our upbringing and the attitudes of our parents, family and later peers. It has already been discussed in Chapter 1 how this form of modelling may affect smoking habits in later life.

The attitudes that a child has do not however solely emerge as a result of copying (modelling) the behaviour and attitudes of others. The whole process of upbringing is a complex system of factors which may and usually does include frequent use of rewards for certain behaviours and lack of reward or punishment for undesirable behaviours. These forms of early conditioning cannot be ignored when discussing attitude formation. It may be worthwhile at this juncture to also mention that indirect experience (in the form of being told by parents that something is good or bad, for example 'do not talk to strangers because it could be very dangerous') has a vital part to play in the early life of any individual.

ATTITUDE MEASUREMENT

The measurement of attitudes is an extremely complicated if not impossible process if we consider the every day use that the term attitude is subjected to. Managers frequently are asked on appraisal forms to comment on a particular individual's attitudes, and indeed some assume that such information can be readily gleaned from an ordinary selection interview.

It has already been noted that it is a rare occurrence for a specific attitude to have a one-to-one relationship with a specific attitude object without interrelationships with other attitudes and with attitude objects. If we take the example of a nurse's attitude to her paediatric experience it can be seen that such an attitude would comprise not only of an attitude towards children, but also of one towards children who are ill and possibly to the children's parents, possibly another to the environment in which they are being cared for, and possibly a whole set of attitudes directed towards different age groups. Just as there are many attitudes, it follows that the foundations of such attitudes may have had many completely separate origins, many of which would be difficult to determine. For instance, has the attitude towards nursing of neonates emerged from second-hand accounts from colleagues, previous experiences in an intensive care setting or even a dislike of the environment in which they are nursed? The reader can no doubt add numerous other possible origins giving an attitude concerning this connection, but the point will remain the same and that is, extreme caution should be exercised when attempting to comment on an individual's attitude towards an attitude object.

The measurement of attitude can to an extent be carried out using various measurement tools, which will be briefly discussed.

OSGOOD'S SEMANTIC DIFFERENTIAL (OSGOOD ET AL., 1957)

The individual is presented with a set of bipolar adjectives and asked to rate their belief or attitude on a seven point scale. One of the most famous examples of this tool being used is the 'least preferred co-worker scale' (Fiedler, 1967) where the individual is asked to think of the person with whom they can work with least well. From this, certain leadership implications can be raised.

The values may range from +3 to −3 with 0 or neutral as the mid-point, rather than 4 as the mid-point on Fiedler's measurement scale.

It is not surprising to discover that the Osgood semantic differential measure is of most use when measuring the affective component of an attitude.

THE LIKERT SCALE (LIKERT, 1932)

The Likert scale is familiar to most of us and is used extensively in market research. Its major use in measuring attitudes is the cognitive component.

Pleasant :__:__:__:__|:__:__:__:__: Unpleasant
8 7 6 5 | 4 3 2 1

Friendly :__:__:__:__|:__:__:__:__: Unfriendly
8 7 6 5 | 4 3 2 1

Rejecting :__:__:__:__|:__:__:__:__: Accepting
1 2 3 4 | 5 6 7 8

Helpful :__:__:__:__|:__:__:__:__: Frustrating
8 7 6 5 | 4 3 2 1

Unenthusiastic :__:__:__:__|:__:__:__:__: Enthusiastic
1 2 3 4 | 5 6 7 8

The 'least preferred co-worker' scale. From Fiedler (1967).

The scale consists of a number of statements, and the individual is asked to respond to each statement in one of five ways, namely, strongly agree, agree, undecided, disagree, and strongly disagree. It is important that the statements are equally divided between opposing points of view, and as with the Osgood's semantic differential measure, the selection of the attitude object needs to be highly specific. An example of the Likert scale is given below:

	Strongly agree	Agree	Undecided	Disagree	Strongly disagree
Professional updating should be compulsory					

It should not be assumed that these tests are a completely accurate assessment of the individual's attitude, as they may not reply to the questions in a true fashion. For instance, they may give responses which they feel are acceptable to the assessor (social desirability), or they may answer consistently in the middle of the scale, or may agree with all statements, or may disagree with all statements; this is known as the response set.

It would seem logical therefore, that any attitude test should be accompanied by other means of assessment, for example direct methods, such as asking the individual to make a story about a picture or even to place them in a situation where an attitude can be demonstrated.

ATTITUDE CHANGE

It is perhaps a preoccupation of most of us to ascertain how we may change someone's attitude, either from an advertising point of view, as mentioned earlier in the chapter, or from a health education point of view, or perhaps more obviously changing someone's attitude towards illness and treatment. The social environment has perhaps received the most attention when considering models of attitude change, and it seems appropriate at this juncture to re-examine the components of attitudes, and their possible role in changing attitudes.

It could be argued that when we attempt to change someone's attitude towards something, then we are ultimately attempting to alter a particular facet (or facets) of their behaviour. If we now return to the earlier discussion, we need to ask some fundamental questions about attitude change. For instance: do we need to change the way a person feels towards a particular object, or do we have to alter or increase their knowledge about it? Perhaps we need to change both or, by changing one component we could hope that the others will follow.

It would appear however, that at least to some extent, the question of what to change is not so immediately pressing as the matter of how to change it, and the key would appear to lie in the manner in which a message is communicated, and also in the characteristics of those involved in such a communication.

COMMUNICATION AND ATTITUDE CHANGE

The subject of which factors may prevent us listening to a message have already been discussed in Chapter 5, and should be borne in mind here. The characteristics of both the 'sender' and 'receiver', in relation to attitude change, will be discussed here, as will the mode of transmission and the structure of the message. If we wish to draw a distinction between the relatively straightforward transmission of a message, and a communication capable of changing an attitude, then we need to view such a communication in terms of its ability to persuade an individual or group.

THE SENDER

The individual who is communicating the message has an influence over the effectiveness of the message, and it will be remembered from Chapter 5 that one of the reasons for not listening is that the sender of the message is not liked, for one reason or other.

It perhaps comes as no surprise that we are more likely to take notice of the message if we perceive the communicator as being attractive, either physically or in relation to personality. Admiration for, and even identification or similarity (Snyder and Rothbart, 1971, Mills and Jellison, 1968) with the sender may actually prove to be more persuasive than the message content itself (Newcomb, 1961). The personality of the sender will naturally have an effect on changing attitudes, but in this case it seems logical to suppose that it is the perceived personality of the sender that will give credibility to the message rather than the sender's actual personality.

Naturally, credibility does not depend only upon whether we perceive the sender as being confident or pleasant (or indeed attractive), but they must also be perceived as being credible in terms of their knowledge and expertise. This effect is diminished when the recipient is strongly involved with the attitude object being discussed (Johnson and Scileppi, 1969). For instance, teachers of nursing may find it easier to change the attitudes of ward staff in a subject that the ward staff feel they have little knowledge of (such as a different speciality), than to change an attitude towards something that they do every day and consider themselves experts in.

THE MESSAGE

Obviously, the sender of the message can have little effect on changing attitudes if the message they are giving is of little worth. It is therefore reasonable to say that the content of the message is of vital importance, but also the message must be attended to, and subsequently understood. The factors that may prevent this have already been discussed in part, and this will be looked at further when discussing the 'receiver'. Amongst other factors, the encoding and decoding of the message are of major importance (see Chapter 5).

The evidence to support or refute various aspects of the importance of message structure and content is considerable, and at times contradictory (Jaspars, 1978). Some facts, however, do appear to emerge as being significant to attitude change.

Much of the research in connection with message content (as well as 'sender' and 'recipient' factors) has been directed towards the study of propaganda. Propaganda is directed towards the manipulation of attitudes, and as such has been studied in several contexts, not least of all from political and advertising viewpoints. Not surprisingly, attractiveness and credibility of the sender once more emerge as important factors, although the questions raised at the beginning of this section have also been considered.

Simple terms used so patient understands

Beliefs

Propaganda directed towards the cognitive component of attitudes has been found to have some effect. This can be observed readily in numerous television commercials where factual information is presented to the audience (e.g. toothpaste, where information is presented about tooth decay or shampoo where information is presented about scalp disorders).

Emotions

The other direction that propaganda may take is towards the affective component, and an approach which attempts to manipulate, or at least evoke

AIDS.
PREVENTION IS THE ONLY CURE WE'VE GOT.

Fig. 8.1 Sometimes, in order to change an attitude, we may need to evoke fear.

emotions, may be used. Certainly, with the above examples, one at least (the toothpaste commercial) may be seen as evoking fear (of loosing teeth through decay) as well as presenting information. The use of fear as a means to bring about attitude change (Leventhal, 1967), is a strategy well known to most of us who have observed certain health education material regarding drug abuse. The effects of fear appear to be limiting, and as such attitude change may only occur in response to a certain amount of fear arousal, after which the degree of attitude change will decline (McGuire, 1966).

One- and Two-Sided Arguments

To state that the message should be directed towards the cognitive or affective components does not tell us how this may be achieved, and therefore some consideration of this aspect is necessary. The presentation of facts, with or without an emotional slant, will need to be structured in such a way as to take account of the existing attitudes of the recipient. If, for instance, the recipient is well disposed towards the sender, a one-sided argument may be more effective than a two-sided argument, which may prove to be more productive when directed towards a more indifferent or antagonistic audience, when the opposing argument needs to be faced and attacked (Niven, 1989). The two-sided argument is also of use when talking to individuals who are familiar with the subject matter.

Drawing Conclusions from the Argument

The question then arises as to what conclusions the audience or individual may come to following the presentation of the argument. Put another way, should the recipients be given the conclusion, or should they be left to form their own? In looking at this problem, we have to consider that we are all individuals with unique perceptions and experiences, and that an obvious conclusion to one person may not be obvious to another. It therefore seems likely that the message should carry its own conclusions in order to be effective in changing atttitudes (Haskins, 1966).

THE RECIPIENT

Naturally, many of the factors which have already been discussed will depend upon the perceptions and experiences of the recipient of the message, and therefore it can be seen immediately that the recipient is a key factor. That this factor is important is plainly apparent, although some implications need to be explored here. Do we always take such factors into account when planning to give advice to a patient or client, or do we plan to give them the same talk on, for instance, smoking that we gave the previous fifty individuals that we came into contact with? Taking this a stage further, do we teach a subject to junior colleagues without adapting it to meet their individual needs?

The chances are that most of us will have preconceived ideas as to how a subject may be broached from a subject matter viewpoint, but have paid little attention to the factors which may affect the recipient's use and interpretation of it. This is not intended as a damning criticism, as it is frequently impossible to know sufficient details about our audience in advance in order to plan effectively; this may only be achieved when we meet the individual.

The fact remains, as we may have observed from our everday lives, that some people are more susceptible to persuasion than others. McGuire (1969) suggested that self-esteem may be related to the amount of attitude change that takes place, inasmuch as a high self-esteem may be positively related to understanding the message, but negatively related to undergoing attitude change as a result.

COGNITIVE DISSONANCE

Festinger (1957), in proposing his now famous theory of **cognitive dissonance** highlighted an important aspect of attitude theory, namely as individuals we normally strive to maintain consistency within ourselves. Put another way, we will strive for cognitive consistency, and hence avoid (whenever possible) situations where we may have to act in a manner contrary to our beliefs.

When such a predicament exists, then Festinger suggests that we no longer have cognitive consistency, but rather will experience a conflict known as cognitive dissonance. The dissonance that the smoker may experience has already been discussed in Chapter 4 in relation to motivation, and the example given provides us with a suitable starting point for the discussion.

Naturally, to learn that something that you enjoy (or just find difficult to give up) is likely to kill you will cause the behaviour and beliefs of the individual to be in conflict, but it would be as well to examine the variables which will determine whether dissonance will occur. The importance of the components can be seen to play a major part, and if the above example is again used, the knowledge that smoking is likely to kill us is important and hence dissonance is created.

Very often, however, the choices that we have to make are between two equally pleasurable options, such as choosing between two cars that we like equally (assuming that the gulf between the car we desire and the one we can afford is not too great). In such circumstances we may, after purchasing one of the cars, begin to emphasise the positive aspects of the one that we have bought and to emphasise the negative aspects of the one we have rejected, and hence lost.

Generally, the greater the difference between the two events or objects, the greater the potential difference. Many of us have experienced this when having to choose a career. We would probably experience greater dissonance if choosing between a career in law and a career in medicine than if

Fig. 8.2 Smoking helps me concentrate.

our choice was between nursing and physiotherapy. Naturally, much of the dissonance that we experience (as we have seen) is the result of personal choice, but often we have no choice but to enter into a situation and to act in such a way as to cause conflict between our beliefs and our actions. In such an instance, the 'reward', if any, that we may receive (e.g. financial, recognition, security) will influence the amount of attitude change that we may undergo (Festinger and Carlsmith, 1959).

WANTED

FOR INCITEMENT TO

MURDER

Fig. 8.3   Propaganda—a particularly powerful way to influence our attitudes, even if it has little basis in fact.

Cognitive dissonance, therefore, is an extremely uncomfortable state that the individual must resolve one way or the other. Certainly, as an agent for attitude change it can be seen as extremely powerful, although the ultimate consonance that the individual may attain may not always be desirable, as was seen with the 'smoker' example given in Chapter 4.

PREJUDICE

Prejudice is a specific type of attitude, and is described by Allport (1954) as: '. . .an antipathy based on a faulty and inflexible generalisation directed towards a group as a whole or towards an individual because he is a member of that group'.

It is a common misconception that a prejudice is always directed against someone (or a group), and indeed this is most certainly not the case. We may be equally inflexible in ignoring negative qualities as we may be in ignoring positive ones, and as such, prejudice can be considered as a continuum from extremely favourable to extremely unfavourable (Reich and Adcock, 1976).

As would be expected, as prejudice is an attitude it has the same basic components, namely cognitive, affective and behavioural. Although the cognitive and behavioural aspects are rather different from those of other attitudes, these will nevertheless be explored.

COGNITIVE COMPONENT

The forming of **stereotypes** is a characteristic of prejudice and really is a more accurate description of this component than to say that it is truly 'cognitive', although stereotyping occurs as a result of the individual acquiring knowledge, albeit very incomplete and one-sided.

Naturally we are rarely in possession of the total amount of information about an object, and hence it is usual for us to act on partial information; however, when the concepts that we hold are over-generalised, ambiguous and inaccurate then the person/group/object may be stereotyped. To an extent, this on its own does not give us too much cause for concern, as we will usually tend to form generalisations about a group or person based on very little information, but the more normal tendency is to continue accumulating information about the object in order to form a more realistic picture. The fact that any information which may disprove our belief (and such information may be overwhelming) may be completely ignored, and further information which may serve to confirm our beliefs is readily accepted, will differentiate it from a normal attitude, and will distinguish it as a prejudice.

BEHAVIOURAL COMPONENT

Behaviourally, prejudice is demonstrated by the prejudiced person as discrimination towards a person or group, and this may include aggressive behaviour. Once again it should be stressed that such discrimination may be in favour of or against the person or group.

The facility to generalise about people and groups is normal; without it we would be somewhat incapacitated in a world which is a perpetually changing set of experiences for the individual. Conversely, because the expectations that emerge from the prejudice tend to be both errorful and ineffective, the social interactions of the prejudiced individual could be crippled.

It can be deduced therefore that prejudice lacks a degree of humanitarianism, rationality is both reduced and resisted, and a sense of justice is reduced.

Having taken a brief look at prejudice, it seems fairly easy to detect a prejudiced person, however this is not always the case. We will judge a person by our standards, which in turn may be prejudiced. In addition to this, social factors for every individual will vary considerably.

CAUSES OF PREJUDICE

The causes of prejudice are a matter of some debate. However, it is generally accepted that it is a learned behaviour, not a biologically based bahaviour. Because it does not have a biological foundation, prejudice is not inevitable, and because it is not inevitable, it would follow that people who have not learned the attitude will not be prejudiced.

Prejudice probably has its basis in the interaction of personal and social factors. During wartime, for instance, prejudice against the enemy will be the norm of that society, and if a person does not conform to the society's prejudice, then prejudice will be directed towards that person for not conforming. On a personal level, a prejudice will occur as a result of a person's life experiences. If life experiences lead to situations of frustration and the individual is unable to release this frustration (which would normally take the form of aggression), then the individual will displace the aggression onto targets which cannot easily retaliate. This has been termed the scapegoat theory of prejudice. Once again it can be seen that the prejudice is learned, however not everyone will react in the same way, and indeed not everyone will develop a prejudice following life experiences. To explain this, it may be useful to look at two different aspects, both of which are concerned with childhood experiences.

The first aspect deals with aggression. Bandura (1973) showed in his experiments just how much aggression can actually be learned by children after watching aggression either live, on film or in cartoons. After watching violence, these children were far more aggressive in their play. If this is continually reinforced, the behaviour continues and the child will come to consider this aggression as normal behaviour.

The second aspect concerns how the child is brought up. Individuals with an authoritarian personality are frequently associated with holding very fixed views on subjects, including groups with various characteristics (e.g.

immigrants, communists, etc.) and these views tend to be definite (i.e. they are either positive or negative). It has been shown (Adorno *et al.*, 1950) that there is a correlation between this type of person and very strict upbringing, teaching obedience and a rejection of anyone not in their group. This is referred to as the personality theory of prejudice.

As an extension of the personality theory of prejudice, it is also possible to learn specific prejudices from parents on the basis of verbal reinforcement alone. Again, these are learned responses.

Prejudice can be attributed to such social factors as community separateness, ignorance, rapid change in the social structure, unemployment, etc. Such social factors, however, may not produce prejudice in a person for two main reasons. Firstly, not all individuals will be brought into significant contact with these factors, but more importantly, going back to the personality theory of prejudice, not everyone will be susceptible to prejudice in this way.

So far, personality theory, scapegoat theory, social factors, learned aggression and life experiences have all been mentioned as possible causes of prejudice. It is now thought far more likely that the tendency towards prejudice is not due to any one of the above, but more likely to be a combination of factors.

One more factor, however, should be taken into consideration, and that is legal restraint. This has been particularly evident in certain countries which have used legal segregation as part of government policy. This and other such laws serve to reinforce prejudice in both groups that are involved in the consequences of such legislation.

Prejudice, however, may actually be a positive attitude possessing many of the qualities of the 'negative' prejudice, such as holding an unsubstantiated bias, or favourable view of a certain group, contrary to logical information. It could be argued that in order to have a prejudice against one group, an individual must have a prejudice in favour of another opposite group.

In order to eradicate a prejudice, because it is an attitude, an attitude change must take place. Paradoxically this is best done using the same factors that originally caused the prejudice, namely legal measures to enforce racial integration, changes in social factors, etc. Unfortunately, evidence has shown that the prejudice often only disappears in the immediate situation, and is still held against groups away from the individual's immediate situation.

The subject of attitudes in relation to health and illness will be discussed in Chapter 13.

LABELLING

It has already been suggested that we all tend to have preconceived ideas about people and groups, and that this helps us to cope with the world that we live in. In order that we may, to some extent, behave appropriately, we categorise people according to a vast array of criteria, such as where they live, their profession, religion, etc. This 'labelling' as it is called can be helpful, but often it leads to incorrect assumptions, and hence incorrect behaviour.

CONCLUSION

Our attitudes towards objects and people will determine our behaviour. The formation of our attitudes is of prime importance when considering the methods that may be utilised in changing them such as in health education, and particularly when considering the origins of prejudice. In terms of acting in a manner contrary to our attitudes, the psychological discomfort that this produces acts as a strong motivator to bring about attitude change, and hence return us to a state of consistency.

SUMMARY

Allport (1935) has defined an attitude as: 'A mental and neural state of readiness, organised through experience, exerting a directive or dynamic influence upon the individual's response to all objects and situations with which it is related'.

An attitude can be viewed as having three components (Secord and Backman, 1964):

(1) Cognitive
(2) Affective
(3) Behavioural

An alternative way of looking at the three-component model is to examine it in terms of expectancy value.

Attitudes are formed in a number of ways, the most obvious of which is by direct experience, and indeed attitudes based on direct experience are more accurate than those based on second-hand knowledge. Attitude formation may also be strongly correlated with our upbringing.

The measurement of attitude can to an extent be carried out using various measurement tools, e.g. the Osgood semantic differential, or the Likert scale.

It could be argued that when we attempt to change someone's attitude towards something, then we are ultimately attempting to alter a particular facet (or facets) of their behaviour. The key would appear to lie in the manner in which a message is communicated, and also in the characteristics of those involved in such a communication.

We all strive for cognitive consistency, and hence avoid (whenever possible) situations where we may have to act in a manner contrary to our beliefs.

When such a predicament exists, then Festinger suggests that we no longer have congitive consistency, but rather will experience a conflict known as **cognitive dissonance**. Cognitive dissonance, therefore, is an extremely uncomfortable state that the individual must resolve one way or the other.

Propaganda directed towards the cognitive component of attitudes has been found to have some effect. The other direction that propaganda may take is towards the affective component.

REFERENCES

* indicates standard texts or articles

Adorno, T.W., Frenkel-Brunswick, E., Levinson, D.J. and Sandford, R.N. (1950) *The Authoritarian Personality*. Harper and Row, New York.*

Allport, G.W. (1935) Attitudes. In: Murchinson, C.M. (ed.), *Handbook of Social Psychology*. Clark University Press, Mass.*

Allport, G.W. (1954) *The Nature of Prejudice*. Addison-Wesley, Wokingham.*

Bandura, A. (1973) *Aggression: A Social Learning Analysis*. Prentice-Hall, Englewood Cliffs, NJ.*

Campbell, D.T. (1963) Social attitudes and other acquired behavioural dispositions. In: Koch, S. (ed.) *Psychology: A Study of a Science*, Vol. 6. McGraw-Hall, New York.

Festinger, L. (1957) *A Theory of Cognitive Dissonance*. Harper and Row, New York.*

Festinger, L. and Carlsmith, L.M. (1959) Cognitive consequences of forced compliance. *Journal of Abnormal and Social Psychology* **58**, 203–210.

Fiedler, F.E. (1967) *A Theory of Leadership Effectiveness*. McGraw-Hill, New York.

Haskins, J. (1966) Factual recall as a measure of advertising effectiveness. *Journal of Advertising Research* **6**, 2–8.

Jaspers, J.M.F. (1978) Determinants of attitudes and attitude change. In: Tajfel, H. and Fraser, C. (eds), *Introducing Social Psychology*. Penguin Books, Harmondsworth.

Johnson, H.H. and Scileppi, J.D. (1969) Effects of ego involvement conditions on attitude change to high and low credibility communications. *Journal of Personality and Social Psychology* **13**, 31–36.

Leventhal, H. (1967) Fear—for your health. *Psychology Today* **1**, 54–58.

Likert, R. (1932) A technique for the measurement of attitudes. *Archives of Psychology* **22**, 1–55.

McDavid, J.W. and Harari, H. (1974) *Psychology and Social Behaviour*. Harper and Row, New York.

McGuire, W.J. (1969) The nature of attitudes and attitude change. In.: Lindzey, G. and Aronson, E. (eds), *Handbook of Social Psychology*, 2nd edn, Vol. 3. Addison-Wesley, New York.

Mills, J. and Jellison, J.M. (1968) Effect of opinion change on similarity between the communicator and the audience he addressed. *Journal of Personal and Social Psychology* **9**, 153–6.

Newcomb, T.M. (1961) *The Acquaintance Process*. Holt, Rinehart and Winston, New York.

Niven, N. (1989) *Health Psychology; An Introduction for Nurses and Other Health Care Professionals.* Churchill Livingstone, London.

Osgood, C.E., Suci, G.J. and Tannenbaum, P.H. (1957) *The Measurement of Meaning.* University of Illinois Press, Illinois.

Reich, B. and Adcock, c. (1976) *Values, Attitudes and Behaviour Change.* Methuen, London.

Secord, P.F. and Backman, C.W. (1964) *Social Psychology.* McGraw-Hill, New York.*

Snyder, M.G. and Rothbart, M. (1971) Communicator attractiveness in attitude change. *Canadian Journal of Behavioural Sciences,* **3**, 377–87.

SUGGESTED READING

Bandura, A. (1973) *Aggression: A Social Learning Analysis.* Prentice-Hall, Englewood Cliffs, NJ.*

Festinger, L. (1957) *A Theory of Cognitive Dissonance.* Harper and Row, New York.* (This classic text is worth more than just a passing perusal!)

Reich, B. and Adcock, C. (1976) *Values, Attitudes and Behaviour Change.* Methuen, London. (This easy-to-read text provides a useful background to the subject. See particularly Chapter 2 (the nature of values), and Chapter 10 which discusses learning theories.)

SECTION

TWO

REACTION TO LIFE EVENTS

CHAPTERS

Again, the more the mind knows, the better is understood its forces and the order of nature; the more it understands its forces or strength, the better it will be able to direct itself and lay down rules for itself; and the more it understands the order of nature, the more easily it will be able to liberate itself from useless things. . .

SPINOZA

INTRODUCTION TO SECTION TWO

A lot of attention has been focused in recent years on the events that may occur in the life of the individual, and the possible effects that this may have on them.

Many different views exist, and the topic can be explored from several different aspects. First, it seems logical to suppose that personality will have a major role to play in how we react, but if this is the case, we will need to consider some different approaches to personality and how these would view the subject. In doing so, the subject of defence mechanisms is covered, but this is by no means the only view. The possible role of birth order and inferiority is introduced, along with a review of the implications for those theories discussed in Chapter 2.

The emergence of our reactions to life events is examined, and in doing so, grieving is discussed, as is prosocial behaviour. The possible responses of the child to separation experiences is looked at, along with some possible implications for health professionals.

The first chapter in this section examines stress, and goes on to discuss how the individual may cope with stress as well as how they may express emotion.

CHAPTER 9

STRESSORS AND
COPING

'Life is the art of drawing sufficient conclusions from insufficient premises'

SAMUEL BUTLER (1835–1902)

INTRODUCTION

It is very easy when reviewing the psychology literature to assume that the individual, when faced with a crisis (or even normal everyday events), will immediately run for cover behind a **defence mechanism**, or will suffer some dire psychological fate as a result of being confronted with such problems. This is clearly not the case, as we are all faced, during the course of our lifetimes, with many difficulties that quite simply do not have a ready solution, and yet we learn to adapt our lives around such difficulties, and to cope in the face of adversity. Similarly, some problems do have a solution, but only by coping with the problem and actively trying to deal with it will the solution evolve.

If we momentarily return to the discussion in Chapter 7, it will be remembered that Allport believed that most individuals will face most problems 'head-on', and only in exceptional circumstances will defence mechanisms be evoked.

The individual's **coping mechanisms** will be discussed later in the chapter, but to start with the subject of stressors, which was covered from a physiological viewpoint in Chapter 3, will be re-examined. The subject of occupational stress will also be discussed.

STRESSORS

The physiological responses to **stress** were discussed earlier in the text, and for the purposes of this discussion possible stressors will be identified. Lazarus and Folkman (1984) define stress in terms of 'a particular relationship between the person and the environment that is appraised by the individual as taxing or exceeding his or her resources and endangering his or her wellbeing'.

Naturally, different events will be considered by the individual to be different in terms of the amount of stress that they may produce for them; this is further discussed in the section below which deals with coping. Although stress is frequently described in terms of its physiological characteristics, to ignore the psychological aspects is to turn our backs on the causes of stress that will result from our interactions with the environment, as well as those factors that may determine our stress reactions. Once again, we cannot ignore the importance of past experiences, together with predictability, physical control over stressors, and social support (Steptoe, 1983).

In considering the factors which may cause stress to the individual, Holmes and Rahe (1967) asked people about the adjustment required for certain life events in order to ascertain their relative importance. These ratings are also known as 'life change units' (LCUs). This 'social readjustment rating scale' is reproduced below.

The social readjustment rating scale

Rank	Life event	Mean value
1	Death of spouse	100
2	Divorce	73
3	Marital separation	65
4	Jail term	63
5	Death of a close family member	63
6	Personal injury or illness	53
7	Marriage	50

Rank	Life event	Mean value
8	Fired at work	47
9	Marital reconciliation	45
10	Retirement	45
11	Change in health of family member	44
12	Pregnancy	40
13	Sex difficulties	39
14	Gain of new family member	39
15	Business readjustment	39
16	Change in financial state	38
17	Death of a close friend	37
18	Change to a different line of work	36
19	Change in number of arguments with spouse	35
20	Mortgage over £10,000	31
21	Foreclosure of mortgage or loan	30
22	Change in responsibilities at work	29
23	Son or daughter leaving home	29
24	Trouble with in-laws	29
25	Outstanding personal achievement	28
26	Wife begins or stops work	26
27	Begin or end school	26
28	Change in living conditions	25
29	Revision of personal habits	24
30	Trouble with boss	23
31	Change in work hours or conditions	20
32	Change in residence	20
33	Change in schools	20
34	Change in recreation	19
35	Change in church activities	19
36	Change in social activities	18
37	Mortgage or loan of less than £10,000	17
38	Change in sleeping habits	16
39	Change in number of family get-togethers	15
40	Change in eating habits	15
41	Vacation	13
42	Christmas	12
43	Minor violations of the law	11

Reproduced from Holmes and Rahe (1967).

WORK AND STRESS

The social readjustment rating scale has been criticised by some researchers, not least of all because it fails to distinguish between positive and adverse events, but rather it assumes that all the events can be viewed as stressors. Be this as it may, it can be seen that one significant group of events, namely those connected to work, have considerable prominence.

The subject of occupational stress is not a new one, and has received considerable research interest. A definition of stress has already been given earlier in the chapter and within the realms of occupational stress this is equally applicable. The relationship between a situation and the individual's ability to deal with the situation is of key importance in this subject (Ivancevich and Matteson, 1984). Once again however, we return to the point made so often in this text, that the reality of the situation is frequently overshadowed by the individual's perception of the situation or events around them as well as their ability to cope with them.

The stress associated with work is not as straightforward as it would at first appear. We could all naturally identify jobs that we think would present stress because of the components of that job and how we would perceive our abilities to cope with it. It is essential, however, that we understand the possible sources of stress in our jobs in order that firstly we may reduce the stress placed on us, but possibly more relevant to the discussion, we may attempt to educate our clients to reduce the stress in their lives and hence minimise the risk of stress-related illness.

In a major study on managerial job stress (Marshall and Cooper, 1979), several sources of job-related stress have been suggested, although at the same time the individualistic aspects have been emphasised. The job itself as well as the working conditions, work load, aspects of the role, role conflict and role responsibility, relationships at work, promotion, job security, career development, and lack of autonomy have all been identified as potential stressors. What is particularly worrying about this collection of possible stressors is that many of us can identify at least one of them that is affecting us, or rather that we perceive as affecting us.

Other studies have confirmed Marshall and Cooper's findings and have gone some way to identifying aspects of jobs which produce stress. An excessive amount of decision making (Sofer, 1970) and making mistakes (Kearns, 1973) are two aspects with which most of us are familiar and it probably comes as no surprise that poor mental health has been directly correlated with poor working conditions (Kornhauser, 1965). Particularly with regard to jobs such as those on assembly lines, a deterioration in physical health has also been identified (Marcson, 1970).

As far as the individual's role in the organisation is concerned, stress is again produced when the individual perceives that their potential to deal with a situation is incompatible or insufficient to deal with the situation in hand. Perhaps the most obvious area where this occurs is where the individual is torn by conflicting demands of the job. Physical manifestations including changes in blood pressure and in electrocardiograph readings have been found in members of a Kibbutz who were experiencing work overload, ambiguity of role, as well as conflict (Shirom et al., 1973).

Job responsibility again appears to be quite straightforward as a stressor although it has now been suggested that it is not only the level of responsibility that produces stress but rather whether the person is responsible for things or people (Wardwell et al., 1964), with the responsibility for people producing the most stress, probably because of the increased amount of interactions that are required. Valid though this finding appears to be, other factors probably intercede. In one study of two occupational groups, airline pilots and air traffic controllers (Cobb and Rose, 1973), it was found that the incidence of ulcers in the air traffic controllers was twice that of the pilots. Perhaps the difference could be explained in terms of the more sustained amount of vigilance over a longer period of time that is characteristic of the air traffic controllers group, or perhaps it may be due to the greater volume of responsibility in terms of the amount of people that they are responsible for.

The assumption that this sort of stress is directly related to coronary heart disease is somewhat tempered by other research which demonstrates that responsibility for people is correlated with heavy smoking (French and Caplan, 1970). Therefore it could be said in this case that the stress is only indirectly related to the illness.

There are a tremendous amount of variables involved. Smoking is just one of them when considering the relationship between occupational stress and illness, and it is perhaps appropriate if we now examine some of the work carried out in order to establish a direct link between the two.

STRESS AND HEALTH CARE

Rather disturbingly, one survey (Nursing Times, 1992) revealed that 93% of nurses feel stressed at work, with an estimated 42% of sick leave being stress related. Perhaps surprisingly, patient-related causes played a relatively minor role in this predicament, with the major causes being related to organisational and mangerial factors. It would appear that the nurses who actually leave the profession do so for reasons other than difficulties with the actual job, with managerial and organisation factors again playing a major role (Williams *et al.*, 1991).

LIFE EVENTS AND ILLNESS

That stress can cause illness (or at least be a significant contributing factor), and that it probably is instrumental in recovery, is strongly argued by numerous researchers. It would appear from the results of some research, that both physical and mental illness may, to an extent, have their causes in stressful life events.

Once again though, we are faced with the complexities of the individual's life, and the risks that drawing unwarranted conclusions from apparently obvious associations will bring. For example, if we were to wander around a cemetery, and were to look for graves where both husband and wife are buried together, we may be struck with the amount of elderly couples who have died within a short space of time of each other. We may draw the conclusion that the surviving partner was so grieved by the loss of a loved one that this led to their own death. There may or may not be truth in such a

hypothesis, but what is certain is that we have ignored vast amounts of data in reaching our conclusion, and indeed such an unwarranted conclusion would be extremely unstable.

The association of life events to illness most certainly has its critics, but as Creed (1992) points out, with the emergence of more refined measures of life events, and with the more careful selection of subjects, a greater understanding of the aetiology is now emerging.

LIFE EVENTS AND PHYSICAL ILLNESS

We have all probably heard, or have even expressed ourselves, the day-to-day associations that people make between certain events and illness. Probably the classic association is between continuous hard work and the onset of a myocardial infarct, or perhaps more often, a duodenal ulcer. We have already discussed the possible relationships between occupational stress and illness. We now need to extend the discussion further to include life events generally.

The evidence for a connection between stressful life events and physical illness is far from clear cut, with apparently well-founded arguments on either side of the debate. In one study of Naval personnel, it was found that there was a positive correlation between a high amount of LCUs and physical illness (Rahe, 1975), although as Bakal (1979) points out, these ailments were extremely diverse, and could well have had other explanations.

Possible **psychosomatic** origins of non-organic abdominal pain and menorrhagia were investigated by Harris (1989), and there was found to be an association with very threatening life events, although no such link was found with organic disease (Craig and Brown, 1984).

Chronic disorders have also been investigated, and with at least one such disorder (multiple sclerosis), a link is strongly indicated between life events (most notably marital and family difficulties) and the onset of the disease (Grant *et al.*, 1989).

LIFE EVENTS AND MENTAL ILLNESS

That certain events in our lives, such as the loss of a loved one, can cause depression is apparent to most of us, although the assumption that traumatic life events invariably lead to depression is probably wrong (Paykel, 1978). Bereavement is however a link which has been made with depression, and it will probably come as no surprise to learn that in one study it was found that patients hospitalised for depression had undergone a bereavement in the previous 6 months, six times as often as the normal average (Parkes, 1964).

It is now relevant to return to a point made earlier in the chapter, namely that one of the criticisms of the social readjustment rating scale (SRRS) is that it fails to distinguish between favourable and unfavourable life events. In attempting to establish whether a link existed between life events and depression, Paykel, (1974) found it necessary to separate the favourable from the unfavourable life events, and hence, using a different tool from the SRRS, they found that patients suffering from depression reported three times as many life events in the 6-month period before the onset of symtoms than did the control group.

Grant *et al.*, (1981) found that unfavourable events were correlated with depression, and that favourable events were more likely to be associated with reduced symptoms. In support of this, Miller *et al.*, (1989) report that an improvement in the depressive state is associated with a reduction of difficulties. Once again, as with the example given above regarding multiple sclerosis, certain types of events were correlated with depression, namely long-term threatening events as distinct from those with short-term consequences (Brown and Harris, 1978), although it should be stated that this study was carried out on women only.

So far, our discussion on depression has centred around **exogenous depression**, and the effects that life events have on its development. Studies have also been carried out on **endogenous depression** and it would seem that life events are also important to the causation of this type of depression (Thompson and Hendrie, 1972).

Depression is not the only condition for which causation has been investigated in relation to life events. Schizophrenia has been researched both in terms of onset and relapse. Results would appear to suggest that both onset and relapse may be related to certain types of event, namely those events which involve the removal of a social support (Dohrenwend *et al.*, 1987).

COPING

In attempting to try and decide what constitutes a **coping mechanism**, it would be as well to remind ourselves that a coping mechanism for one individual may turn out to be a nightmare for anyone else in the same predicament. For instance, one individual, when confronted with a relationship problem, may insist on having 'things out in the open' in order to 'clear the air'. To another individual, such an approach to the problem would create rather than alleviate stress.

Quite how we search for answers to, and eventually resolve problems, is therefore a highly individual phenomenon, and although we can often identify how the individual has arrived at their optimum set of behaviours to cope with a problem, the end result is far from predictable.

We can, however, identify some of the more common mechanisms that the individual may use. When considering such mechanisms, it should be remembered that the factor that distinguishes them from **defence mechanisms** is their orientation towards reality, as distinct from the distortion of reality which is the characteristic of a defence mechanism.

A coping mechanism should therefore, if successful, help to reduce the stress created by a problem, in one way or another. This does in fact appear much easier than it actually is. These basic facts will direct us to conclude that coping mechanisms may have distinct functions, depending upon how the individual perceives the problem. One model which attempts to explain not only the functions but also the process of coping is discussed below.

A COGNITIVE MODEL OF COPING

It can be deduced from the earlier definition that the degree of stress cannot be predicted from the intensity of the stimulus or from the resources of the individual but rather depends on the relationship between them. For example, the same situation could be presented to two individuals, such as giving a teaching session to a group of people. The session would be the same one with the same audience but to the experienced teacher, the demands of the session would not exceed the resources available to them and hence may not be viewed as stressful. The inexperienced teacher, never having given the session before, or who is generally inexperienced at teaching, may find that the gulf between her personal resources and the demands of the session is too great and hence stress is increased.

Appraising Stress

Lazarus and Folkman went on to describe a **cognitive appraisal process** which attempts to evaluate the amount of stress (if any) that a given situation may present to the individual. They described three forms of appraisal.

Primary Appraisal. With this first form of appraisal the individual is concerned with categorising the situation in terms of their own well-being. The situation may be regarded as stressful in which case the individual has perceived it as either potentially or actually harmful to them. They may however define the situation as benign positive, in which case the individual views the situation as actually or potentially beneficial to them. It may well be of course that the individual sees no relevance to them in terms of a threat to their well-being, either actual or potential or in terms of benefit to their well-being and therefore the situation is viewed as irrelevant.

Secondary Appraisal. Having ascertained that a situation is or is potentially threatening to their well-being the individual will then need to decide upon a course of action. The coping strategy that the individual will actually use should aim at reducing the gulf between the individual's resources and the demands placed upon it, and hence the level of stress in a given situation evolves from the relationship between demands and resources to the relationship between primary appraisal and the secondary appraisal of coping options.

Re-appraisal. It is rare to find any given situation which will remain static even from a demand or a resources point of view and for this reason the individual would continually reappraise the situation in the light of further information and perceptions; hence their behaviour may change accordingly.

Coping Process

Lazarus and Folkman (1984) suggest that coping fulfils two major functions.

Problem-focused coping. This is directed towards altering the relationship between the demands of the situation and the resources available. Naturally problem-focused coping will only come into existence if the individual perceives that either the problem they are facing or the resources they have available are changeable, but further that they can bring about such change. Life is full of examples of problem-focused coping and indeed most of us are familiar with the scenarios of leaving a job which we may have perceived as stressful or even going to college to learn more about a subject in order that we may feel more comfortable in our practice at work. It must be said however, that to state that we would only ever encounter problems for which we may see a solution is to deny the existence of a group of problems which will have no answer or solution.

Emotion-focused Coping. It may be the case that we are faced with a problem which genuinely has no solution and in any case is totally outside of our control. For instance, a relative who is dying in hospital will die regardless of what we do, and hence we can do nothing to change the stressful condition. What we can do however is to alter our emotional response to such a situation; this can be done either behaviourally or cognitively.

Behaviourally we may change, for instance, by increasing our social contact with friends and loved ones, in order to gain some support; engrossing ourselves in work so we think of the situation less; or even turn to alcohol, drugs etc., in order to alter our state of consciousness and awareness.

Alternatively, we may attempt to cognitively reappraise the situation in order to reduce the amount of stress that it is inflicting upon us. For instance, with a dying relative, we may tell ourselves that it is not a tragedy and that it is a good thing that the person is dying because they will be relieved of further suffering. We may reduce the importance of a job or even an exam by altering the emphasis that we originally put upon it, so that we may be of the opinion, the night before the exam, that passing the exam is not really so important, despite that fact that we have worked consistently hard because of our underlying belief that the exam was extremely important.

It is highly likely however, that rather than having such clear-cut distinctions as problem-focused coping and an emotion-coping strategy, both are used in conjunction with each other for at least part of the time.

Coping Mechanisms
Although the model proposed by Lazarus and Folkman provides us with a good set of general principles, its high level of generality can be a disadvantage (Stroebe and Stroebe, 1987), and therefore a more specific view of coping mechanisms will be discussed here. The reader may notice that most if not all of the following examples of coping mechanisms can be categorised into the problem- or emotion-focused coping models proposed by Lazarus and Folkman.

Gaining Control. The concept that we cope with a situation by actively intervening to alter the intensity of the problem or to increase the amount of resources that we have available to deal with it has already been discussed. There are occasions, however, where we do not have immediate control over the problems nor can we easily deal with it by changing our behaviour or cognition. One such example of this could be the individual who is experiencing pain and discomfort following surgery or as part of an illness. There are few resources available to them to deal with the pain, if they are hospitalised and indeed they cannot alter the nature of the problem. It is an admirable ethic of medical and nursing practice (most notably in hospice care) that the patient should be kept pain free, as opposed to being given analgesia when the pain actually starts.

Hinton (1984) suggests that demands placed upon medical staff and nurses make it difficult to give ideal treatment at the right time, and indeed delays in prescribing and administering the appropriate analgesia may vary from a few minutes to many days in the case of waiting for further laboratory results, etc. Clearly, in this situation the individual will lose all control over his pain management and so an alternative method of pain relief (if we are seriously considering reducing their stress levels) should be considered. One such method is self-administration, where a predetermined quantity of the analgesic (to a maximum dose over a period of time) can be administered intravenously in small metered doses through an *in situ* cannula, by the patient activating a control device when they have pain.

The subject of pain will be covered in more depth in chapter 14.

For a much wider perspective the concept of self-care can be viewed as giving the individual a large amount of control over his treatment and care (Gammon, 1991). In his research Gammon demonstrated the strong relationship between self-care and how an individual copes with cancer in terms of promoting a sense of control, higher **self-esteem**, and lower levels of **anxiety** and depression. Naturally, we also need to consider other factors which may influence the individual's ability to carry out self-care, for instance, whether they have an internal or external **locus of control**, the part played by personality, and whether self-esteem has an effect.

Information Control.   To an extent seeking information about the stressor can give the individual a form of control, insofar as they are able to define more accurately the nature of the stressor and hence are better able to deal with it. Cohen and Lazarus (1973) found that those patients with the least knowledge or awareness of their condition were the ones most likely to show avoidance or denial of emotional or threatening aspects of their medical experience, and this was termed an **avoidance coping style**.

Conversely, Cohen and Lazarus also described a vigilant coping style, where the individual is very aware of the possible emotional or threatening aspects of their medical experience and will actively seek knowledge about it.

In any event, as the discussions in Chapters 12, 13, 14 and 15 will indicate, giving the necessary information to a patient is essential in order to reduce (to some extent) the inevitable **anxiety** that some patients may experience.

Logical Analysis.   It may be the case that the individual will attempt to systematically break down the problem and carefully analyse each aspect in order to identify the actual rather than the perceived situation and hence to make realistic plans to deal with it. Many of us are aware of such a mechanism when faced with difficult decisions, when we take a piece of paper, draw a line down the middle of it and on one side of the paper we write all of the items which suggest we should adopt one course of action and on the other side of the paper all the things which suggest we should favour an alternate course of action. Alternatively, we can look at the problem in terms of 'plusses' and 'minuses'.

Once again this cannot be applied to the whole population; very far from it, as many other factors will come into play which will determine whether the individual will be able to act on their own analysis.

Direct Action. It is of course not beyond the realms of possibility that some problems can be solved by directly going to the source of the problem, as was mentioned at the beginning of the chapter. It would indeed be convenient if we could all go to the source of our problems and resolve them straight away, but this regrettably is not possible on some occasions.

It may be that the individual concerned may have sustained too much emotional damage to themselves in the process of sorting out such a problem and hence will draw away from such an action. For instance, a close friend may have inadvertantly caused an upset to us and caused us some amount of hardship. We may feel extremely stressed at this and it would seem the only way to relieve this stress is to point out to the friend what they have done and the effects that their actions have had. Some individuals will do this, but others will weigh up the 'pros and cons' of the situation and will come to the conclusion that the loss of the friendship would be more damaging than to allow the misdemeanour to go unchallenged.

So many different coping mechanisms have been described by different authors that it is difficult to take account of them all here and indeed, this would be ill advised, partly because of the number of them and also because some are difficult to substantiate by research.

DEFENCE MECHANISMS AS A COPING MECHANISM

Strange as it may seem the **defence mechanisms** discussed in Chapter 10 can be viewed as coping mechanisms in their own right, although humanistic psychologists would argue that anything significantly greater than an isolated retreat into a defence mechanism could indicate that an individual requires help.

Certainly, one way to deal with a problem which cannot be faced is to attempt to distort it in one form or another, and it will be remembered from the earlier discussion that the most obvious way of doing this is denial. For a more in-depth account, the reader is directed to Chapter 10.

EXPRESSION: AN INDICATION OF STRESS?

One of the problems facing the health professional concerns the ability to be able to recognise the expression of emotion and hence to be better equipped to help the individual to deal with stressful life events (if at all possible).

When considering how the individual expresses fear, the most obvious place to start is with how the individual actually looks (Gray, 1987). This is readily recognised by most of us, although the culture of the individual and that of the observer may affect the effectiveness of such a recognition. There are now thought to be several universal facial expressions which reflect the following emotions: happiness, anger, disgust, sadness and fear/surprise (Evans, 1989).

It seems likely that since there does exist such universality of expression that some form of innate responses to certain stimuli is probable, and will continue to occur without a cognitive structure having to be built up. Some dilemma could arise however when describing the expression associated with pain. It would seem a reasonable assumption that fear is strongly related to pain, and hence the expressions should be fairly similar. This is not the case. The emotional expression that allies itself with pain is in fact anger (Izard, 1971), and this may well be misconstrued by those attempting to assess the individual's pain. The expressions that may accompany pain will to an extent have a cultural foundation which may in some cases lead to little or no expression of pain, whereas with others, the converse may be true.

Fig. 9.1 Who is having blood taken and who is on a fairground ride?

Fig. 9.1 (continued)

CONCLUSIONS

The subject of stress and how we cope with it concerns us all greatly, and many of us have tried and trusted methods of dealing with certain situations. As we have seen in this chapter, however, coping is highly individual, and we should hesitate in making judgements of how an individual is going to cope with any given event.

To give advice is all to often to persuade an individual to adopt our own coping mechanism in order to resolve a situation, and as we have already observed, this can turn out to be a nightmare for the recipient of such advice. To allow the individual the security and even the time to mobilise their own resources in order to be able to cope with stress, and to help them to accept their individuality without putting our own conditions on them, is probably the most significant help that we can render.

SUMMARY

Lazarus and Folkman (1984) define stress in terms of 'a particular relationship between the person and the environment that is appraised by the individual as taxing or exceeding his or her resources and endangering his or her wellbeing'.

With regard to occupational stress, it is the job itself as well as the working conditions, work load, aspects of the role, role conflict and role responsibility, relationships at work, promotion, job security, career development and lack of autonomy that have all been identified as potential stressors.

It would appear from the results of research, that both physical and mental illness may, to an extent, have their causes in stressful life events.

Lazarus and Folkman described three forms of appraisal in coping: primary appraisal, secondary appraisal, and re-appraisal.

Lazarus and Folkman (1984) suggest that coping fulfils two major functions: **emotion-focused coping** and **problem-focused coping**.

There are now thought to be several universal facial expressions which reflect the following emotions: happiness, anger, disgust, sadness and fear/surprise (Evans, 1989).

The emotional expression that allies itself with pain is anger.

REFERENCES

Bakal, D.A. 91979) *Psychology and Medicine*. Springer, New York.

Brown, G.W. and Harris, T. (1978) *Social Origins of Depression: A Study of Psychiatric Disorder in Women*. Free Press, New York.

Cobb, S. and Rose, R.M. (1973) Hypertension, peptic ulcer, and diabetes in air traffic controllers. *Journal of the American Medical Association* **224**, 489–492.

Cohen, F. and Lazarus, R.S. (1973) Active coping processes: coping dispositions and recovery from surgery. *Psychosomatic Medicine*, **35(5)**, 375–87.

Craig, T.K.J. and Brown, G.W. (1984) Goal frustration and life events in the etiology of painful gastrointestinal disorder. *Journal of Psychosomatic Research* **28**, 411–421.

Creed, F. (1992) Life events. In: Weller, M. and Eysenk, M. (ed.), *The Scientific Basis of Psychiatry*. Baillière Tindall, London.

Dohrenwend, B.P., Levav, I., Shrout, P.E., *et al.*, (1987) Life stress and psychopathology; progress on research begun with Barbara Snell Dohrenwend. *American Journal of Community Psychology*, **15**, 677–715.

Evans, P. (1989) *Motivation and Emotion*. Routledge, London.

Fitzpatrick, R., Hinton, J., Newman, S., Scambler, G. and Thompson, J. (1984) *The Experience of Illness*. Tavistock, London.

French, J.R.P. and Caplan, R.D. (1970) Psychosocial factors in coronary heart disease. *Industrial Medicine* **39**, 383–397.

Gammon, J. (1991) Coping with cancer: the role of self-care. *Nursing Practice*, Vol. 4, No. 3 (supplement to *Nursing Standard* **5(3)**, 11–15).

Grant, I., McDonald, W.I., Patterson, T. and Trimble, M.R. (1989) Multiple sclerosis. In: Brown, G.W. and Harris, T.O. (eds), *Life Events and Illness*. Guilford Press, New York.

Grant, I., Sweetwood, H.L., Yager, J. and Gerst, M. (1981) Quality of life events in relation to psychiatric symptoms. *Archives of General Psychiatry* **38**, 335–339.

Gray, J.A. (1987) *The Psychology of Fear and Stress*. Cambridge University Press, Cambridge.

Harris, T.O. (1989) Disorders of menstruation. In: Brown, G.W. and Harris, T.O (eds), *Life Events and Illness*. Guilford Press, New York.

Hinton, J. (1984) coping with terminal illness. In Fitzpatrick *et al.*, *The Experience of Illness*, Tavistock, London.

Holmes, T.H. and Rahe, R. (1967) The social re-adjustment rating scale. *Journal of Psychomatic Research* **11**, 213–218.

Ivancevich, J.M. and Matteson, M.T. (1984) A type A-B person-work environment interaction model for examining occupational stress and consequences. *Human Relations* **37(7)**, 491–513.

Izard, C.E. (1971) *The Face of Emotion*. Appleton-Century-Crofts, New York.

Kearns, J.L. (1973) *Stress in Industry*. Priory Press,

Kornhauser, A.W. (1965) *Mental Health and the Industrial Worker*. Wiley, New York.

Lazarus, R.S. and Folkman, S. (1984) *Stress, Appraisal and Coping*. Springer, New York.

Marcson, S. (1970) *Automation, Alienation and Anomie*. Harper and Row, New York.

Marshall, J. and Cooper, C.L. (1979) *Executives Under Pressure*. MacMillan, London.

Millcr, P.Mc., Kreitman, N.B., Ingham, J.G. and Sashideran, S.P. (1989) Sclf esteem, life stress and psychiatric disorder. *Journal of Affective Disorders*

12, 73–88.

Nursing Times (1992) High anxiety. Vol. 88, No. 12, 18 March 1992.

Parkes, C.M. (1964) Recent bereavement as a cause of mental illness. *British Journal of Psychiatry* **110**, 198–204.

Paykel, E.S. (1974) Recent life events and clinical depression. In: Gunderson, E.K. and Rahe, R. (eds), *Life Stress and Illness*. Thomas, Illinois.

Paykel, E.S. (1978) Contribution of life events to causation of psychiatric illness. *Psychological Medicine* **8**, 245–253.

Rahe, R.H. (1975) Life changes and near future illness reports. In: Levi, L. (ed.), *Emotions—their Parameters and Measurement*. Raven, New York. (Quoted in Bakal, D.A. (1979) *Psychology and Medicine*. Springer, New York.)

Shirom, A., Eden, D., Silberwasser, S. and Kellerman, J.J. (1973) Job stresses and risk factors in coronary heart disease among occupational categories in Kibbutzim. *Social Sciences and Medicine* **7**, 875–892.

Sofer, C. (1970) *Men in Mid-Career*. Cambridge University Press, Cambridge.

Steptoe, A. (1983) Emotion and stress. In: Weller, M. (ed.), *The Scientific Basis of Psychiatry*. Bailli`ere Tindall, London.

Stroebe, W. and Stroebe, M.S. (1987) *Bereavement and Health*. Cambridge University Press, Cambridge.

Thomson, K.C. and Hendrie, H.C. (1972) Environmental stress in primary depressive illness. *Archives of General Psychiatry* **38**, 309–314.

Wardwell, W.I., Hyman, M. and Bahnson, C.B. (1964) Stress and coronary disease in three field studies. *Journal of Chronic Diseases* **17**, 73–84.

Williams, C., Soothill, K. and Barry, J. (1991) Why nurses leave the profession. *Nursing Standard* **5(39)**, 33–35.

SUGGESTED READING

Bakal, D.A. (1979) *Psychology and Medicine*. Springer, New York. (Chapter 3 provides a useful overview of stress and illness.)

Brown, G.W. and Harris, T.O. (eds) (1992) *Life Events and Illness*. Guilford Press, New York. (This is an excellent text which explores many different facets of life events.)

Creed, F. (1992) Life events. In: Weller, M. and Eysenk, M. (ed.), *The Scientific Basis of Psychiatry*. Bailli`ere Tindall, London. (Chapter 28 gives an overview of the possible psychiatric implications of life events as well as an account of their measurement.)

Evans, P. (1989) *Motivation and Emotion*. Routledge, London. (Chapter 10 provides some interesting insights into the expression of emotion and the construction of emotion.)

CHAPTER 10

ANXIETY

'Life is just one damned thing after another

ELBERT HUBBARD, A Thousand and One Epigrams (1856 1915)

INTRODUCTION

Personality theorists have long been associated with the question of how the individual may react to events that may occur in their lives, and once again a considerable diversity of opinion exists. The discussion on personality in Chapter 2 centred around the nature and development of personality. In this chapter, the discussion will be directed towards the different perspectives that some of the theorists have on the subject of **anxiety**, and more especially, how we cope with anxiety.

In this chapter we will attempt to examine some of the 'classical' ideas that have been put forward regarding the origins and nature of anxiety. As with the discussion on personality in Chapter 2, the following account should be regarded as far more than a journey through classical theories that constitutes little more than a history lesson. Instead, each theory should be regarded as a building block which contributes to our overall perception of the subject area.

Beginning with the individual psyschology of Alfred Adler which gives us some insight into our early interactions with others and its possible consequences, the discussion turns to psychoanalytic and neoanalytic theories of anxiety as well as examining briefly other perspectives on the subject.

INDIVIDUAL PSYCHOLOGY (ALFRED ADLER)

Once a prominent Freudian, Alfred Adler developed his theory of 'individual psychology' which was to direct the thinking of many. Alder's theory was the first to acknowledge and describe the social determinants of personality, and although his name is not now generally recognised by the general public (in contrast to Freud), at least two of his terms ('**inferiority complex**' and 'life style') have been incorporated into everyday speech.

Despite the many criticisms which have been levelled against it, the theory has had an enormous impact upon many theorists (not least of all Horney and Sullivan who will be discussed later in the chapter). Also, it does give considerable insight into the possible origins and nature of anxiety.

SOCIAL INTEREST

Adler not only believed in the importance of interpersonal relationships, but also postulated that human beings have an innate aptitude to relate to other human beings. This phenomenon he termed '**social interest**' (or to be more precise, 'Gemeinschaftsgeful', which has proved difficult to translate), and considered it to be of immense importance not only to the individual, but more especially to society in general.

Social interest is important in terms of the co-operation and social culture which are vital to the existence of mankind, but although its potential is innate, social interest does not exist as a complete entity, but rather has to develop within the child's perception of the social context (Adler, 1929). Put another way, 'The term social interest denotes the innate aptitude through which the individual becomes responsive to reality, which is primarily the social situation' (Ansbacher and Ansbacher, 1955). The development of social interest begins with the relationship with the mother, and is thereafter further guided by other environmental factors such as education.

INFERIORITY AND SUPERIORITY

To feel secure, to achieve perfection and superiority are the ultimate goals of human endeavours. It would appear at a first glance that 'striving for superiority' could lead to something other than the co-operation needed for the existence of mankind. It is, however, guided by social interest which is mindful of the interests of others.

This unconscious striving for superiority emerges from the feelings of inferiority that the child experiences when comparing himself with the adults around him. In order to compensate for this feeling of inferiority, the child may, if he acknowledges it, strive to adjust to a superior level. Hence, this inferiority is not undesirable, but rather an essential component of development.

Naturally, the degree of inferiority is dependent upon the individual's environment and all the variables that it may entail. Adler also maintained that gender was an important factor, inasmuch as we may attempt to live up to **stereotyped** images of one sex or another.

Our physical characteristics may also lead to feelings of inferiority, particularly if the individual perceives themselves as being unattractive, or if they have a physical abnormality. In this case, the individual may attempt to compensate by developing aspects of their character, for instance, the obese person may develop interpersonal skills that others perceive as joviality. It is perhaps an appropriate juncture to reiterate a point made several times already throughout this text, namely that the individual's perceptions and the actual realities may be quite different.

BIRTH ORDER

One of the major determinants to the degree of inferiority that the individual feels is the order in which they are born in the family, such as being eldest, second born, youngest or being an only child (Adler, 1931).

The first born, or eldest child, was described by Adler in several different ways. The major difficulty that this child will have is the threat of 'dethronement' by younger children, particularly if the gap between the first and second is less than 3 years. In such circumstances, the child may perceive that he has lost the sole attention of the parents and particularly of the mother. The child may attempt to fight against the mother, having first attempted to pull the mother's affection back. If the mother attempts to 'fight back', the child may become disobedient, bad tempered and critical. It may be that they do, however, feel secure and sure of their parents' affection, in which case the event of a birth in the family will pass without too many ill effects, as will be the case if the gap between the children is 3 years or more.

The second child is in an altogether different situation. They are born into a situation where they will not receive sole attention, and hence are rather nearer to 'co-operation' from the start. They will tend to compete with the older child with considerable energy as if they are continually trying to catch

Fig. 10.1 Does the order in which we are born affect the way we develop?

up with the eldest child. As the child grows older, they may find the leadership and dominance of others difficult to tolerate.

The youngest child will always have someone to compete with, and will often want to excel at everything they attempt. This child may suffer from more inferiority feelings than the other children, quite simply because they are surrounded by older brothers and sisters who have more skills than they do.

The only child will normally compete against the father, and be pampered by the mother (which Adler sees as a serious misdemenaour). In some ways, this child resembles the eldest child inasmuch as they may fear the arrival of younger siblings. Being the centre of attention is all very well when young, but this may lead to difficulties in later life. In families where the births have spread over a long period with large gaps between each birth, then each child may, to an extent, be like an only child.

INFERIORITY AND SUPERIORITY COMPLEXES

In the normal course of events inferiority is dealt with effectively, but it may be that the feelings of inferiority may overwhelm the individual, and certainly do not contribute to development. In some circumstances the reverse is true, with development being severely impeded. This inadequacy can occur even in the pre-school years, and was termed an '**inferiority complex**' by Adler.

The world of an individual with an inferiority complex is not a pleasant one, and may lead to timidity, lack of confidence and even distrust. Such a complex is unpleasant. As has been mentioned, development is impaired, and hence the individual may attempt to disguise it by developing a '**superiority complex**' in which false feelings of being superior to others are experienced, hence further preventing development by denying the inferiority that needs to be overcome.

ANXIETY

Anxiety, like many other terms used in pscyhology, has been misused, and often depicts a state that certain (**stereotyped**) individuals will work themselves up to in response to certain situations. Interestingly, although such a person may evoke our pity or even our ridicule, it is probably the apparently upright, unshakeable individual that should give us cause for concern. We often compare ourselves to this apparent font of human strength, wondering how they 'carry on' regardless of life's traumas, and admiring their 'stiff upper lip'. To say that this person never has any concerns or that they can resolve all crises as they arise would quite naturally be ridiculous, so what happens to their anxieties? Do they simply evaporate, or are they neatly filed into some kind of psychological 'pending' tray to receive attention at the appropriate time?

In order to find some answers to these questions, or to be more precise, to find out how anxiety is dealt with, we will firstly need to discuss some important concepts of anxiety. Such concepts are found in many different theories. Psychoanalytic and 'neoanalytic' theories have a considerable amount to say about how the individual may react to the stresses of everyday living, and it is perhaps a good starting point for this chapter to examine the subject of anxiety in more detail.

The 'individual psychology' of Alfred Adler has been reviewed and the implications for the individual as far as the possible reasons for their reactions to life events has presented us with not only a view on how we are motivated, but also on how such factors as birth order may direct our action.

It may be of use at this point to 'revisit' some of the personality theories discussed in Chapter 2 in order to gain a variety of perspectives on the subject of how we react to stress.

PSYCHOANALYSIS AND ANXIETY

One of the most important concepts of Freud's psychoanalytic theory is anxiety. It is of importance in the development of personality and is also an integral part of his theories of the psychoses and neuroses, and consequently also of dreams. In fact it is in repressed sources of anxiety that Freud saw the most significant roots of mental pathology.

Freud attempted to differentiate between different types of anxiety and eventually described three types. These were **neurotic anxiety**, **objective anxiety** and **moral anxiety**.

Although Freud thought that there were significant (but unknown) differences in our experiences such as those arising from tensions resulting from bodily needs, he was convinced that they were both occurring only in the **conscious** (although conflicts could occur in the **unconscious** resulting in neurotic anxiety). A person is able to distinguish subjectively between anxiety and the results of other tensions. The reason for the anxiety, however, may be unknown to the person.

In the early 1890s, Freud thought that anxiety was physically derived from **libido**, a theory that he completely reversed in 1926 when he attributed the origins of anxiety to a reaction of the ego. To take this one step further, Freud ascribed to anxiety the function of a 'signal' warning the ego to suppress certain instinctual processes or to avoid certain danger situations.

To return to the distinctions that Freud made between the different types of anxieties, it may be useful to discuss them all in more detail.

REALITY (OBJECTIVE) ANXIETY

Firstly, **objective** (or **reality) anxiety**, which Freud considered to be synonymous with fear, results from a perception of danger in the external world. There could be a number of reasons for reality anxiety, i.e. it could be an innate response to a situation from past generations, or it could come about as a result of previously experiencing the danger.

Returning to Freud's revised theory of anxiety whereby he attributed the origins of anxiety to a reaction of the **ego**, it would logically follow that if anxiety is acting as a signal to the ego to cope with (suppress) certain instinctual processes or avoid dangerous situations, then if a person's ego is immature and he is physically helpless and thereby unable to cope with the situation this would lay the foundation for a whole complex of fears. Such is the case in infancy and childhood. The young child or infant has not a sufficiently developed ego to cope with these situations and to take appropriate action. Therefore it could be said that fears are all related to and derived from early experiences of helplessness, including birth trauma.

NEUROTIC ANXIETY

Neurotic anxiety, Freud believed, results from an unconscious conflict between id impulses (mainly sexual and aggressive) and the constraints enforced by the ego and the **superego**, and can take three main forms — apprehensiveness, phobias and panic.

The apprehensive person, i.e. the typically nervous person, fears that his ego will fail to cope with and attempt to rationalise a fear and that the id will take over, thereby rendering him helpless. A person who has an irrational fear of something may, on analysis, be found to have a fear of wanting to do something which he considers to be immoral and he then may be considered to have a phobia. The person exhibiting panic behaviour, i.e. 'discharges behaviour which aims to rid the person of excessively painful neurotic behaviour by doing that which the id demands', is often seen as displaying impulsive behaviour.

MORAL ANXIETY

Moral anxiety is very much like neurotic anxiety in that it comes about as a result of the conflict between the **id** and the superego and ego, and is experienced as feelings of guilt and/or shame. The conscience is in a way punishing a person for transgressing from the 'ego' ideal. People actually do things such as break windows or commit other more serious crimes with the intention of being caught and punished in order to compensate for their feelings of guilt.

ANXIETY DREAMS

Apart from the main types of anxiety that Freud described in connection with personality disorders and development, in 1900, after much deliberation, he developed a theory of '**anxiety dreams**', which was not significantly altered by his reversal of his theory of anxiety in 1926. Indeed the anxiety dream theory (out of all the five unpleasurable dreams) appears to be the only one which 'fits' both his early and his revised theories.

Anxiety dreams are wishful dreams which upon interpretation usually prove to be of a sexual nature, where libido has been transformed into neurotic anxiety. Therefore anxiety dreams are an integral part of Freud's theories on the neuroses. Freud put forward three separate formulaes for anxiety dreams, two sexual and one non-sexual. The first formula consists of an anxiety which is already present before the dream and the dream seizing upon the anxiety in order to express a disguised wish. In his second formula, Freud thought that an anxiety dream could arise from a 'repressed (erotic) wish in a dream being openly fulfilled without sufficient disguise'. At this point some of the libido in the dream is converted into anxiety. His third formula, a bodily disturbance (non-sexual) such as a chronic illness generates anxiety-like symptoms during sleep. These symptoms are in turn converted into an appropriate anxiety dream by a pre-existing suppressed wish.

The Freudian concepts of anxiety have been further developed by other psychoanalysts. One such psychoanalyst was Melanie Klein. Klein, whilst agreeing with many of the Freudian traditions nevertheless emphasised the importance of the aggressive drives rather than the sexual drives. Our inborn aggression is a reflection of the death instinct.

Klein considered that anxiety was the ego's response to the expression of the death instinct, and is reinforced by separation which is caused by leaving the womb at birth and by bodily needs being frustrated. The death instinct is seen as the primary cause of anxiety in the form of persecutory fears.

ADLERIAN PERSPECTIVES OF ANXIETY

For Adler, the term anxiety is usually used to describe a conscious system such as phobias, although he also described anxiety as 'increased feelings of inferiority'. It was left principally to Karen Horney (see below) to provide a more concrete idea of the nature of anxiety.

NEOANALYTIC VIEWS OF ANXIETY

The psychoanalytic concepts of anxiety are by no means the only viewpoints on the subject. Principally, Harry Stack Sullivan and Karen Horney have contributed to our understanding of personality, but also of anxiety. Both have stressed the importance of social and cultural factors, with interpersonal relationships making a crucial contribution to the development of personality. Therefore, both Sullivan and Horney are, initially at least, from the Adlerian mould, although their theories differ in many respects, both from each other and from Adler's original work.

BASIC ANXIETY

Horney (1950) described neurosis as being derived from disturbed interpersonal relationships in childhood which results in the emergence of '**basic anxiety**'. Basic anxiety has three major characteristics, namely helplessness, aggressiveness and detachment.

As far as the development of basic anxiety is concerned, Horney suggests that adults are so diverted by their own neuroses that the love that they should be giving to the child is left wanting, with the result that the child fails to develop a sense of belonging and in its place will experience insecurity and apprehensiveness. As a result, instead of developing their true innate capacities (self-realisation), the child may be deflected from this path in favour of a concerted drive for safety. There are three 'neurotic' solutions to this basic anxiety, and these solutions are through the exaggeration of one of the three major characteristics of basic anxiety mentioned above.

The first of these neurotic solutions, helplessness, will result in 'moving towards people' by seeking their protection and by compliance with other people. As the term would suggest, the individual attempts to comply with the wishes of others and to show a sincere interest in them, whilst at the same time having repressed feelings to the contrary. Sooner or later the individual's repressed feelings will emerge as they perceive that others have responded unfavourably to their concerns, usually in the form of an angry outburst of some kind, which is rarely expected by the person on the receiving end!

The second type of neurotic solution, aggressiveness, results in 'moving against people', and is characterised by attempts to dominate and exploit others, using the assumption that other people are hostile and generally unpleasant. The repressed feelings of helplessness contrast markedly with their behaviours, which seek to exemplify power and selfishness. Affection from others is something that will usually elude this individual because of their beliefs about the nature of others and also because of the 'power' ethic that they attempt to live by.

The third type of neurotic solution, detachment, results in 'moving away from people', and is characterised by the avoidance of others. Although this individual needs love and affection as anyone else would, they attempt to evade contact with others by striving towards isolation. This individual may even deny their own needs. The conflicts that may arise in such an individual result from their repressed need for dependency and love.

TENSION AND ANXIETY

Sullivan postulated that as well as striving towards mental health, the individual strives to reduce tensions, the most important cause of which is anxiety, with the others being physicochemical needs (the needs to eat, drink, breathe, eliminate waste, maintain body temperature and to fulfil sexual desire), the need to sleep, and the need experienced by a mother (or other principal caregiver) to fulfil a need which she perceives her infant as having.

Anxiety is viewed as a harmful emotion with its most prolific causes in the relationship with the mother. Anxiety in the mother induces anxiety in the infant, and it therefore follows that anxiety may be relieved by contact with non-anxious individuals, thus providing the infant with 'interpersonal security' (Sullivan, 1954). For Sullivan, anxiety is closely related to what he terms as '**uncanny emotions**' which encompass such emotions as horror, dread, awe and loathing. Anxiety, in its most extreme form, resembles such uncanny emotions and, as would be expected, underlies them.

Anxiety is responsible for preventing, to varying degrees, the satisfaction of the individual's needs such as the maintaining of meaningful interpersonal relationships, which in turn may lead to further anxiety. Other needs such as eating, sleeping and sexual activity may also be impaired. Anxiety may also be induced by other factors such as those factors which the indivudal may construe as threats.

Sullivan attributes much of our difficulties in life to anxiety, and suggests that it is responsible for much of the disturbed and inadequate behaviours that are observed in so many individuals.

HUMANISTIC PERSPECTIVES ON ANXIETY

The '**humanistic**' approach to anxiety and defence is, as would be expected, notably different from those discussed earlier. Rogers (1951) considers that psychological tension arises when the individual cannot assimilate their experiences into their current self-structure.

PERSONAL CONSTRUCT THEORY AND ANXIETY

Kelly (1955) has a different approach to the subject of anxiety which asserts that anxiety is 'not necessarily evil', but rather that 'some measure of anxiety is seen as a correlate of adventure', and it is only when 'anxiety stifles adventure must action be taken'.

Anxiety is seen by Kelly as being the result of the individual having a 'construction system' that fails them because certain experiences lie outside the scope of existing constructs, and as a result future events are difficult to anticipate.

DEFENCE MECHANISMS

Whatever the exact origins and nature of anxiety, it is clear that it is potentially damaging to the individual, and that it may not always be possible to deal with the causes of our anxieties in order to reduce or eliminate their potential effects. Most of the theorists that have been discussed in this chapter have postulated the existence of mechanisms to deal with anxiety.

An understanding of the possible origins and nature of anxiety will go a long way towards providing us with an understanding of neurotic behaviour. Defence mechanisms as such should not be regarded as abnormal, but when anxiety is so overwhelming that such mechanisms are 'resorted to in a massive way, symptoms may develop and adult behaviour may to some extent become maladaptive' (Wolff, 1969).

The mechanisms of defence described by Sigmund Freud and later by Anna Freud (1946) will be discussed firstly, followed by the standpoints of some of the other prominent contributors on the subject.

REPRESSION

Repression is probably the best known, and arguably the most important of all the defence mechanisms in psychoanalytic theory. We do not consciously repress potentially threatening matter from our conscious, but rather we unconciously remove it so that it is no longer possible to recall it on demand. The material that is represssed may be a wish or impulse originating from the **id**.

Repression is seen in Freudian theory as originating from the unconscious part of the ego. Most significant repressions occur in early childhood. Although they may protect the individual from external threats they nevertheless can prevent the individual from facing problems. Repressions are usually permanent, and persist into later life, possibly leading to neurotic symptoms in adult life.

REGRESSION

When faced with an unsafe situation, the individual may **regress** to a time of their lives that they perceive as being safer. Enuresis as part of an (**uncon-**

scious) response to moving school or the birth of a sibling is an example of regression.

REACTION FORMATION

When confronted with unpleasant feelings and urges, the individual may replace them with opposite feelings and beliefs. As such, **reaction formation** and repression will usually occur together, and both originate from the unconscious part of the ego.

The aggression that a child may feel towards a parent who is domineering may turn to affection, hence the aggression is repressed. On first impression, the behaviours brought about by reaction formation appear sincere, but they are usually exaggerated and compulsive in nature. The repression which is so often a characteristic of reaction formation will frequently ensure that reality is not faced and once again neurotic symptoms may emerge.

DENIAL

Probably the most obvious of all the mechanisms of defence is to deny that something unpleasant exists at all. As will be seen in Chapter 11, **denial** may play an important part in the grieving process, whether it be towards bad news, illness or death. This ego protection is important inasmuch as it enables us to proceed with life in greater psychological comfort, because consciously we are only believing what we want to believe, not necessarily what actually exists.

DISPLACEMENT

When it is dangerous, or we feel guilty about directing impulses and feelings towards the object of our frustration and anger (such as a child being annoyed by his father), then these may be directed towards 'safer objects' such as toys, or a less threatening person such as another child, or even ourselves ('turning against the self'), i.e. **displacement**.

PROJECTION

Dangerous impulses that we may harbour can be **unconsciously** dealt with by attributing them to someone else. This **projection** can take on several forms, including the belief that someone wishes to harm us when, in reality, it is us that wishes to harm them.

ISOLATION

When feelings and emotions are separated from an experience or thought, the term isolation is used. Wolff (1969) gives the example of the child who is fastidious about cleanliness but is apparently oblivious to the smell and mess from soiling his pants. Such 'splitting' is unconscious and is usually associated with intellectualisation.

INTELLECTUALISATION/RATIONALISATION

The **intellectualisation of** threatening thoughts can result in the individual being able to talk about unpleasant experiences, with the apparent air of a detached analytical observer. In order to do this, their threatening thoughts have been repressed, with all the possible implications of that mechanism.

Rationalisation is in many ways closely akin to intellectualisation insofar as we may reduce our feelings of guilt at having illicit feelings towards others by giving such feelings and impulses rational explanations in order to justify them.

FANTASY

Fantasy is a mechanism well known to most of us. It consists of the individual attempting to gratify unfulfilled needs by imagining that they have been fulfilled.

SUBLIMATION

Many of the impulses and feelings that we have are totally unacceptable to society, and these may be sublimated to acceptable behaviours. For instance, violent impulses that we may harbour can be sublimated into sports. **Sublimation** is also unconscious, although most of us will be aware to a small degree that we feel less aggressive after playing contact sport, or even after a strenous 'work out' at the gym. May of us will be directed towards such activities because of the calming feelings that such activities may produce.

Fig. 10.2 The acceptable face of aggression.

HORNEYAN PERSPECTIVES ON DEFENCE MECHANISMS

Whilst lending some support to the Freudian concepts of fantasy, rationalisation, isolation and projection (which Horney calls 'externalisation'), repression and denial, Horney also suggests that the neurotic may develop an 'idealised image' (Horney, 1950) that hides their more painful conflicts by the belief in a virtually unattainable **self-concept**.

Such an image prevents the individual from facing reality, and may lead to further problems when the neurotic realises that such an image can only exist in fantasy. In pursuit of the actualisation of the idealised image, the neurotic individual may develop inner commands which direct their behaviours; these commands are known as 'shoulds'. Shoulds are responsible for the apparently irrational striving towards an impossible goal.

It is said that 'no man is an island', and the **idealised image** of the neurotic individual involves other people in that they will develop 'claims' that they believe other people or society in general should fulfil. For example, an individual who is indecisive and ineffectual and who has a physical illness may believe that regardless of any other person's needs they should have priority.

HUMANISTIC PERSPECTIVES ON DEFENCE

For Rogers, the individual whose experiences highlight incongruences between their self-concept and organismic experiences may eliminate such experiences from their awareness, although it is more probable that they will 'defend' against such experiences by distortion. The individual who believes that she is the best footballer may blame the state of the pitch or her team mates for her failure to score a goal. The individual who believes that he he academically superior may blame the person who marked his paper for his failure. We can probably all cite examples where such distortion has taken place, even within ourselves.

Allport (1968) to a great extent supports the Freudian view of defence mechanisms and agrees that we all have such mechanisms. However, Freud's view of the illicit impulses of the id is not shared by Allport. Hence the perspective towards defence mechanisms is somewhat different, as he does not regard such mechanisms as an integral part of healthy development, to such an extent that he views the personality dominated by these mechanisms as being abnormal. For Allport, the **proprium** is capable of meeting problems realistically and finding solutions to them.

OTHER PEOPLE'S ANXIETY; HOW WE REACT TO IT

Understanding that people have anxiety in response to life events, and the knowledge that we all react in different ways to different situations, should help us to care for people under our care more effectively. However, we really need to ask ourselves whether this knowledge does in fact help us to plan and implement care on an individual basis, or whether we just assume that certain situations are anxiety inducing and that the patient/client requires reassurance.

There is certainly a plethora of theories on the subject of anxiety, but one or two facts do emerge that are accepted by most theorists. Firstly, anxiety, in its more extreme forms at least, is a threatening emotion which may seriously impair the ability of the individual to function effectively. Certainly if the anxiety itself is not problematic enough, the dependence on mechanisms of defence to protect us from either internal threats from the id, or unpleasant experiences in our environment may lead to abnormal behaviour.

If we are to plan our care to take account of any possible anxieties that the patient/client may have, then we must keep an open mind as to its manifestation. It has been shown that anxiety is not necessarily manifested by obvious signs, and that an outwardly calm individual may be harbouring extreme anxieties.

The discussion on defence mechanisms provides us with perhaps the most significant clues as to the recognition of the signs of anxiety. To the untrained eye, defences such as repression are virtually impossible to detect, although the patient who talks about his terminal illness in an apparently detached and logical manner only hours after receiving the news that he was suffering from it may have a greater need of support than the individual who responds immediately in a more 'emotional' way. At least the second example, distressing though it may be to the carers, is meeting the problem face to face and may at least reach some partial acceptance of the situation. The first individual however, in intellectualising their predicament is using, to some degree, represssion to help them cope, and resolution and acceptance will be much more difficult.

A certain amount of vigilence is most certainly required when listening to the individual's comments and questions regarding other people, as in such remarks may lurk the fears and anxieties of the person who themselves fear the fate that they may predict for others. For instance in talking about, particularly repeatedly, the elderly lady who lives next door, and how her eyesight is failing because of untreated cataracts, the elderly individual may well be expressing their own anxieties. A more generalised story may also emerge when talking about the elderly in general and the problems they may have.

Perhaps more obviously, anxiety (according to Sullivan) may interfere with the physiocochemical needs of the individual such as eating and elimination, as well as other needs such as sleeping. It may be the case that disturbances of how such needs are met could give some clue to possible anxiety.

It would be a mistake to assume that all patients and clients are suffering from anxiety, and that hospitalisation and treatment are always the inevitable cause of such anxieties. There must indeed be many instances when coming into hospital and receiving treatment will at least provide the individual with the potential to be able to predict more accurately the possible future that they have to face, even in the case of confirming the existence of terminal illness.

Once again we have to return to the discussion in Chapter 5 which dealt with communication, for it is in communicating with the individual in such a way that they feel safe enough to self-disclose, and in such a way that the information is understood, that anxiety may most likely be revealed.

CONCLUSIONS

Anxiety is probably the term that is in commonest usage when describing an individual's mental state. The various approaches to the study of anxiety, although varied, on the whole yield the conclusion that its origins are at times far from straightforward, and its effects may be far reaching. Certainly, the individual who is suffering from anxiety may respond in a multitude of ways, some of which will not be on a conscious level.

SUMMARY

Adler's theory was the first to acknowledge and describe the social determinants of personality.

Adler not only believes in the importance of interpersonal relationships, but also postulates that human beings have an innate aptitude to relate to other human beings. This phenomenon he terms '**social interest**'.

To feel secure, to achieve perfection and superiority are the ultimate goals of human endeavours. The unconscious striving for superiority emerges from the feelings of inferiority that the child experiences when comparing himself with the adults around him.

One of the major determinants to the degree of inferiority that the individual feels is the order in which they are born in the family, such as being eldest, second born, youngest or being an only child.

In the normal course of events, inferiority is dealt with effectively, but it may be that the feelings of inferiority may overwhelm the idividual. This inadequacy can occur even in the pre-school years, and was termed an '**inferiority complex**' by Adler.

Freud attempted to differentiate between different types of anxiety and eventually described three types. These were neurotic anxiety, objective anxiety and moral anxiety.

Klein considered that anxiety was the ego's response to the expression of the death instinct.

Horney (1950) described neurosis as being derived from disturbed interpersonal relationships in childhood which results in the emergence of '**basic anxiety**'. There are three 'neurotic' solutions to this basic anxiety, and these solutions are through the exaggeration of one of the three major characteristics of basic anxiety.

Sullivan postulated that as well as striving towards mental health, the individual strives to reduce tensions, the most important cause of which is anxiety. Anxiety is viewed by Sullivan as a harmful emotion with its most prolific causes in the relationship with the mother.

Rogers (1951) considers that psychological tension arises when the individual cannot assimilate their experiences into their current self-structure.

Anxiety is seen by Kelly as being the result of the individual having a 'construction system' that fails them because certain experiences lie outside the scope of existing constructs, and as a result future events are difficult to anticipate.

Defence mechanisms as such should not be regarded as abnormal, but when anxiety is so overwhelming that such mechanisms are 'resorted to in a massive way, symptoms may develop and adult behaviour may to some extent become maladaptive' (Wolff, 1968).

REFERENCES

All of the following have become standard texts in their own right, and whilst being rather 'old', will nevertheless provide a valuable insight into the subject.

Alder, A. (1929) *Problems of Neurosis*. Routledge and Kegan Paul, London.

Adler, A. (1931) *What Life Should Mean to You*. Little Brown, Boston.

Allport, G.W .(1968) *The Person on Psychology; Selected Essays*. Beacon Press, Boston.

Ansbacher, H.L. and Ansbacher, R.R. (1955) *The Individual Psychology of Alfred Adler*. Basic Books, New York.

Freud, A. (1946) *The Ego and Mechanisms of Defence*. Hogarth Press, London.

Horney, K. (1950) *Neurosis and Human Growth: The Struggle Towards Self-Realisation*. Norton, New York.

Kelly, G. (1955) *The Psychology of Personal Constructs*, Vol. 1. Norton, New York.

Lansdown, R. and Benjamin, D. (1985) Development of the Concept of Death in Children Age 5–9 years. *Child Care*, No. 11, pp 13–22.

Rogers, C.R. (1951) *Client-centered Therapy, Its Current Practices, Implications and Theory*. Houston, Boston.

Sullivan, H.S. (1954) *The Psychiatric Interview* (Reprint Norton, New York (1970).)

Sulloway, F.J. (1979) *Freud, Biologist of the Mind*. Basic Books, New York.

Wolff, S. (1969) *Children Under Stress*. Penguin, London.

SUGGESTED READING

The reader is directed to all of the above texts which will give a complete account of the theories discussed, but principally the following:

Sulloway, F.J. (1979) *Freud, Biologist of the Mind*. Basic Books, New York. (This text gives a particularly good account of Freud's theory. See particularly Chapter 4.)

Wolff, S. (1969) *Children Under Stress*. Penguin, London. (An excellent introduction to the subject.)

CHAPTER 11

SOCIAL
LEARNING AND
LIFE EVENTS

'If life had a second edition, how would I correct the proofs'?'

JOHN CLARE (1793 1864)

INTRODUCTION

Many experiences will shape our lives and indeed 'social learning theory' suggests that our social environment is responsible for shaping all our behaviour, 'where there is a continuous and reciprocal interaction between a behaviour and its controlling conditions' (Jenner, 1992). A stormy relationship may make us behave differently in subsequent relationships, exam successes may prompt us to take further exams, and indeed a traumatic experience in hospital may make us wary of hospitals in the future, even if it is only as a visitor.

The nature and complexities of our experiences are so vast that the permeations for each individual make generalisations rather difficult. In this chapter, however, some behaviours will be examined along with their possible causes; it must be stressed, as always, that human beings do have a habit of not conforming to the behaviours predicted in any given circumstance. This does not mean that they will not have tendencies to behave in a certain direction, and hence some prediction is possible. However, as health care professionals, we must always be aware that what would affect one individual in a certain way will not necessarily affect another in the same way. It would indeed be a comfortable world for the health professional to predict the patient/client's behaviour to any given stimulus and considerable restraint must be exercised in order to prevent this from happening. Certainly, when dealing with physical illness, it has to be the case that the more accurate prediction and indeed the more long range the prediction, the more likely the patient is to recover as treatment can be instigated at an early stage and prophylactic therapy can be commenced.

Although this can be done to an extent with a patient's psychological reactions, considerable damage can be done if the individual's unique set of responses are ignored, with regard to, for instance, bereavement.

Having warned against the precarious nature of behaviour prediction it is as well to examine some of the events that may occur in individual's lives along with their possible consequences. As ever, childhood experiences must play a vital role in determining not only behaviour at the time, but also behaviour in later life. Such events should never be seen in isolation and will usually be modified by other events which may be occurring simultaneously, or may occur later.

A good starting point for this discussion may be to examine some childhood experiences which the health care professional may encounter, indeed that most of us have experienced. As with all such discussions, it is useful to examine our own past and try to remember how such events affected us at the time and whether we have carried such effects into adult life.

ATTACHMENT, SEPARATION, LOSS AND THE EMERGENCE OF THE CONCEPT OF DEATH

The concept of death develops from early childhood, and its association with reactions to separation in the early months is a close one. As will be seen during the following discussion, although the concept of death is to a great extent a matter of consideration in its own right, once such a concept is formed, it is difficult to completely extricate the reactions it may elicit from the more global concept of 'loss'.

Nagy (1948) considered the development of the concept of death as occurring in three stages:

(1) Under 5 years—death conceived as reversible and is seen as a departure or separation.
(2) 5–9 years—death is final, but not inevitable. Usually personified and is destructive.
(3) Over 9 years—death is viewed as final, inevitable and universal.

The findings that Nagy put forward have been challenged many times since, although the development of the concept of death in stages is accepted by most psychologists. A brief account of these stages, as seen by other researchers, will lay the foundation for later discussions.

THE NEONATE TO 2 YEARS

It would appear that one important factor in the formation of attachments is **person permanence**. Object permanence has already been discussed in Chapter 6. Person permanence is similar inasmuch as the infant will need to develop the concept that a person may exist even when they are out of sight. Such a concept should be complete by about the age of 2 years.

Some further points need to be considered when looking at attachment in the early months. Firstly, does the infant recognise the characteristics of his caregivers rather than the actual person? Researchers investigating the perceptions of the infant with regard to their principal caregivers and others have indicated, for instance, that the infant as young as 12 weeks may become distressed if the mother leaves by an unusual exit (Stayton, 1973). One question that may emerge from such research is: does distress occur at this age as a result of separation or as a result of the disruption of the infant's expectations? If the latter is the case, and further findings suggesting that an infant of up to 15 months will not become distressed if left with a stranger (Stayton, 1973) are accepted, then we may be looking at the situation in which the carer in a hospital setting should be attempting to replicate the actions of the principal caregiver as much as possible.

Secondly, and perhaps most pertinent to the following discussion, is the question of whether attachment is instinctual (which would have an effect on how we view Stayton's work), or whether it emerges as a result of the interactions between the principal caregiver and the infant.

SIX MONTHS TO 2 YEARS

Many of us can remember early separation experiences, either through hospitalisation, divorce or parental illness. In observing animals such as cats or dogs we may observe the distress experienced by their young when taken away from their mother. Indeed the basis of separation reactions could be construed as a survival mechanism which will bring about a strong reaction.

Probably the most famous researcher in this field was John Bowlby, who despite approaching the subject from a psychoanalytic point of view, also considered the ethological point of view (Bowlby, 1981). Bowlby considered that attachment is a result of instinctual responses which are necessary for the survival of the species.

The emotion which associates with separation is grief, and within such a framework can be seen the beginnings of our responses towards the death of a loved one in later life.

Bowlby, in his original work, found that many of the delinquent adolescents whom he was treating showed a particular aspect in common, namely that they had had traumatic separation experiences early in life. He then went on to investigate separation experiences in young children (2–3 years old) and found that a trend did in fact begin to emerge. Most of us with children will recognise these stages, particularly the first one, which is protest. This is followed by despair and detachment. A more complete account of separation experiences is given in Chapter 14.

Bowlby's theory, although important, is by no means the last word on the subject, and researchers such as Michael Rutter, whilst accepting the importance of the maternal bond, also stress the care prior to the separation as well as the loss of familiar people and objects (Rutter, 1980). Parke (1981) stressed the important role played by the father, and rejected Bowlby's relegation of the father to a secondary role. Other studies have suggested that the notion of 'attachment' has outlived its usefulness. Clarke and Clarke (1976) suggested (as did Rutter) that the effects of early separation experiences were reversible.

The circumstances under which a child may be separated from its mother are many and varied. Hospitalisation has already been mentioned, as has divorce and parental illness, but further to these causes is the whole question of removing the child from the family environment and putting them into some form of care, or fostering situation, which may last for days, weeks, months or even years.

TWO TO 5 YEARS

Up to about 3 years of age the child is likely to view separation and death as synonymous (Vaughan and Litt, 1990), and hence separation may still be distressing (as indeed it may be for some time to come). Regression in particular may be manifested by a return to a previous (safe) state, and bed wetting and thumb sucking may return. After this time (or earlier) a more definite distinction begins to emerge.

Curiosity about death is common at this age (Rochlin, 1967) and indeed they may even experiment with death by killing insects and showing considerable interest rather than fear at the sight of a dead mouse or bird. Even so, the concept of the finality of death may not be complete for some time, probably due to inadequate prior experience and adult explanations. Raphael (1982), investigating bereaved 2–8 year olds, found that some of them believed that the deceased parent was hidden somewhere. The resulting reactions that this may bring, along with the child's incomplete concept of finality, may lead the surviving parent to believe that the child is relatively unaffected by the loss.

The clue to understanding the child's images of death may lie in a phenomenon discussed in Chapter 6, namely the way that a child deals with events when they only have minimal experience and information. It will be remembered that Piaget suggested that the child will assimilate and accommodate data into schemas, and in the process will use the limited structure of their schemas to explain events such as death. For instance, a child may believe that by being well behaved, the deceased parent will return to them. Hence the child is attributing the removal of the parent to something that they have done (and hence have attempted to explain by cause and effect). By being 'good' they may instigate another effect, namely the return of a loved one.

Another explanation could be a phenomenon known as '**magical thinking**' which, broadly speaking, is the explanation of events past, future or present (or indeed the path to a resolution of a particular crisis) by 'supernatural' factors.

THE SCHOOL CHILD

Between the ages of 5 years and adolescence, many changes will take place with regard to how the child views the world and the events that occur around him. The concept of death will usually become complete at this time. Nagy, as has been seen, suggested that the child has a realistic understanding of the concept by about the age of 9 years of age. Later researchers have put the age as much earlier, with Lansdown and Benjamin (1985) judging that up to 60% of 5-year-old children had a complete or nearly complete conceptualisation, although most other researchers put the age at around 8 years.

The child will attain knowledge from many different sources, not least of all from asking questions. The media may also be a source of information, although the character that is so dramatically killed in one television programme may miraculously reappear in another an hour later! The reversibility of death gives way to the emergence of death's finality, although in the early stages of this age group, until about 8 or 9 years, this is not applied to their own lives.

Although the biological facts of death may have been established, the causality of death, up to the age of about 8 years, may still present problems inasmuch as they may see themselves as responsible in some way for the death of a parent.

It is perhaps pertinent at this stage to consider that although the egocentricity that centres the causes of so many events such as death around the child is so evident at this and earlier ages, it can also be seen, albeit in a modified form, in later life. We will often see the death of a loved one as partly due to our actions, even though logic may tell us otherwise.

THE PRE-ADOLESCENT

From about 8 or 9 years of age, the biological and causality concepts of death are nearly or totally complete, although their reaction to death in the family may be akin to that of a much younger child, particularly in relation to denial, which may lead to the child appearing to others as untouched by the experience. Anger may also be evident at this age.

The realisation that death may come to them and those they love makes death something to be feared, and hence they are vulnerable to unfounded fears of their own death. The beginnings of the adult response to loss and the remnants of childhood separation reactions are both seen in this age group.

The emergence of long-term psychological problems of children in this age group, as well as earlier ones, to the loss of an attachment figure is much debated. Brown (1982) concluded that early parental loss increases the risk of depression in adult life, while Brown and Harris (1978) concluded that maternal loss before the age of 11 years is strongly related to how the individual copes with stressful events in later life. Other reviewers, on the other hand, remain less convinced of the link between early bereavement and later psychiatric illness (Birtchnell, 1980; Crook and Eliot, 1980).

THE ADOLESCENT AND ADULT REACTION TO LOSS

The reaction to the death of a loved one by the adolescent is generally assumed to be similar to that of the adult, although little research has been done in this direction (Vaughan and Litt, 1990).

It is important at this stage to stress that 'loss' does not only refer to the loss of a loved one. Within the concept of loss must also be considered the impending death of the individual themselves, the impending death of a loved one, as well as separations that do not involve death, but are nevertheless traumatic (such as divorce). The grieving process bears a strong resemblance to the reactions seen in early childhood, and it may be appropriate to return to the work of John Bowlby, this time in relation to the adult grieving process.

Bowlby (1973) described the grieving process as having four stages:

(1) **Denial**
(2) Sensation of loss
(3) Restitution
(4) Resolution.

Denial
The loss may be denied to such an extent that the individual may appear to be able to continue functioning in a relatively normal way. The emotions that such a loss may evoke appear to be put on hold. Eventually, the disbelief that accompanied the loss will be overwhelmed by the evidence surrounding them, therefore steering the individual to the next stage.

Sensation of Loss

In some ways, this stage resembles the protest stage of the infant, in that the individual, having experienced and recognised the loss, may respond with anger, frustration and crying. The individual may feel helpless and emotionally numb.

Restitution

The multitude of jumbled emotions that accompany loss are worked through by the individual, often leading to an over-emphasis of good or bad aspects of the lost loved one. Such a process is not an easy one to work through, and opportunity must be given to the individual to talk through their feelings.

Resolution

Resolution may occur when the individual has accepted the loss and has resolved their feelings towards the loss. Relationships with others may resume that may have been neglected in favour of coming to terms with their loss.

STAGES OF GRIEVING—ELIZABETH KÜBLER-ROSS

Probably the most widely read and most widely publicised account of grieving is by Kübler-Ross (1970), who describes grieving as occurring in five stages:

(1) **Denial**
(2) Anger
(3) **Bargaining**
(4) Anger/depression/acceptance
(5) True acceptance.

Kübler-Ross, whilst identifying these stages, nevertheless asserts that not all individuals will go through them, no time limit can be put on any stage, and that some individuals will never truly accept the loss (or impending loss).

Denial

This is similar in nature to Bowlby's stage of denial, although it may recur throughout the coping process.

Anger

Anger may be directed towards themselves, their loved ones, or those involved in their care. Such anger can alienate carers from the individual if they take it at face value It may be manifested as complaints against staff, irrational apportionment of blame, as well as envy and resentment towards others.

Bargaining

This stage resembles the 'magical thinking' described earlier in this discussion. The individual may attempt to change their behaviour in the hope that the inevitable may not happen. They may even be changing their behaviour in order to aid the return of a loved one who has died.

Anger/Depression/Acceptance

Anger may again be experienced when death appears to be inevitable or the finality of the loved one's death becomes apparent. The individual may be asking the question 'why me'; this may in part be a form of bargaining, as though the individual is attempting to build a case for not dying, and that an outcome, when it is realised that he does not deserve to suffer, could be that his burden may be removed (?by God). If we now extend the 'why me' to 'why me, and not him', then this provides the basis for further anger and resentment.

In order for the individual to be angry about their predicament, a certain amount of acceptance must exist, although inevitably depression will accompany this stage.

Acceptance

An acceptance of the situation may be achieved over time and given the right support. This stage may be characterised by the individual wishing to spend time alone, and perhaps later by re-establishing contacts and relationships with others in order that the problem can be faced together with a sharing of emotions.

PERINATAL DEATH

Grieving following a perinatal death may present its own difficulties. Lewis and Bourne (1989) described such difficulties under the following headings:

(1) Unreality: due to the conflict between life and death, increased by abnormal circumstances such as a general anaesthetic, congenital abnormalities of the infant, etc.
(2) Anger: similar to that described above.
(3) Jealousy or possessive fury: feelings of betrayal. May be viewed as a 'broken promise' and may lead to psychotic symptoms at a later date, possibly after the birth of a subsequent child.
(4) Envy: for those with babies, and even for the dead. May lead to phobias of harming or stealing other peoples' babies.
(5) Shame: feelings of inferiority, humiliation and defilement. May withdraw from contact with others.
(6) Guilt: may be associated with the feeling that they have done wrong and deserve to be punished. May be manifested by shoplifting and hence inviting more punishment.
(7) Triumph: feelings of joy at being alive possibly being seen as illicit. Can lead to a vicious circle of guilt and manic overactivity.

CULTURAL ASPECTS OF GRIEVING

Our emotional reaction to many events is learned (Ekman, 1971), and although the subject of 'expression' is covered in some depth in Chapter 9, it is nevertheless important to consider at this juncture that demonstrating grief by crying, the support received from friends and relatives, and society's reactions to life events such as death and divorce may be, to an extent, culturally determined.

Fig. 11.1 & 11.2 Cultural variations in the funeral ceremony.

FOSTERING AND ADOPTION

It is perhaps stating the obvious that, in an ideal world, the best place for a child to be is with her natural parents. Unfortunately we do not live in such an ideal world, and as a result we have to aim for continuity, security and the physical and emotional well-being of the child, sometimes in a setting away from her natural parents.

This is not to say that extensive efforts have not been made to keep the child's family together; indeed, the question of fostering and adoption is sometimes considered at too late a stage to prevent a disastrous outcome. Therefore, we should recognise that a child who is being cared for by persons other than her natural parents has (with her family) been the subject of much scrutiny and the final decision, quite apart from usually being the last resort, has not been taken lightly. On a more positive note, the child will often form strong attachments to her new caregivers, and this can only be to her advantage. This is recognised by the various agencies involved when reaching their decisions as to the child's future.

Studies have been carried out into the psychological effects of adoption on the child. Bowlby's work has already been discussed, and if his theory is considered in the light of long-term fostering and adoption from an early age, along with his assumption that such experiences can produce lasting adverse effects, then fostering and adoption could do untold damage.

Bowlby's findings have been challenged on several occasions, and Tizard and Hodges (1978) go as far to suggest that early separation experiences provide no reason for lasting effects. Rutter (1981), in reviewing the available literature, suggested that delinquent behaviour was more likely to occur when the child was reared by the biological parents who themselves had a problem such as alcoholism or criminal behaviour, rather than by adopted parents.

Tizard and Hodges considered that any effects of separation in the long term were at least partly offset, quite simply because the 'adopted parents' worked harder at being parents than did the 'biological parents'.

THE CHILDREN'S ACT 1989

The latest Children's Act which applies to England and Wales acknowledges the importance of maintaining contact with the parents, although the overriding aim of the act is to promote and safeguard the welfare of children. The local authorities are encouraged to maintain the participation of adults in the family in the care of the child even if the child is being looked after away from the family home. The only time that this would not apply is if it is considered that such a contact would be detrimental to the child's welfare.

The acknowledgement of the importance of parental involvement in the upbringing of the child is needless to say an important one. It is coupled with the assertion that early intervention in the cases of neglect and abuse, including psychological trauma, should lay the foundation for problems to be tackled at an early stage before they become unresolvable.

At the time of writing the laws pertaining to adoption are under review as are other aspects of family law. For a more comprehensive view of the Children's Act 1989 the reader is directed to the document itself which although lengthy will provide them with a coherent and well-written text.

FEAR AS A LEARNED RESPONSE

The physiological basis of fear, and indeed its definition, has already been discussed in Chapter 3, but it will be re-examined here in terms of how fear may be acquired, and its possible innate origins.

The debate as to whether fear is innate or acquired has centered mainly around animal studies, although some studies have been carried out on humans. In considering such research, the incidence of fear occurring at a certain age which was not present at an earlier age needs to be considered. Gray (1987) encapsulates the argument thus:

'The temptation is to assume that the animal learnt in the interval that the stimulus is dangerous. But this need not be the case at all. In many instances what happens is that the neural mechanisms mediating the behaviour are not fully functioning at an early age, but undergo further development (maturation) by the later age'.

Fear of the dark and animals (Valentine, 1930), fear of heights (Bertenthal *et al.*, 1984), and others have been attributed to this process, although the possibility that such behaviour is either learned through experience or from others has been used to counter such arguments.

FEAR STIMULI

Gray suggests that five principles need to be considered when discussing fear stimuli:

(1) Intensity (e.g. loud noises).
(2) Novelty (e.g. fear of strangers).
(3) Special evolutionary dangers (fear which may develop over many generation into an innate fear of a particular successful predator).
(4) Stimuli arising during social interaction.
(5) Conditioned fear stimuli (see below).

One of the most prevalent theories of how fear is learned arises from the work originally carried out by the behaviourist Watson (1913). Discussion concerning classical conditioning can be found in Chapter 6; such a form of conditioning in early childhood is thought by some psychologists (e.g. Jacobs and Nadel, 1985) to form the basis of many human fears, as many such fears can be eliminated using conditioning techniques.

It would seem most likely, as Gray points out, that learning and innate mechanisms co-operate in order that the organism is best adapted to the environment.

In considering the fear of the individual who is ill, in particular if they are hospitalised, it is worth identifying the possible foundations of such fear. It would seem that at least part of the explanation lies in a fear of the unknown..

AGGRESSION

The concept of aggression from a psychoanalytic viewpoint has already been discussed in Chapter 2 and again in Chapter 9. The origins of aggression as a learned response have been investigated extensively, particularly in childhood.

As far as a clear definition of aggression is concerned, this is not as straightforward as it seems. As Evans (1989) puts it, such a task is a 'definitional minefield'. He goes on to discuss whether an aggressive behaviour need be an active one. Is it an aggressive behaviour not to tell someone of impending danger? Taking this a step further, is cheating an aggressive act? As Evans says: 'it is difficult to avoid including some reference to intention in any definition'.

With these cautions firmly in mind, some origins of aggression need to be considered. That aggression may be an innate phenomenon has already been discussed in terms of psychoanalytic theory elsewhere in the text, although difficulties emerge in substantiating such a hypothesis.

Parental influence could well be a factor in the development of aggression, especially if such behaviour is praised, or at least allowed to proceed uncorrected. There are certainly times when aggression is actively encouraged, such as in sports. Peer influence may also be a contributing factor.

One theory that has remained popular since its first appearance in the 1930s is the 'frustration–aggression' hypothesis (Dollard *et al.*, 1939) which states that aggression is the consequence of frustration. In other words, when a desired goal cannot be attained, then aggression may be directed towards the obstacle that has prevented the goal being attained. In terms of health care, it may be the case that a health professional is perceived as the 'obstacle' in certain situations (such as in a casualty department), in that the individual may see them as preventing the attainment of their goal of receiving the treatment that they perceive as being necessary (such as a prescription for certain drugs). It must always be remembered that the removal of objects may not be possible, and in such a case aggression may be directed towards an unrelated object (displacement) such as a loved one.

AGGRESSION AND THE MASS MEDIA

One of the areas of child development that has received considerable attention is the possibility of a child learning to be aggressive from what they watch on the television. It would appear that media violence could have, broadly speaking, one of two effects. Firstly, it was once thought to have a cathartic effect (Berkowitz, 1964). In several studies it was suggested that any violent behaviour which resulted from watching violence seemed to arise as a result of disinhibition—namely the releasing of something already in the emotions, rather than the acting out of something learned.

Alternatively, it has been suggested that violence seen through the media actually is the initiator of violent behaviour. This type of theory generally comes from the social learning theorists (e.g. Bandura), and suggests that

Fig. 11.3 Sometimes, such as in sport, aggression is actively encouraged.

the viewer actually learns aggression. This has lead to the speculation of three further consequences, namely that it may:

(1) Help us learn new forms of expressing aggression.
(2) Lead to an increase in aggressive behaviour.
(3) Increase tolerance of violence.

Learning New Forms of Aggression
Bandura *et al.*, (1961) arranged for nursery children to watch a film of an adult beating a rubber doll (with a weighted base). The film was shown to each child individually. The adult was shown hitting the doll with an axe, hammer, cursing the doll, etc. Prior to watching the film, each child had played with the doll, and was then given the doll to play with after the film. Behaviour and methods of aggression were far different after watching the film (aggression was an imitation of the adults)'.

Increase in Aggressive Behaviour
Meyer (1972a) measured the immediate effects of watching violence on punitiveness. The experiment was in two phases.

Phase I—a naive subject (NS) and a stooge (ST) were used. The NS writes an essay and the Stooge reads it and gives the NS electric shocks if he didn't like it.

Phase II—The stooge writes an essay, with the NS evaluating. ST takes too long. Experimenter walks in and says he has a colleague doing some work on visual appraisal, and would the NS mind helping while he is waiting. One group of NSs are shown a violent film, the other half a non-violent film. The ST has finished his essay by the time the film has finished. Those showed the violent film gave the ST far more electric shocks than those watching a non-violent film.

Hence, punitiveness changes. Verbal violence also leads to the same thing. As well as an increase of violence, studies have been done to investigate T.V. violence in the long term. Stein and Friedrich (1972) investigated a nursery school with children aged 4–6 years in a poor area who watched television frequently. The children were divided up into three groups and each group was shown films, three times weekly. One group was shown 'prosocial' films only, one group was shown 'neutral' films, e.g. flower pressing, and one group was only shown prosocial aggression (e.g. 'Batman'). Those children shown prosocial films became more helpful and less aggressive, those shown the neutral films showed no difference in behaviour, and those shown prosocial aggression were less helpful and more aggressive. When these children were followed up several months later, the above effects were still apparent.

Another explanation was offerred by Kniveton (1973). He suggested that the children did not become more aggressive, merely more active (hence they annoy people and create conflicts, etc.)

Increased Tolerance of Violence
Drabman and Thomas (1974) worked with 7 and 8 year olds. They allowed the children individually to watch one of two films, either a cowboy film or a non-violent film. They were told afterwards that they were going to be asked questions, but that before this, the experimenter had to make an important phone call. The child was put in one room and told that another two children were going to arrive in the next room (wired with T.V.). The child was asked to keep an eye on them, and if there was any trouble to go and get the experimenter. The two children started drawing and playing with 'Lego'. Sooner or later, they begin to quarrel. Those children who had watched the non-violent film sought assistance far quicker.

This experiment was replicated in 1975 with a larger age group to test to see whether it was excitement, content or aggression that caused the phenomenon. One group this time watched a basketball game, and the other a violent detective story. The results, however, were still the same.

When considering the features of the programme, its violence realism and justification of violence must be examined. Noble (1973) observed about 50 6–7 year olds. Each was observed briefly to see firstly how constructive they were, and secondly how aggressive their play was. Following this, the children then went and watched one of two war pictures, one newsreel and one fictional. Children who watched the fictional film changed very little in their play, however thoese who watched the newsreel became more aggressive and less constructive.

Meyer (1972b), using undergraduates, told them that they would be taking part in a literary appraisal (appraising essays before and after a newsreel film) showing an American ambush on the Viet Cong, where one Viet Cong was clubbed to death. Two different soundtracks were used: one said that the Viet Cong group had been raping and murdering, and that the Americans had been looking specifically for them, during which they captured their leader, and therefore his killing was justified; the other soundtrack emphasised the brutality of the act. It was found that the viewers who had seen the justified version were more punitive.

Kniverton and Stephenson (1973) attempted to find out if it is always the same individual that is affected. They showed children aggression towards the BoBo doll, and observed to see how many imitated the aggression. They returned 6 months later and showed a different film, namely depicting destruction (not aggression), showing a child breaking toys. Then the children were given the same types of toys to play with and they observed whether the same children were affected. There was a high correlation, hence they concluded that there are individual differences in susceptibility.

PROSOCIAL BEHAVIOUR

One of the more attractive aspects of human behaviour is that of 'care giving' (nurturance) which, along with 'care seeking', are the most common types of prosocial behaviour. Naturally, both behaviours lie at the centre of health care, and may help us to further understand the behaviours of both carers and those they care for. Whilst considering the behaviours of each, it should be stressed that a vast amount of caring and being cared for occurs outside the domain of the health professional. The most obvious example is the family or person who provides care for a sick or disabled relative at home, often with the bare minimum of help from outside agencies.

DEPENDENCY AND NURTURANCE

Care-seeking behaviour (dependency) may be a means for the individual to attain something (such as food, comfort, relief of pain, treatment of symptoms) which may not be achieved independently for one reason or another (**instrumental dependency**), although it may also be sought for purely pleasurable ends (**emotional dependency**). It can be seen that there is an immediately obvious link between these dependent behaviours and infancy. An example of instrumental dependency could be when the child has to have his mother dress him because he lacks the dexterity to fasten buttons. On the other hand, he may allow his mother to dress him for the attention that this brings, even though he is perfectly capable of dressing himself, and in this case he is exhibiting emotional dependency. Further it can be seen that there is a complementary relationship between dependency and nurturant behaviour. Such links can be seen as the early emergence of social interaction.

As we grow older, emotional dependency becomes less tolerated by society, although instrumental dependence continues to be socially acceptable, probably due to the inevitability of a loss or independence at some time during our lives through illness, disability or old age. Emotional dependency does occur however, and could be associated with a period of illness where instrumental dependence may have been passed through, or even in the convalescent stage. It is not altogether unknown for an individual who has passed the point of requiring active nursing care to continue to be demanding and to seek attention. The reasons for this dependence could be a regression to a childlike state which may for instance occur in terminal illness (Hinton, 1984), or perhaps more obviously it could be that they lack warmth and understanding in their relationships.

The nature of care giving is not as straightforward as it as first seems, and it may be helpful to consider the subject in terms of the consideration for the well-being of other individuals (altruism).

ALTRUISM

We all admire the person who we perceive as being truly **altruistic**, in other words those who will help others without thought of personal gain. The emergence of helping behaviour in children has been investigated in two main areas, namely 'donation responses' and 'rescue activity' (Bryan, 1972). Donation responses could involve the child giving a prized article to a charitable cause, and rescue activity refers to helping someone in distress.

It would seem that there is a positive link between observing a positive model of helping behaviour (such as a parent) and the child's behaviour, although mere verbal reminders of social responsibility have not been shown to have any such effect (Bryan, 1971), although it may be that a child's rescue activity may serve to reduce their own empathy-induced anxiety. There does appear to be a difference in childhood and adult behaviour in this direction, as will be seen in the following discussion, although perhaps, to an extent, role modelling may still be having an effect into the adult years.

THE BYSTANDER EFFECT

There has been much attention given to the behaviour of the individual who observes another who is in trouble. Many of us have said at some time or another: 'You could die here and no one would notice!' Many such flippant remarks about workplaces, towns and even whole countries are commonplace, but is there any truth in them? It would be clearly impossible to come to any such conclusions about individual environments without the appropriate research, regardless of what our instincts may tell us. More generalised findings may serve to give us an idea as to how we react towards a fellow human who is in trouble.

Perhaps some of the most dramatic findings have come from research into real life incidents as distinct from controlled experiments. One such piece of research concerned the murder of Kitty Genovese. In order to emphasise the importance of the findings (Darley and Latane, 1968) a brief account of the incident as quoted by the authors is given:

'Kitty Genovese is set upon by a maniac as she returns home from work at 3 a.m. Thirty eight of her neighbours...come to their windows when she cries out in terror; none come to her assistance even though her stalker takes over half an hour to murder her. No one even so much as calls the police. She dies.'

This dreadful incident and others are quoted by the authors, and they concluded, from subsequent interviews of bystanders of this and other incidents, that in an emergency they have to make a series of decisions.

Firstly, the bystander must actually notice that an emergency has occurred. This will depend on whether the individual is so pre-occupied with their own thoughts that they do not actually see it happening, or may actually feel that it is impolite to look! More especially her actions will depend on the reaction of other bystanders around her, therefore suggesting that a crowd can enforce inaction by imposing the wrong definition of the situation on those around them. This second stage, interpreting the situation, is often determined by a group rather than by the individual coming to their own conclusions, but even if the individual interprets the emergency independently, they may come to a wrong conclusion. A collapsed person may be construed as a drunk rather than the victim of trauma or illness.

Interpreting the situation and the next stage may be strongly related. For instance, an attack on a person may be construed as a domestic argument that has got out of hand, and the bystander may come to the conclusion that they have no responsibility in such an incident. Once again though, other bystanders may have an effect on us if everyone has defined the situation as an emergency. Diffused responsibility between the bystanders could mean that each one thought the others were going to do something about it, or that they felt that someone else should take the responsibility.

The decision to intervene (or not) could be based on the decisions arrived at from the previous stage, but could also include considerations for personal safety, and even an evaluation as to what the bystander would gain from such an intervention. The evidence to suppport the theory that the bystander did not wish to become involved (for many of the above reasons) has received support from several pieces of research (e.g. Darley and Latane, 1968; Latane and Darley, 1968; Latane and Rodin, 1969), and has come from both real life incidents and experimentation.

CONCLUSION

The study of grieving, naturally important in terms of death and dying, has many other associations. This is particularly the case if we consider it as a separation reaction rather than as a unique phenomenon. If viewed in this way it can be seen that events such as a prolonged hospital stay may, particularly for younger patients, bring undesirable effects. It has been discussed that a child learns about death and gradually forms accurate concepts about it, and there is some evidence to suggest that the same may be the case with aggressive and prosocial behaviour. Certainly, as health care professionals, we should examine the concept of prosocial behaviour in terms of the occupations we have chosen, and perhaps try to identify how our professional and personal lives may be governed by it.

SUMMARY

The concept of death develops from early childhood, and its association with reactions to separation in the early months is a close one.

Bowlby, in his original work, found that many of the delinquent adolescents whom he was treating showed a particular aspect in common, namely that they had had traumatic separation experiences early in life.

Clarke and Clarke (1976) suggested (as did Rutter) that the effects of early separation experiences were reversible.

Bowlby (1973) described the grieving process as having four stages:

(1) **Denial**
(2) Sensation of loss
(3) Restitution
(4) Resolution.

Kubler-Ross (1969) describes grieving as occurring in possibly five stages:

(1) **Denial**
(2) Anger
(3) **Bargaining**
(4) Anger/depression/acceptance
(5) True acceptance.

Grieving following a perinatal death may present its own difficulties.

Studies have been carried out into the psychological effects of adoption on the child. Tizard and Hodges considered that any effects of separation in the long term were at least partly offset quite simply because the 'adopted parents' worked harder at being parents than did the 'biological parents'.

Gray suggests that five principles need to be considered when discussing fear stimuli:

(1) Intensity (e.g. loud noises).
(2) Novelty (e.g. fear of strangers).
(3) Special evolutionary dangers (fear which may develop over many generation into an innate fear of a particular successful predator).
(4) Stimuli arising during social interaction.
(5) Conditioned fear stimuli.

One of the areas of child development that has received considerable attention is the possibility of a child learning to be aggressive from what they watch on the television.

Care-seeking behaviour (dependency) may be a means for the individual to attain something (such as food, comfort, relief of pain, treatment of symptoms) which may not be achieved independently for one reason or another (**instrumental dependency**), although it may also be sought for purely pleasurable ends (**emotional dependency**).

The emergence of helping behaviour in children has been investigated in two main areas, namely 'donation responses' and 'rescue activity' (Bryan, 1972).

There has been much attention given to the behaviour of the individual who observes another who is in trouble. Interpreting the situation and the next stage may be strongly related. For instance, an attack on a person may be construed as a domestic argument. The decision to intervene (or not) could be based on the decisions arrived at from the previous stage, but could also include considerations for personal safety.

REFERENCES

* indicates standard texts or articles

Bandura, A., Ross, D. and Ross, S.A. (1961) Transmission of aggression through imitation of aggressive models. *Journal of Abnormal and Social Psychology* **67**, 601–607.

Berkowitz, L. (1964) Aggressive cues in aggressive behaviour and hostility catharsis. *Psychological Review* **71**, 104–122.

Bertenthal, B.I., Campos, J.J. and Barrett, K.C. (1984) Self-produced locomotion: an organiser of emotional, cognitive and social development in infancy. In: Erride, R.N. and Harmen, R.J. (eds), *Continuities and Discontinuities in Development.* Plenum, New York.

Birtchnell, J. (1980) Women whose mothers died in childhood. *Psychosocial Medicine* **10**, 699–713.

Bowlby, J. (1973) *Attachment and Loss. Vol. 2. Separation, Anxiety and Anger.* Hogarth Press.*

Bowlby, J. (1981) *Attachment and Loss. Vol. 3. Loss: Sadness and Depression.* Penguin Books, Harmondsworth.*

Brown, G.W. (1982) Early loss and depression. In: Parkes, C.M. and Stevenson-Hind, J. (eds), *The Place of Attachment in Human Behaviour.* Basic Books, New York.

Brown, G.W. and Harris, T. (1978) *Social Origins of Depression: A Study of Psychiatric Disorder in Women.* N.Y. Free Press, New York.

Bryan, J. (1971) Model affect and children's imitative behaviour. *Child Behaviour* **42**, 2061–2065.

Bryan, J. (1972) Why children help: a review. *Journal of Social Issues* **28(5)**, 87–103.

Clarke, A.M. and Clarke, A.D.B. (1976) *Early Experience: Myth and Evidence.* Open Books, London.

Crook, T. and Elliot, J. (1980) Parental death during childhood and adult depression: a critical review of the literature. *Psychological Bulletin* **87**, 252–259.

Darley, J.M. and Latane, B. (1968) Bystander intervention in emergencies: diffusion of responsibility. *Journal of Personality and Social Psychology* **8**, 377–383.*

Dollard, J., Doob, L.W., Miller, N.E., Mower, O.H. and Sears, R.R. (1939) *Frustration and Aggression.* Yale University Press, New Haven.

Drabman, R.S. and Thomas, M.H. (1974) Does media violence increase children's tolerence of real life aggression? *Developmental Psychology* **10**, 418–421.

Ekman, P. (1971) Universal and cultural differences in facial expressions of emotion. In Levin, D. (ed.) *Nebraska Symposium on Motivation,* Univ. of Nebraska Press, Lincoln, Nebraska.

Evans, P.E. (1989) *Motivation and Emotion.* Routledge, London.

Gray, J.A. (1987) *The Psychology of Fear and Stress*. Cambridge University Press, Cambridge.*

Hinton, J. (1984) Coping with terminal illness. In: Fitzpatrick, R., Hinton, J., Newman, S., Scambler, G. and Thompson, J. (eds), *The Experience of Illness*, Tavistock, London.

Jacobs, W.J. and Nadel, W. (1985) Stress induced recovery of fears and phobias. *Psychological Review* **92**, 512–531.

Jenner, S. (1992) Psychological interventions and techniques: how to promote learning and reduce the adverse effects of handicap. In: Thompson, A. and Mathias, P. (eds) *Standards and Mental Handicap – Keys to Competence*. Bailli`ere Tindall, London.

Kniverton, B.H. (1973) The efect of rehersal delay on long term imitation of filmed aggression. *British Journal of Psychology* **64**, 259–265.

Kniverton, B.H. and Stephenson, G.M. (1973) *British Journal of Psychiatry*, **122**, 53–57.

Kubler-Ross, E. (1970) *On Death and Dying*. Tavistock, London.*

Latane, B. and Darley, J.M. (1968) Group inhibition of bystander intervention in emergencies. *Journal of Personality and Social Psychology* **10(3)**, 215.*

Latane, B. and Rodin, J. (1969) A lady in distress: inhibiting effects of friends and strangers on bystander intervention. *Journal of Experimental Social Psychology* **5(3)**, 189.*

Lewis, E. and Bourne, S. (1989) Perinatal death. In: Oates, M.R. (ed.), *Psychological Aspects of Obstetrics and Gynaecology*. Baillie`re Tindall, London.

Meyer, T.P. (1972a) Effects of viewing justified and unjustified real film violence on aggressive behaviour. *Journal of Personality and Social Psychology* **23**, 21–29.

Meyer, T.P. (1972b) *A.U. Communication Review* **20**, 160–169.

Nagy, M. (1948) The child's theories concerning death. *Journal of Genetic Psychology* **73**, 3–27. (Quoted in Vaughan, V.C. and Litt, I.F. (1990) *Child and Adolescent Development; Clinical Implication*. W.B. Saunders, Philadelphia.

Noble, G. (1973) Effects of different forms of filmed aggression on children's constructive and destructive play. *Journal of Personality and Social Psychology* **26**, 54–59.

Parke, R.D. (1981) *Fathering*. Fontana, London.*

Raphael, B. (1982) *The Anatomy of Bereavement*. Basic Books, New York.

Rochlin, G. (1967) How younger children view death and themselves. In: Grollman, E.A. (ed.), *Explaining Death to Children*. Beacon Press, Boston.

Rutter, M. (ed.) (1980) *Scientific Foundations of Developmental Psychiatry*. Heinemann Medical, London.

Rutter, M. (1981) *Maternal Deprivation Reassessed*. Penguin, Harmondsworth.*

Stayton, D.J. (1973) Infant responses to brief everyday separations: Distress, following and greeting. Paper presented at the meeting of the Society for Research in Child Development (Quoted in Atkinson, R. Atkinson, R.C., Smith, E., and Benn, D.J. (1990) *Introduction to Psychology* (10th Edn), Harcourt Brace Jovanovich, London.

Stein, A.H. and Friedrich, L.K. (1972) Television content and young children's behaviour. In: *TV and Social Behaviour* (Vol. 2), US Govt Printing Office, Washington D.C.

Tizard, B. and Hodges, J. (1978) The effect of early institutional rearing on the development of eight year old children. *Journal of Child Psychology and Psychiatry* **11**, 177–86.

Valentine, C.W. (1930) The innate bases of fear. *Journal of Genetic Psychology* **37**, 394–419.

Vaughan, V.C. and Litt, I.F. (1990) *Child and Adolescent Development: Clinical Implications*. W.B. Saunders, Philadelphia.

Watson, J.B. (1913) Psychology as a behaviorist views it. *Psychological Review* **20**, 158–177.

SUGGESTED READING

Bowlby, J. (1984) *Attachment and Loss*, Vols 1, 2 and 3. Hogarth Press.* (This standard text provides the reader with a superb resource. Controversial. The reader is also directed towards Rutter and possibly Clarke and Clarke (see above).)

Kubler-Ross, E. (1970) *On Death and Dying*. Tavistock, London.* (A very readable text.)

Rutter, M. (1981) *Maternal Deprivation Reassessed*. Penguin, Harmondsworth.*

Stroebe, W. and Stroebe, M.S. (1987) *Bereavement and Health*. Cambridge University Press, Cambridge. (See Chapter 3 (Cultural Variations) and Chapter 4 which looks at depression models and grief.)

The reader is directed to the following for an account of the bystander effect.

Latane, B. and Darley, J.M. (1968) Group inhibition of bystander intervention in emergencies. *Journal of Personality and Social Psychology* **10(3)**, 215.

Latane, B. and Rodin, J. (1969) A lady in distress: inhibiting effects of friends and strangers on bystander intervention. *Journal of Experimental Social Psychology* **5(3)**, 189.*

HEALTH
CARE
INTERVENTION

CHAPTERS

. . .we refilled our glasses, lit our pipes, and resumed the discussion on the state of our health. What it was that was actually the matter with us, we none of us could be sure of; but the unanimous opinion was that it —whatever it was —had been brought on by overwork

JEROME K. JEROME *Three Men in a Boat*

INTRODUCTION TO SECTION THREE

Health care professionals come into contact with individuals who are ill, receiving treatment and/or are hospitalised. Additionally, many individuals who are bereaved or dealing with other stressful life events may seek the help of health care professionals. Individual differences have been discussed in Section 1, and the individual's possible responses to certain life events has been reviewed in the second section.

In considering stress, anxiety and coping, we have already begun to look at responses to illness treatment and hospitalisation, and these shall be expanded upon in this section. The subjects covered in earlier chapters need to be considered in order to gain some insight into the individual's possible responses, and it is in this section that they can be drawn together within the context of health care.

Naturally, in discussing these subjects many factors will be considered, not least of all age differences, and of course the individuals past experiences deserve the health care professional's close scrutiny. Beginning with the individual's responses to illness and treatment, the discussion then moves on to examine how the individual's attitudes may affect their responses in the health care setting. Not only will the attitudes of those receiving or requiring health care be examined, but also the attitudes of those providing care. Hospitalisation, its possible effects and how they may be overcome is the subject of Chapter 14.

CHAPTER 12

ILLNESS AND TREATMENT

'Cur'd yesterday of my disease, I died last night of my physician.'

MATTHEW PRIOR (1664–1721)

INTRODUCTION

There can be few subjects which affect the day-to-day working of the health professional more than the reactions of individuals to their illness. It is not uncommon for us to ask ourselves questions like 'How will they take the news?', or 'How will they cope with their disability?'. Nurses who advocate a 'self care' approach to nursing may ask themselves 'to what extent, and in which context should the health professional intervene?'.

All these questions, and countless others besides, infer that to a large extent, we are asking 'how is the individual reacting to their illness?', or perhaps more accurately in some cases 'how is the individual reacting to their illness now that we have diagnosed it and explained it to them?'

Immediately we can begin to connect the grieving processes described in Chapter 11 with the individual who is terminally ill, or who will suffer loss (such as through surgery). But naturally, the picture is left substantially incomplete if we apply only this reaction to the individual. To return to the discussion in Chapter 7, illness could be considered in terms of the changes that may occur in the individual's self-image. Certainly, the roles that we have in our everyday lives may change dramatically in the light of illness.

On perhaps a more obvious note, the reactions that the individual may have to pain are a serious consideration, as are the controls that we may or may not have over the relief of such pain. The discussion on pain leads to the function of giving adequate information to the patient, and this theme is further developed in the discussion on the effects of communication, and finally on adherence to treatment. Some models of health (e.g. locus of control—Chapter 4) are to be found elsewhere in the text, primarily because they are pertinent to the subject area of the chapter concerned.

The starting point for our discussion in this chapter, and one which will incorporate topics covered in other chapters, addresses the question of how we may react, in terms of roles, when we are ill.

ROLES

When considering the whole subject of roles, it may be useful to draw comparisons between real-life situations and the acting profession. We all know that when an actor plays a role, that they are repeating lines which are usually learned from a script, and are behaving in a way in which the character they are playing demands. The next day, or week, they may be playing a different role altogether, bearing little resemblance to the previous one.

In our everyday lives, we all play a number of roles, often within the same day, and like the actor we play these roles in accordance with certain rules, only this time it is society that defines them rather than a producer or director. These rules (and sometimes even the things we are alllowed to say) are sometimes very strict, although at other times they are more liberal.

Roles are, in essence, components of a social system, and although interlinked with our personalities, with each having an effect on the other, they are nevertheless a collection of actions and words rather than 'people'. By saying of someone 'they are only doing their job', when for instance we are stopped by the police for a traffic violation, is to acknowledge that the role and the person may be separated.

Most of the roles that people play have certain characteristics in common with others who play similar roles. For instance, the roles may be governed by our occupation, relationships, gender, or even the qualifications that we possess. The rules for such roles are frequently violated in minor ways by individuals, and this is frequently viewed as favourable by others. For example, we often admire the individual who does not always do things 'by the book', but who will use their initiative to solve a problem in a novel way, often at the cost of straying outside the norms for that role. It has to be said though, that although such minor violations may bring us the admiration of others, throwing the proverbial 'book' away altogether could have the opposite effect. The manager may admire the individual who uses their initiative, but may take an entirely different view if such an initiative involves changes in practice from the rest of the staff without the manager's involvement or sanction.

ROLE CONFLICT

It is rare indeed to find an individual who has only one role in life, and at this juncture it may be useful to consider how many different roles we may have. This is an exercise that the reader may like to try for themselves, as it would be useful for the purposes of reflection later in the chapter. Below is an example of one individual's most important roles.

(1) Father
(2) Son
(3) Brother
(4) Nurse
(5) Friend
(6) Husband.

Each one of these roles has its own set of norms, and at times the individual concerned may have to play several roles simultaneously, for example when taking his family to visit his parents and brothers and sisters. Normally, this should present no significant problem, and he could play the roles of father, son, brother, and husband without much difficulty. Conflict may occur, however, if there are different 'prescriptions' for the same event (inter-role conflict).

If for instance the grandmother's response towards one of the children having a tantrum is to pick them up and cuddle them, and the father's response is to ignore it, then a potential for inter-role conflict could occur, with the father having to assert his authority over his own mother in order for the desired behaviour to occur. This may indeed be a long-standing problem which happens on every visit, and it will come as no surprise to learn that such conflicts are diminished by geographical distances!

Another type of conflict that may occur is 'intra-role' conflict, which could emerge as a result of disagreement on the behaviour of role occupants. Put another way, if two or more people have the same role, then conflict can occur as a result of the perceptions of the accepted behaviours of that role differing.

ROLES AND ILLNESS BEHAVIOUR

When sickness intervenes in our lives, it may well be the case that we will behave in a particular way. Naturally, some illnesses, such as a light cold or a toothache, usually mean that life goes on as normal with only minor adjustments. It has been suggested that most symptoms do not result in any form of consultation, and this has been termed the '**illness iceberg**' (Last, 1963). Subsequent research has indicated that up to a third of symptoms will go unreported (Scambler et al., 1981). Generally speaking though, illness behaviour is usually taken to mean those behaviours which the individual, who percieves himself as ill, may undertake in order to ascertain his state of health and also to uncover possible remedies.

Parsons (1951), in the now famous theory of **sick role** behaviour, suggested that the individual, when suffering from an illness, may behave in certain ways in order to facilitate recovery. For instance, they may stay off work, or avoid social contacts and normal responsibilities, and will normally seek medical attention. Just as with other roles, however, certain criteria must be set before society would deem it appropriate for the individual to adopt a sick role:

(1) Society must recognise their disorder as an illness.
(2) There should be something to validate the difficulty e.g. a physical symptom or the sanction of an expert (usually a doctor).
(3) It has to be accepted by the individual concerned.

It would be a wrong assumption that the individual automatically takes on the sick role in response to an illness. There are in fact a number of different responses that the individual may make in terms of the sick role:

(1) They may adopt the sick role readily, and surrender it on recovery.
(2) They are reluctant to adopt the sick role, but when they do they are reluctant to surrender it.
(3) They do not adopt it at all.
(4) They adopt the sick role and do not give it up.

Naturally, many factors are involved in such a mechanism, and we need to look at social pressures such as family commitments and pressure of work.

The individual's **self-image**, which will include their **body image** and of course their self-esteem, can all be affected by illness, and indeed the reverse may also be true, with their reactions to their illness (or operation) being determined by their self-image. In the discussion in Chapter 7, it was suggested that the individual who has an ideal image which is attainable is likely to be in a better position than one whose self-image and ideal image are miles apart. It is conceivable that the individual's ideal image is based on physical achievement, in which case the occurrence of debilitating illness or surgery could have a more marked effect.

The roles that an individual plays in their everyday life will usually undergo some modification during illness, but for the individual described with such a wide gulf between the actual and ideal self, it is possible that a 'sick role' could act as a temporary respite during which roles, both current and desired, are re-evaluated and perhaps adjusted. It seems likely that such an adjustment may bring with it some form of grieving reaction, as the loss of roles is mourned (see Chapter 11).

PAIN

The physiological mechanisms of pain were discussed in Chapter 3, and some reference to at least one of those theories, namely gate theory, needs to be made when discussing the psychological aspects. It was stated that psychological factors take on an important role when considering the messages descending from the brainstem and the cortex, and that emotional conditions such as anxiety can serve to open or close the gate, as can depression or excitement.

The notion that psychological factors can open or close the 'gate' appears to have some foundation and could provide an explanation for some of the phenomena observed in recent years. A couple of pieces of recent research have highlighted the probable importance of psychological factors.

POST-OPERATIVE PAIN

One of the pieces of research to have had a major impact, particularly on nursing practice, was carried out by Hayward (1975) and considered the effects of giving information about the physical experiences which may be expected post-operatively to patients about to undergo surgery. The effect, generally, was that post-operative pain was reduced, and this appears to complement the gate theory to some extent at least. However, other variables must also be taken into consideration (Johnson *et al.*, 1978), which leads us to suppose that a detailed assessment of the individual is important in the subsequent management of pain, and further that a more detailed assessment of the pain that the individual is experiencing is also necessary (Walding, 1991).

A detailed assessment of the individual who is in labour may also reveal interesting correlations between past experiences and the level of pain that will be experienced (Niven, 1991), with correlations between previous pain in childbirth and the current labour, and also less pain being reported by those women who had severe dysmenorrhea prior to conception. This at least can lead us in the direction of considering that the perception of pain is an extremely personal phenomenon, and that to some extent it may be based on a cognitive as well as an innate framework.

There is some support for the suggestion that to reduce the individual's feelings of powerlessness could be an important component of pain control (Walding, 1991), and it has been found that to give the responsibility of analgesia administration to the individual who is experiencing the pain could reduce analgesia consumption by up to 50% (Dallison, 1991); it should be mentioned that this study only concentrated on those individuals who had undergone abdominal hysterectomy.

DISCUSSION: WHO DECIDES ON PAIN CONTROL?

As far as post-operative pain is concerned, therefore, psychological factors do seem to play a major role in its control. The suggestion of giving the individual some control over their own analgesia is an interesting one, and it does raise some questions as to why it appears (at least at this stage of the research) to be successful.

Firstly, the perception of those who traditionally assess the pain in order to administer the analgesia should be questioned. All of us involved in health care should ask ourselves whether the assessment that we carry out truly reflects how the individual is feeling, or whether we are using some form of unsubstantiated method of pain measurement based on our own experiences. For instance, do we make assumptions about the level of pain that should be expected with certain types of surgery, and dispense analgesia accordingly? Given a choice between two or more prescribed analgesics, do we make a choice based upon the assumption that pain on the third day post-operatively is less or different from that on the first day?

Of course, as health professionals we all need to make decisions about analgesics, and the assumptions quoted above are in some circumstances at least partly acceptable, but perhaps if the individual who is experiencing the pain is better informed about their condition and the analgesia that is available, then we may find that the pattern of analgesia consumption meets the individual's needs more closely.

Secondly, we need to consider whether the pattern of pain is related to the times that the drugs are traditionally made available (usually the times of the medicine round). It is a possibility that the individual may ask for analgesia when in fact they may not need it, just because they will not be offered it again for another 4 hours, and they may not want to bother the nurses in between rounds. This is not to say that the individual should suffer pain—this is clearly unacceptable—but it is interesting to note that in Dallison's study, analgesics were never taken at the times of the drug rounds.

Finally we should consider whether, as Walding suggests, the element of control that self-administration brings with it reduces anxiety and hence the amount of pain experienced.

CHRONIC PAIN

The control of pain for long-standing conditions is a problem which confronts many health professionals, not least G.P.s who will have to carefully adjust medication to give the maximum amount of relief with the minimal amount of side effects. The situation can of course be carefully monitored in a hospital setting, with due regard to the points raised in our earlier discussion.

The management of the individual who is suffering from pain from a long-standing condition such as osteoarthrosis is frequently a problem in the community. The world of the individual who has to live with severe chronic pain can be one of despair, with little hope of relief. Behaviour towards those around them may become uncharacteristically irritable, until at last their whole world will seem to concentrate around their pain (Sternbach, 1974).

Psychological factors will most certainly play a part in the perceptions of their pain, and it is perhaps pertinent here to draw a distinction, as Bakal (1979) does, between organic and psychogenic pain. The term 'organic' pain refers to pain that has been found to have a definite organic cause. 'Psychogenic' pain, on the other hand, is generally taken to mean that it is due to psychological causes.

It seems plausible that the two types of pain may be interrelated, especially when considering chronic pain, and indeed the occurrence of psychogenic pain is in keeping with the gate control theory. It should not be assumed that psychogenic pain hurts any less than purely organic pain—it certainly does not, and indeed it may even have arisen from an existing organic cause. To suggest to the individual that their pain may be all in the mind is of no help whatsoever, and instead the pain should be considered for what it really is, namely something that is real, and perhaps more pertinently, something that hurts.

In a study which looked at chronic pain in the elderly in the community, the link between psychological and organic factors has been highlighted (Walker, 1991). The variables that were identified as directly determining coping with the pain were:

(1) Feeling the pain to be under control.
(2) Being occupied.
(3) Feeling informed about the painful condition.
(4) Having regrets.
(5) Non-pain-related problems (especially bereavement).

It seems that considerable variation exists between acute and chronic pain sufferers in terms of the neurotic disturbances (Sternbach *et al.*, 1973), but it appears that these may not have been present at the onset of the condition, and that 'they reflect a preoccupation and extension of the pain symptoms' (Bakal, 1979).

CHILDREN AND PAIN

The ways that a child will cope with pain, or even how they tell us about pain, confronts the health professional with a completely different situation. In describing pain, for example, the young child may describe it verbally. Wilkinson (1988), in a review of the literature, observes that children may report the same sort of pain that other members of their families do, and this has been found with different types of pain including abdominal and dental pain.

As far as their reactions to pain are concerned, it seems that children in the approximate age group from 8 months to 4 years are the most vulnerable (Bergmann and Freud, 1966), because they no longer feel totally protected by their parents, and also because of their vulnerability to separation reactions. It has been discussed, primarily in Chapter 6, that the level of the child's understanding of the cause of the pain may lead to further anxiety, and hence the situation is compounded.

Repeated painful experiences may lead to a **regression** in behaviour, and be manifested by regressing to an earlier stage of mobilising, eating, and of course bowel and bladder habits. This type of reaction is thought to be an attempt on the part of the child to retreat to a safer stage in their development.

Naturally, the preparation required by the child for painful procedures should be dependent upon their stage of development, and as such should be in a language that they can understand. The language that the child itself utilizes should be used and built upon when giving explanations. As with adult patients, a complete assessment of the pain, which should include all previous experiences, should be made in order that certain fears may be allayed. It is not beyond reason to expect that previous unpleasant experiences of pain will be applied to the situation in hand, and this may lead to misconceptions and unnecessary anxiety. Once again, if possible, those responsible for the everyday care of the child should also have an explanation appropriate to their understanding, as conflict may arise if each party is giving a completely different explanation.

The assessment of pain in any individual should not be based on assumptions, or merely what is observed, although this naturally has its place.

Assessment of pain in children, and moreover preparing them for painful procedures, is something that should not be left to chance. Possibly more education of those responsible for such as assessment should be undertaken (Price, 1991), as there could be a tendency for some (in this case student nurses) to view pain as a purely physical phenomenon.

THE EFFECT OF COMMUNICATION

The amount of information that we give an individual who is ill has been investigated by several researchers, and not surprisingly it has been found that generally individuals feel most distressed when they have little or no idea what is happening to them. This is by no means a statement borne out of the theoretically obvious, but rather the result of numerous studies in several different specialities which have attempted to examine the possible causes of patient dissatisfaction.

COMPLIANCE

As health professionals, we are not only concerned with the individual's response to illness, but also their response to treatment. Naturally, one of the determining factors in the success or failure of any treatment regime is the degree of compliance with it by the individual.

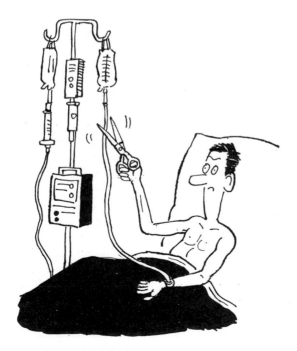

The overall picture that emerges from numerous studies into compliance with treatment is not a particularly hopeful one in many respects. In one American study (McKenny and Harrison, 1976), it was found that 10% of patients on a medical ward of a large teaching hospital were there because of non-compliance with the medical regimen. Ley (1988), in reviewing the literature, observes that between 10% and 25% of patients are admitted to hospital because of non-compliance.

This picture is certainly not just confined to compliance with drug regimen. It has been shown to be even more dramatic when considering such therapies as psychotherapy (Foulks *et al.*, 1986), where over 50% of clients may decide to discontinue therapy against advice.

Harvey (1988) points out that non-compliance (or non-adherence as he terms it) may be due to the following factors:

(1) Volitional non-adherence—the individual decides rationally not to follow advice.
(2) Accidental non-compliance—the individual may forget or misunderstand the instructions they have been given.
(3) Circumstantial non-compliance—the treatment may be prematurely ended by severe or unpleasant side effects.

The remedies for non-compliance would naturally be fairly easy to identify if all such instances were accidental. Several studies (e.g. Ridout *et al.*, 1986) indicate that there is a need for further work to be done in terms of new information tools and their effectiveness in drug prescription and use. It is conceivable that a more vigorous effort to provide coherent explanations could prevent non-compliance in other areas, although at the same time, as Foulks points out, a significant amount of clients discontinued psychotherapy following discussion.

Non-compliance with treatment regimen is a serious and prolific problem which by its very definition costs vast amounts of money every year. It does seem reasonable to assume that by communicating with the individual at an appropriate level (see the discussion in Chapter 5 on encoding) and by using appropriate methods that non-compliance may be reduced (see Chapter 6). Certainly, as far as possible, the patients' understanding and perceptions of their treatments should be of prime importance.

CONCLUSION

The individual's reaction to illness and treatment should not be considered in isolation from their individual differences. Having said this, there does appear to be parameters within which most of us will behave when ill, from not seeking medical advice at all to a complete sick role. Not surprisingly, the individual's perceptions of illness and treatment must be assessed accurately in order to minimise the possible psychological effects of illness and to maximise compliance with treatment.

SUMMARY

It has been suggested that most symptoms do not result in any form of consultation, and this has been termed the '**illness iceberg**' (Last, 1963).

Parsons (1951), in the now famous theory of **sick role** behaviour, suggested that the individual, when suffering from an illness, may behave in certain ways in order to facilitate recovery.

It would be a wrong assumption that the individual automatically takes on the sick role in response to an illness.

The individual's **self-image**, which will include their **body image** and of course their self-esteem, can all be affected by illness.

The roles that an individual plays in their everyday life will usually undergo some modification during illness.

There is some support for the suggestion that to reduce the individual's feelings of powerlessness could be an important component of pain control.

The perception of pain is an extremely personal phenomenon, and to some extent may be based on a cognitive as well as an innate framework.

The world of the individual who has to live with severe chronic pain can be one of despair, with little hope of relief.

The term 'organic' pain refers to pain that has been found to have a definite organic cause. 'Psychogenic' pain, on the other hand, is generally taken to mean that it is due to psychological causes.

It seems that considerable variation exists between acute and chronic pain sufferers in terms of neurotic disturbances.

Children may report the same sort of pain that other members of their families do, and this has been found with different types of pain including abdominal and dental pain.

Repeated painful experiences may lead to a regression in behaviour.

The language that the child itself utilizes should be used and built upon when giving explanations.

Non-compliance with treatment regimen is a serious and prolific problem which by its very definition costs vast amounts of money every year.

REFERENCES

Bakal, D.A. (1979) *Psychology and Medicine.* Springer, New York.

Bergmann, T. and Freud, A. (1966) *Children in the Hospital.* International Universities Press, New York.

Dallison, A. (1991) Self administration of oral pain relief. *Nursing* **4(35),** 30–31.

Foulks, E.F., Persons, J.B. and Merkel, R.L. (1986) The effects of patients' beliefs about their illness on compliance in psychotherapy. *American Journal of Psychiatry* **143,** 340–344.

Harvey, P. (1988) *Health Psychology.* Longman, New York.

Hayward, J. (1975) *Information: A Prescription Against Pain*. London, Royal College of Nursing.

Johnson, J.E., Rice, V.H., Fuller, S.S. and Endress, M.P. (1978) Sensory information, instruction in a coping strategy, and recovery from surgery. *Research in Nursing and Health 1*, 4–17. (Quoted in: Niven. N. (1989) *Health Psychology*. Churchill Livingstone, London.)

Last, J. (1963) The iceberg: completing the clinical picture in general practice. *Lancet* **2**, 28–31.

Ley, P. (1988) *Communicating with Patients*. Chapman and Hall, London.

McKenny, J.M. and Harrison, W.L. (1976) Drug related hospital admissions. *American Journal of Hospital Pharmacy* **33**, 792–795. (Quoted in: Ley, P. (1988) *Communicating with Patients*. Chapman and Hall, London.)

Niven, K. (1991) Excellence in nursing: the research route. In: Faulkner, A. and Murphy-Black, T. (eds), *Midwifery*. Scutari, London.

Parsons, T. (1951) *The Social System*. Free Press, New York.

Price, S. (1991) Student nurses and children's pain. *Nursing Standard* **5(29)**, 25–28.

Ridout, S., Waters, W.E. and George, C.F. (1986) Knowledge of and attitudes to medicine in the Southampton community. *British Journal of Clinical Pharmacology* **21**, 701–712.

Scambler, A., Scambler, G. and Craig, D. (1981) Kinship and friendship networks and women's demands for primary care. *Journal of the Royal College of General Practitioners* **26**, 746–750. In: Fitzpatrick, R., Hinton, J., Newman, S., Scambler, G. and Thompson, J. (1984) *The Experience of Illness*. Tavistock, London.

Sternbach, R. (1974) *Pain Patients: Traits and Treatments*. Academic, New York.

Sternbach, R., Wolf, S.R., Murphey, R.W. and Akeson, W.H. (1973) Traits of pain patients. The low-back pain loser. *Psychosomatics* **14**, 226–229.

Walding, M.F. (1991) Pain, anxiety and powerlessness. *Journal of Advanced Nursing* **16(4)**, 388–397.

Walker, J.M. (1991) The management of elderly patients with pain. *A Community Nursing Perspective*. Unpublished.

Wilkinson, S.R. (1988) *The Child's World of Illness*. Cambridge University Press, Cambridge.

SUGGESTED READING

Bakal, D.A. (1979) *Psychology and Medicine*. Springer, New York. (Chapter 5 gives a comprehensive account of pain.)

Fitzpatrick, R., Hinton, J., Newman, S., Scambler, G. and Thompson, J. (1984) *The Experience of Illness*. Tavistock, London. (Chapter 3 of this extremely readable text gives a good account of consulting behaviour.)

Ley, P. (1988) *Communicating with Patients*. Chapman and Hall, London. (Chapter 4 gives a comprehensive account of compliance.)

Wilkinson, S.R. (1988) *The Child's World of Illness*. Cambridge University Press, Cambridge. (Although geared towards doctors, this text is applicable to all health professionals. Chapters 8 and 9 give a particularly good insight into how a child views illness and pain.)

CHAPTER 13

ATTITUDES AND ILLNESS

"He that believes all, misseth; he that believes nothing, hits not'

PROVERB

INTRODUCTION

The subject of **attitudes** and **prejudice** was covered generally in Chapter 8. It was stated in the introduction to that chapter that our behaviour towards objects or people will often depend upon our attitudes towards them. Certainly, considering people's behaviour towards their own illness or hospitals as well as seeking medical advice and keeping themselves healthy, the individual's attitude cannot be ignored.

That attitudes are formed by direct experience as well as the influence of parents, family, peers, and generally those people close to us is well known, but also it has to be considered that the media in all of its forms can have a considerable impact. It should also not be ignored that one of the greatest influences upon the individual is the culture in which they live, and for many their religion. Attitudes to dying, further treatment, transplantation, and even medical examination may all be regulated by religious and cultural factors.

It is not particularly difficult to uncover the source of misguided attitudes towards health care if we consider that many attitudes are formed as a result of indirect experience, which will come about by interactions with other people who have undergone the experience directly, and who have possibly misunderstood certain procedures and explanations. They may have been deeply shocked and may have related their experiences whilst in this state. Important though it is to discuss the effects that an individual's attitudes may have upon their own health care, two further considerations need to be taken in to account.

Firstly, we need to consider the effects that other people's attitudes have on the recognition and even the direction of treatment. In this context the role of parents in connection with their child's symptoms and possible treatment will be discussed.

Secondly, it is important to remember that health care professionals themselves have attitudes which will affect the way that they behave and in this case may affect the way in whcih they carry out their care of patients. Certain key areas are highlighted in the following discussion, primarily nurses' attitudes towards the elderly and also health professionals' attitudes towards mental handicap and mental illness.

If the quality of care that we provide is governed in any way by prejudice or misconceptions, then obviously this needs to be understood, but it is the recognition that such attitudes may exist and that some of us may hold them, that may eventually lead to change. It has even been suggested (Monchy, 1990) that the formation of the right attitudes in doctors should be facilitated in the curriculum because the traditional humane and interpersonal aspects of the practice of medicine have been neglected in recent times.

CHILDREN AND ILLNESS

In Chapter 6, the formation of schema was discussed in relation to Piaget's work. It was suggested that a child will assimilate information and accommodate it within a framework, and that such a framework is dependent upon their stage of development, and the various characteristics of those stages was described. Examples were given regarding its possible application to health care and it may be as well to build upon these concepts here.

CHILDRENS CONCEPTS OF ILLNESS

Perhaps one of the more illuminating studies on the child's conception of illness in relation to Piaget's developmental stages was carried out by Bibace and Walsh (1980). The categorisation of children's beliefs in this study were found to parallel preoperational, concrete and formal operational thought. Briefly, the categorisation was found to be:

Preoperational Thought

Category 1: *Phenomenism*—Illness is seen as having an external unrelated cause. Causation cannot be elaborated upon beyond stating the phenomenon. The child sees the illness in terms of the 'here and now' rather than future or past, and explanations should be given in this context for children in both this category and category 2.

Category 2: *Contagion*—Illness is seen as being caused by an object in their proximity (but not in contact with them) by magical means.

Concrete Operational Thought

Category 3: *Contamination*—Illness is still seen as being external, although now the child will attribute the illness as being caused by physical contact or by engaging in harmful activities.

Category 4: *Internalisation*—The child perceives the illness as being within the body, although still describing it in non-specific terms, and its cause may still be described as external. Explanations to the child may therefore include some elementary detail on body functions and processes, based on their existing knowledge.

Formal Operational Thought

Category 5: *Physiologic*—Illness is seen as being caused by some form of disordered physiology of organs. Systematically describes events associated with illness.

Category 6: *Psychophysiologic*—This is the highest level of understanding of the causation of disease, and may not only include a greater understanding of the physiological processes involved but also the psychological effects. May feel some control over both the disease process and treatment. The explanations to adolescents in both these categories should involve the principles of relevant physiological functions, if necessary in 'lay' terms. Current implications as well as future progression needs to be discussed, and their involvement sought in terms of adapting care and treatment to their needs.

HOSPITALISATION OF CHILDREN

For most of us, the experience of hospitalisation and serious illness is a relatively rare one, which may only occur two or three times throughout our lifetime. For many of us the experience of hospitalisation for instance, may have occurred in childhood, and this could form the basis of our later attitudes towards hospitals. This attitude in its turn may be inaccurate and based upon only the limited data that were available to us at the time.

Naturally, most of us will continue to add to our store of available information about hospitals as we observe and talk to other people who have had such experiences. It is perhaps relevant to remind ourselves of the strength and relevance of direct experience in this context. Even as adults, if one or perhaps two bad experiences occur, then it becomes very difficult for anybody to convince us that the next experience will be any different.

For example, if we have had perhaps two or three painful experiences whilst visiting the dentist, we will tend not to visit again on a regular basis as our previous experiences told us that such visits were synonymous with pain and discomfort. Our decision not to visit the dentist regularly, as a result of our previous experiences, may be construed as foolish or at the very least inadvisable, but at least we can see that there has been a logical link based upon real and experiental information, i.e. a substantial link between a cause and effect.

For children, particularly the younger age groups, such associations may not follow such a logical pattern, and indeed may remain hidden permanently with the result of considerable psychological trauma. The child who for instance has observed a loved one going into hospital for an operation, and who has subsequently returned to the home environment disfigured in some way, such as with an amputated limb, may form the link of operation as meaning to lose a leg or an arm, and upon going into hospital themselves, for instance for removal of adenoids, may have a fear that because it is an operation, they will have to lose an arm or leg. This will obviously affect their attitudes towards hospitalisation and may also affect their attitudes towards people who provide the care.

Certainly, those who try to question the child by suggesting that if they don't be quiet either a nurse or doctor will come along and give them an injection, may actually cause considerable trauma to the child by reinforcing or even creating the link between doctor/nurse and pain.

It is important therefore to ascertain as far as is possible the child's attitude towards both hospitalisation and illness. If possible, health professionals should attempt to rectify any misconceptions that they may have, but perhaps more importantly, they should attempt to rectify any misconceptions that the care givers may have.

PARENTS, ILLNESS AND TREATMENT

One of the most powerful ways in which we may learn attitudes in our early years is of course from our parents or care givers. Although this may lead to us forming attitudes which may be difficult to change, it may also lead to behaviours on the part of the parent which may affect the treatment and even possibly the diagnosis that the child will receive.

An interesting explanation for parental pressure for their children to have certain operations has been put forward by Downey (1967) who suggests,

within the context of what he terms the 'cultural inertia theory', that once the explanation for something has become dominant within the society, it will tend to persist regardless of its consequences. This would suggest that such misconceptions have acted as a conditioning agent on parental attitudes.

In terms of having a tonsillectemy and adenoidectomy operation (Crown, 1982; Long and Smith, 1985), many parents believe that such operations will cure a multitude of different illnesses, an attitude that has come about from 'casual conversations with friends and relatives'. It is difficult to imagine that a parent could go through the process of visiting the G.P. and gaining a referral to a specialist, and then go on to receive inappropriate treatment but if Downey's theory is to be believed it seems likely that there may be some effect on that child's perceptions and attitudes towards the illness and treatment.

MASS SOCIOGENIC ILLNESS

Some evidence for parents' attitudes towards an illness being reflected in a child's behaviour, even to the point of demonstrating certain symptoms, has been shown to exist. The study which examined an apparent outbreak of an epidemic from toxic exposure to gas at a school (Philen *et al.*, 1989) described an interesting phenomenon. Although no actual toxic levels of gas were detected by systematic and meticulous investigation, parents never-theless reported symptoms in their children, such as headaches, dark shad-ows under their eyes, etc., which in some cases necessitated the child being sent home. It is interesting to note that a large amount of children demon-strated such symptoms to such an extent that the parents even picketed the school and employed a lawyer to deal with their complaint. The interesting point about this study is that it would appear to be the parents who were complaining of symptoms in their children, rather than a more accepted pat-tern where people report symptoms in themselves. This phenomenon was named by the authors '**mass sociogenic illness by proxy**'.

The phenomenon of mass sociogenic illness is not a new one and as Philen reports it has the following characteristics:

(1) Any age group can be affected.
(2) Either sex can be affected, although most reported cases have been females.
(3) Transmission occurs from a social or family network and can occur by line of sight or audio-visual means; even a telephone call is enough.
(4) Illness does not occur amongst those who do not belong to the group and membership of the group is defined by the group itself.
(5) A stressor such as a threat to the group's integrity triggers or starts the event.
(6) No clinical or laboratory evidence of illness is detected.
(7) Physical symptoms may vary but they are usually in a combination which cannot be readily interpreted biologically.
(8) Illness can recur in the setting of the original outbreak.
(9) The time frame of the outbreak can be acute and shortlived, lasting less than a day, with rapid spread and rapid resolution, or chronic and long-lasting, spanning several months.

Mass sociogenic illness and perhaps more pertinently mass sociogenic ill-ness by proxy gives us a powerful example as to how beliefs of a group in the first instance may affect, even to the point of producing symptoms, the behaviour of the rest of the group, and, as with MSI by proxy, may even affect the recognition of symptoms in a different group (parents recognising children's symptoms). It has to be said that such occurrences are usually trig-gered by some form of stressor (Hocking, 1987), and certainly the dynam-ics of the group appears to be a key factor.

ATTITUDES TOWARDS HEALTH AND ILLNESS IN OLDER AGE GROUPS

The reasons why we have the attitudes we have have already been dis-cussed, both at the beginning of this chapter and in Chapter 8, and the atti-tudes which may lead the adult to seek or avoid treatment are very diverse. Our attitudes towards acute and chronic illness, disfiguring disorders or treatments, and infections such as AIDS, may all be tempered by those around us and as in the case of MSI, may lead to inappropriate behaviours.

The attitudes of parents following acute myocardial infarction for instance, strongly influenced compliance with regard to diet, smoking and stress prescriptions, in a study which examined regimen compliance 2 years after the event (Miller *et al.*, 1990). This raises the point that even in the face of direct experience of having suffered a disorder known to be strongly correlated with certain behaviours, these behaviours may persist. Perhaps the explanations offered in Chapter 8 with regard to cognitive dissonance and smoking have some relevance in this instance. It is interesting to note that the authors of this study highlighted the probable importance of the perceived beliefs of others in the patients' compliance.

ATTITUDES OF HEALTH CARE PROFESSIONALS AND SOCIETY

As health professionals we are not immune from negative and even harmful attitudes, towards illness, treatments, or even categories of patients. We may have a particularly negative attitude towards those people who attempt suicide by taking an overdose of drugs, or towards elderly patients with dementia, and it can be seen that both will affect the quality of care that we may provide. From another point of view, it has been found that at least as far as antenatal care is concerned, the clients' written comments on the care that they receive has a marked effect on carers (Stirrat and Golding, 1990).

It becomes apparent, therefore, that to examine the health beliefs of patients is not sufficient, but that the beliefs of health professionals must also be taken into account (Eachus, 1991). Many studies have been carried out to examine the effects of such attitudes on patient care, and a few of these will be reviewed briefly here. The attitudes of the society that we live in will of course have an impact on the health care that certain individuals may receive, particularly in the case of mental illness and mental handicap, as well as those diseases which are perceived as 'socially unacceptable'.

CARE OF THE ELDERLY

Described frequently as one of the poor relations to health care, the units in our hospitals which provide care for the elderly have been the subject of considerable research in recent years, into the possible effects of attitudes on health care (particularly from nurses) and on the quality of care provided. It has been suggested (Tatham, 1982) that the formation of nurse learner's attitudes towards care of the elderly may be from four distinct sources:

(1) View of the elderly held by contemporary society.
(2) The individual learner's previous experience with the elderly.
(3) The attitudes of trained clinical nursing staff.
(4) The attitudes of tutorial staff.

Fig. 13.1 The attitudes of both the new resident and the carer will contribute to the quality of care.

These sources would fit in with our earlier statement that attitudes may be either directly or indirectly learned. It should be emphasised that, particularly with the individual's previous experience with the elderly, this could include their own elderly relatives. Naturally the field of caring for the elderly is quite a formidable one and much of the research carried out has been directly concerned with the elderly who are confused or suffering from dementia.

As Armstrong-Esther *et al.* (1989) point out 'it is reasonable to suppose that attitudes held by professional workers will help to determine the quality of care given to old people'. It would appear that those responsible for the teaching of junior nurses have a considerable impact in decreasing the learner's stereotypical attitudes towards the elderly (Wilhite and Johnson, 1976). The effect of education on the care of elderly patients has also been highlighted by Thomson (1991) who found that for nurses, negative stereotype acceptance was reduced after they had undergone an education process which involved sessions on normal growth and development throughout the lifespan.

On a more pessimistic note it has been found that nurses interact significantly less with confused elderly patients than with lucid elderly patients (Armstrong-Esther and Browne, 1986; Armstrong-Esther *et al.*, 1989). Indeed a generally less positive attitude has been found amongst nurses who choose to work with adults under the age of 65 or who prefer not to work in surgical areas (Armstrong-Esther *et al.*, 1989). A preference for working for the elderly, to further compound the situation, is not always the motivation for applying for a vacancy in such an area, with one study suggesting that less than one-third of nurses working with the elderly were doing so out of preference (Bowling and Formby, 1992).

The implication that less interaction takes place with confused elderly patients is particularly damaging since interaction is such a key part of their care in an ideal setting. Perhaps more disturbing is the fact that the elderly confused patients were observed as being inactive for about 80% of the time, probably because, as the author suggests, the nursing staff regard their care priority as physical care rather than psychosocial interaction.

Of course it cannot be discounted that the reason why there is less interaction with confused elderly patients than with lucid elderly patients is that the nurses concerned quite simply do not know how to deal with confused patients; or indeed it could be that they have a negative attitude towards mental disorders.

CARE OF PATIENTS WITH MENTAL DISORDERS

The socialisation of nurses has also been highlighted, in respect of psychiatric nursing, as being an important contributing factor which affects the care provided. In terms of carrying out nursing assessments, it has been suggested (Savage, 1991) that nurses tend to gather physiological information about patients whilst effectively ignoring psychosocial indices.

Health professionals outside the field of psychiatry may show a reluctance to interact with mentally ill patients on any prolonged basis, but once again this may be due to lack of knowledge; however it may also be due to the **stereotypical** concept of mental illness.

Prescribing of tranquillisers by general practitioners in relation to emotional disturbances in their patients has also been associated with attitudes (Melville, 1980). Those who believed that such disturbances were due to a lack of control on the part of the patient, or that there was not yet any more effective treatment, were more likely to prescribe tranquillisers more readily.

MENTAL HANDICAP

Many people feel uncomfortable when confronted with mental handicap. This is perhaps stating the obvious, but such stereotypical attitudes appear to originate as early as childhood, and children with a mental handicap tend to occupy a lower social status than non-handicapped children (Jenkinson, 1983).

Some insights into the possible reasons for society's views on those individuals with learning difficulties are suggested by Wolfensberger (1975), who suggests eight social role perceptions of such individuals. These are:

(1) As subhuman.
(2) As sick.
(3) As holy innocents (being regarded as without original sin).
(4) As an eternal child.
(5) As an object of pity, and a burden of charity.
(6) As an object of ridicule.
(7) As a menace.
(8) As an object of dread.

Wolfensberger's list makes very depressing reading if we consider that such beliefs are held by society, and they must have immense implications for the care that those individuals will receive, particularly if such attitudes are to be found in unenlightened health care personnel.

Care in the community, receiving schooling in mainstream education, or even just being the parent of a handicapped child may all be affected by the perceptions of others.

Fig. 13.2 Mentally handicapped clients using imagination and thus encouraging self expression, communication, mobility and confidence. Can society overcome its prejudices so that they may use their abilities to the full?

DISCUSSION

The attitudes of health care professionals towards certain groups of individuals has been shown to affect the care that they may receive.

The effect that education has been found to have towards the care of elderly patients would indicate that in this speciality at least, by concentrating on the cognitive aspect of the attitude (see Chapter 8) care can be enriched, with even negative stereotypical attitudes being changed. Perhaps the question needs to be asked as to why this education was not forthcoming in the first place, or more likely, what went wrong with the education they received. As far as the care of the elderly is concerned, we do not have to look far to see that it probably has had a stereotyped image in that it is 'labour intensive' in many cases, and it has been all to easy for nurses in particular to see themselves as just 'pairs of hands', dealing with dependent people (Copp, 1981).

It has already been mentioned earlier in the chapter that one of the ways that nurses' attitudes towards the elderly are formed is through the views of the elderly held by contemporary society. Garrett (1984) considers that the views that the elderly are no longer 'economically productive' and that their parenting functions are redundant are just two of the attitudes held by society that may have contributed to the phenomenon now known as 'ageism', which is a process of stereotyping and discrimination against the elderly simply on the grounds of age.

In the hospital environment, is it possible that a highly specialised form of ageism may exist? It may be possible, and indeed seems likely that a 'local ageism' may be based on the experiences to be gained on working on a care of the elderly unit, and even more likely by the experiences of others working there before us. We may for instance view the prospect as offering us nothing in terms of our education, or in terms of our development generally, and may at best put it down as experience of 'basic care', an attitude that has been fostered over many years.

Education has already been mentioned as an important agent of attitude change in nurses undergoing a 'care of the elderly experience', but as Garrett goes on to point out, the involvement with elderly individuals who are healthy will also help to change attitudes.

CONCLUSIONS

The individual's attitudes frequently remain hidden until they are confronted with the object or persons that their attitudes are directed towards, and as such, behaviour may be difficult to predict. The effect of the individual's attitudes towards health and the attitudes of those who care for them may direct the outcome of the disease and may well prove to be of crucial importance in the success (or otherwise) of any treatment regimen, whatever form it may take. The attitudes and prejudices of society at large may affect how certain groups of individuals (such as the mentally handicapped) are treated.

SUMMARY

Attitudes to dying, further treatment, transplantation, and even medical examination may all be regulated by religious and cultural factors.

'Cultural inertia theory' suggests that once the explanation for something has become dominant within the society, then it will tend to persist regardless of its consequences.

Some evidence for parents' attitudes towards an illness being reflected in a child's behaviour, even to the point of demonstrating certain symptoms, has been shown to exist.

Mass sociogenic illness and perhaps more pertinently mass sociogenic illness by proxy gives us a powerful example as to how beliefs of a group in the first instance may affect, even to the point of producing symptoms, the behaviour of the rest of the group.

Even in the face of direct experience of having suffered a disorder known to be strongly correlated with certain behaviours, these behaviours may persist.

The attitudes of the society that we live in will of course have an impact on the health care that certain individuals may receive.

It would appear that those responsible for the teaching of junior nurses can have a considerable impact in decreasing the learner's stereotypical attitudes towards the elderly.

It has been found that nurses interact significantly less with confused elderly patients than with lucid elderly patients.

It has been suggested (Savage, 1991) that nurses tend to gather physiological information about patients whilst effectively ignoring psychosocial indices.

REFERENCES AND SUGGESTED READING

Armstrong-Esther, C.A. and Browne, K.D. (1986) The influence of elderly patients' mental impairment on nurse patient interaction. *Journal of Advanced Nursing* **11,** 379–387.

Armstrong-Esther, C.A., Sandilands, M.I. and Miller, D. (1989) Attitudes and behaviours of nurses towards the elderly in an acute care setting. *Journal of Advanced Nursing* **14,** 34–41.

Bibace, R. and Walsh, M. (1980) Developmental concepts of illness. *Pediatrics* **66(6),** 912–917.

Bowling, A. and Formby, J. (1992) Nurses' attitudes to elderly people: a survey of nursing homes and elderly care wards in an inner London health district. *Nursing Practice* **5(1),** 16–23.

Copp, L. (1981) *Care of the Ageing.* Churchill Livingstone, Edinburgh.

Cowan, D.L. (1982) Tonsils and adenoids. In: Birrell, J.F. (ed.), *Logan Turners Diseases of the Nose Throat and Ear,* 9th edn. Wright, Bristol.

Downey, K.J. (1967) Public images of mental illness: a factor analytic study of causes and symptoms. *Social Science and Medicine* **1,** 45–65.

Eachus, P. (1991) Multidimensional locus of control in nurses. *Journal of Advanced Nursing* **16(2),** 165–171.

Garrett, G. (1984) Caught and not taught. *Nursing Times,* 24 October.

Hocking, N. (1987) Anthropologic aspects of occupational illness epidemics. *Journal of Occupational Medicine* **29,** 526–530.

Jenkinson, J.C. (1983) Correlates of sociometric status among EMR children in regular classrooms. *American Journal of Mental Deficiency* **88,** 332–322.

Long, C.G. and Smith, D.H. (1985) Parental pressure for tonsillectomy: attitudes and knowledge of parents accompanying their children to an ear, nose and throat clinic. *Psychological Medicine* **15,** 689–693.

Melville, A. (1980) Reducing whose anxiety? In: Mapes, R. (ed.) *Prescribing Practice and Drug Use.* Croom Helm, London.

Miller, Sister P., Wikoff, R., Garrett, M.J., McMahon, M. and Smith, T. (1990) Regimen compliance two years after myocardial infarction. *Nursing Research* **39(6),** 333–336.

Monchy, C. de (1990) More attention should be paid to the formation of attitudes in doctors. *Medical Teacher* **12,** 339–344.

Philen, M.R., Kilbourne, E.M., McKinley, T.W. and Parrish, R.G. (1989) Mass sociogenic illness by proxy: parentally reported epidemic in an elementary school. *Lancet* **2,** 1372–1376.

Savage, P. (1991) Patient assessment in psychiatric nursing. *Journal of Advanced Nursing* **16(3),** 311–316.

Stirrat, G. and Golding, G. (1990) Maternal attitudes to antenatal care: changes over time. *Health Trends* **22(1),** 27–31.

Tatham, S.A. (1982) Factors which affect learners attitudes to the elderly. *British Journal of Geriatric Nursing* **1(5),** 12–13.

Thompson, H. (1991) Attitudes to old people; a review part 2. *Nursing Standard* **5(31),** 33–35.

Wilhite, M. and Johnson, D. (1976) Changes in nursing students' stereotypic attitudes towards old people. *Nursing Research* **25(6),** 430–432.

Wolfensberger, W. (1975) *The Origin and Nature of Our Institutional Models.* Human Policy Press, New York.

CHAPTER 14

EFFECTS OF HOSPITALISATION

'It is not lack of care that grieves me. No houses could be fairer for those who desire to be healed. But I cannot live in sloth, idle and caged.'

J.R.R. TOLKIEN *The Lord of the Rings*

INTRODUCTION

Our reactions to being in hospital are dependent upon many different variables. It may be the case that we have waited so long for treatment for a painful disorder that to be in hospital is a relief. It may also be the case that the fear of the unknown overshadows everything. It certainly cannot be denied that the individual's responses to their illness, treatment and hospitalisation are strongly linked, but this gives us little reason for failing to understand the effects of hospitalisation in its own right.

Our responses will be affected by past experiences, the nature of the illness (and indeed whether the admission was planned or in an emergency) and perhaps most importantly, what awaits us when we arrive! This is the variable over which the health professional has considerable influence (if not control). Before we decide how the environment of a hospital can be more conducive to psychological comfort, we need to discuss how individuals at various stages of the life span may react to hospitalisation, and to suggest some ways of reducing the adverse effects.

In considering the problem in an age-related fashion it is tempting to compartmentalise various problems to particular age groups only, and this is clearly not an advisable strategy. Fear of the unknown, for instance, is a problem which appears to occur in most age groups, the major differences being how the individual deals with the situation and of course how the health professional attempts to reduce its effects.

THE INFANT

The infant's responses to being with strangers and to being in a strange environment have already been discussed in Chapter 10, although a brief examination of this age group in relation to hospitalisation and possible psychosocial consequences is merited here.

A 'revisiting' of Erikson's theory (see Chapter 2) could serve to throw some light on the possible consequences of hospitalisation (as it may also do later in the discussion), in terms of the possible disruption of the relevant psychosocial relationship through separation, changes in the relationship that may occur, and the implications of being in a strange environment.

Some of the possible implications of hospitalisation in the first year of life have already been discussed in Chapter 2, and family-centred care was advocated, but there are some other points which must be raised. Firstly, in the eyes of the infant, is the mother who accompanies them the same as the mother in their normal home environment? This question is not as ridiculous as it at first appears if seen from the view that an infant has not yet fully developed person permanence (Chapter 10) in the first few weeks of life, and may rely on the recognition of behaviours/characteristics of the mother rather than the person. Within the hospital setting such behaviours may, for a time, be disrupted.

This disruption may occur for a number of reasons. Treatments and investigations may prevent normal feeding patterns, not to mention other nurturing behaviours such as cuddling. The mother may feel that, being in a strange environment, she cannot follow her normal patterns of behaviour with her child, and it is conceivable that (particularly if she is a 'new' mother) she may feel reluctant to carry out the simplest care for her child in case she does it wrongly. There is some evidence to suggest that mothers who are given information as to what to expect in hospital experience less anxiety and may expend less effort coping with stressful events (Schepp, 1991).

Further disruption may occur as a result of maternal anxiety, particularly when the child is an emergency admission. The care of the child, including basic items such as feeding, may be placed outside her control and she may feel unable to provide spontaneous care.

THE PRE-SCHOOL YEARS

The effects of separation were briefly described in Chapter 10, but here it is appropriate to discuss such effects in more detail, and so we return to John Bowlby's work on separation. To reiterate, such effects are divided into three stages: protest, despair and detachment.

PROTEST

It comes as no surprise that the first thing that Bowlby noticed in children who were separated from their mothers was a stage of protest, which can be seen quite vividly by the mother merely leaving the room, particularly when a child is in a strange place. Many parents have had the experience when, for instance, leaving their toddlers with a babysitter for the first time, and certainly when leaving their children in hospital and not being able to stay at least initially with them.

To return to our original points in this chapter, it would be a mistake to assume that all children will react in this fashion, as some children are used to being left with childminders and with other relatives, and in some cases with relative strangers, whilst the parents go out to work or engage in other social activities. Generally, however, the child will react to such separation with tears and crying and associated displays of emotion such as refusing to sit down in the cot, refusing to eat, difficulty in sleeping, and so on. They are difficult to pacify and within a hospital environment this becomes immensely difficult for both carer and child. The only way that this can be at least partially abated is to begin to form a trusting relationship with the child. This becomes particularly hazardous in a ward situation where nurses change shifts, have to go off and do other tasks, or even have days off, perhaps on the second day of the child's admission.

To become a mother substitute is not the intention of such trusting relationships, but rather to become the child's friend and offer some security in a strange world. The toddler is unable to rationalise the experience of hospitalisation and illness in several directions. Firstly, if the child has come in as a routine admission, for an operation such as tonsillectomy, they will be able to find little reason behind the well-wisher's assertion that such an experience will make them better, when at that time they do not feel ill. For the child who is admitted as an emergency, and whose mother cannot stay with them, a lack of understanding of the situation may result from a sudden disruption of trust towards the person who had always kept them from harm.

As far as the understanding of peripheral events is concerned, the child will not have sufficient experience or understanding to comprehend where the mother goes when she leaves the ward, and indeed their concept of time is such that a reassurance of her return within 2 or 3 hours will be of little comfort to him.

Perhaps the most dramatic illustration of how the child feels at this time is to compare what our feelings would be if a very close loved one were to die, and hence cease to exist. For the 2–3 year old, such a 'ceasing to exist' could well occur when they are left alone in a strange place. The toddler's protests may last for up to several days (Bowlby *et al.*, 1952). It probably comes as no surprise that alongside the protest is a considerable amount of anger, which may be identified as tantrums, and may elicit the appropriate responses from those who are caring for the toddler.

Probably, the cardinal sin to commit at this stage is to lie to the child in order to pacify him. For instance, the nurse may say to the child that his mother will be back in a couple of minutes and has just gone for a cup of tea, when in fact she knows perfectly well that the mother has gone home, perhaps a long distance, to look after her other children and will not be back until the next day. In such circumstances, when the promise of an early return is not fulfilled, the child protests and anger will become more prolonged. The more the lie is perpetuated the longer and more distressing this stage will be.

It is understandable how such lies emerge, as it is far easier to pacify the child by giving this sort of information than telling the truth. However if she tells the truth, that the mother has gone home to look after the younger brother and sister and that she will be back in the morning when he wakes up, after she has prepared the breakfast, then at least he can relate to this sort of explanation. Although it will bring very little response at first, if the story is repeated and indeed if it happens the way the child has been told, then at least a trusting relationship may begin to emerge.

Keeping an article of, for instance, the mother's clothes, such as a scarf or a handkerchief may at least give the child some comfort that she will return.

DESPAIR

Protest is easy to identify and it is difficult not to be moved by such an emotional display. The next stage however is, along with the third stage, frequently misinterpreted by health care professionals and as such the child's anguish can be multiplied. A toddler will become much quieter and indeed may even begin to play, though if observed such play will not usually typify that of a toddler. The child may become a very solitary figure who prefers to play on their own rather than mix with other children, and further, this stage may alternate, particularly in its early stages, with periods of protest and anger.

Already a pattern appears to be emerging which many of us may relate to as occurring in later life. Bowlby himself recognised such similarities. Think back for a moment to the relationship that we did not wish to end, but did in fact come to perhaps an unexpected conclusion. Many people will report feelings of anger, crying, and pacing up and down the room, followed by feelings of despair when they wanted to be left alone, and feelings of desolation and hopelessness.

DETACHMENT

The third and final stage is detachment, or disinterest and may be typified by the child appearing to lose interest in the mother and even perhaps failing to show recognition of her when she appears after a long absence. It is not difficult to see that the people caring for the child during the separation may wrongly interpret this as the child having finally settled down and being happy in his new surroundings. Nothing could be further from the truth on many occasions, and the child is quite simply attempting to avoid further hurt. As adults we hear this time and time again from people who have had disrupted or traumatic relationships, when they say they will never become involved in a relationship again. What they are saying and what the child is saying are very similar, that is, 'I will not show my love because last time I showed my love I was hurt.'

This of course does not necessarily mean, and in fact rarely does mean, that the child has ceased to love their mother, it merely means that they will cease to show their love and affection for their mother for a period of time. This apparent unresponsiveness may last for several days after the child is reunited with its mother, and although the child may show signs that they do not wish to be picked up and cuddled, or they will not show signs of outward emotion towards the parent, nevertheless tell-tale signs of their underlying love for the mother are evident. For instance, when leaving the child to visit the toilet, the mother may open the door only to trip over a toddler sitting outside.

After the initial period of unresponsiveness the child will often display periods of extreme emotion with outbursts of rage without much apparent cause.

The views that Bowlby originally held, that long separation experiences may show detrimental effects in life, possibly in the form of delinquency in adolescence, have been challenged by other researchers (e.g. Rutter, 1971). If we consider the effects of separation for a moment not as being a solely unconscious response to traumatic events, but rather as responding to future events based on what we can remember from childhood and how those events evolved and how we felt at the time, then there can be little doubt that traumatic experiences such as separation will have an effect in later life. Naturally the nature and intensity of such reactions is extremely variable, but nevertheless pertinent.

Bowlby's theory, although important, is by no means the last word on the subject, and researchers such as Michael Rutter, whilst accepting the importance of the maternal bond, also stress the care prior to the separation as well as the loss of familiar people and objects (Rutter, 1981). Rutter (1987) suggests that 'protective factors' and 'protective measures' can transform hospitalisation into an experience that will make them more resilient when confronted with stress in the future, and hence a positive outcome could emerge from a not altogether pleasant experience.

Parke (1981) stressed the important role played by the father, and rejected Bowlby's relegation of the father to a secondary role. Other studies have

suggested that the notion of 'attachment' has outlived its usefulness (e.g. Cohen, 1974). Clarke and Clarke (1976) suggested that the effects of early separation experiences were reversible, although significant support for Bowlby's findings has come from the research of Douglas (1975), who found correlations between pre-school hospitalisation and later problems in adolescence.

The duration of the hospitalisation is of course a key factor in the amount of disturbance experienced both during and after the child's stay. A single period of hospitalisation lasting less than a week is unlikely to produce any lasting effects, although multiple hospitalisations may result in problems lasting much longer (Quinton and Rutter, 1976; Douglas, 1975).

As Kent and Dalgleish (1986) point out, most of the difficulties that a child has with hospitalisation are with unfamiliar surroundings and unfamiliar people. This may be reduced by allowing the child to control the encounter by waiting for them to approach medical staff instead of the other way round (Illich, 1977).

REDUCING THE EFFECTS OF HOSPITALISATION

Written Information
Other factors which may reduce the possible effects of hospitalisation cannot be ignored. These include the amount of information given to the child prior to admission, either through books that the child and parents can look through at home, or even during the hospital stay. Family information leaflets may serve, along with verbal instruction, to promote family-centred care, although without a more personal approach to augment them they will seldom meet the needs of their audience (Glasper and Burge, 1992).

Pre-admission Preparation and Visits
The use of non-hospital-based 'orientations' (such as nurses talking about hospitals in schools) is common in some areas, but although supported by many health professionals it possibly requires more research before its benefits (or otherwise) can be fully evaluated (Hunsberger, 1989).

The use of pre-admission visits has been found to be of considerable use in recent years, although Goslin (1978) suggests that the younger children of this age group may not benefit greatly from the experience. Whatever the qualifications may be as regards research into preparation for pre-school child hospitalisation, this should not be disregarded out of hand, particularly when considering that preparation can begin with the parents at home, and that this may, along with playgroup and nursery school involvement, ensure that the child's individual needs are catered for.

The use of related play therapy prior to hospital admission has been shown by some researchers (e.g. Schwarz et al., 1983) to increase co-operation and to decrease upset. Storytelling has been suggested as a way to help the child cope with hospitalisation (Hahn, 1987) although perhaps on a more practical note, by reducing the amount of medical stressors during the hospital stay the child is likely to suffer less distress (Saylor *et al.*, 1987).

Day Surgery
Reducing the period of hospitalisation would appear to be the immediate answer to solving problems associated with the effects of hospitalisation, and it is now more common than ever to see hospitals setting up 'day' surgical units for children (and indeed for adults). The minimal period of hospitalisation and hence possible separation is seen as a major advantage (Morton *et al.*, 1991), although it has been seen by some researchers as leading to inadequate preparation of the child for the hospital experience (Kernaghan, 1985).

THE SCHOOL CHILD

The responses of the school child to hospitalisation are, for the younger members of this age group, similar to those of the pre-school child. Fear of the unknown and separation from loved ones will still cause anxiety, although some other related factors are of importance. The comments already made with regard to preparation for hospitalisation are, of course, still valid for this age group, as is the importance of play, and may serve to reduce fears and anxieties.

SOCIAL SHAPE

In considering that the quality and content of a child's interactions are having an effect on their development, Collins (1985) describes them as having a 'social shape' inscribed around them as a result of their interaction with the communities in which they live. Long-term illness and hospitalisation may distort this 'social shape', and the health professional, being a critical part of the sick child's community, through their actions and in what they say to the child may be the determinants of how the child emerges from the experience.

THE HOSPITAL COMMUNITY

The experiences of school and the importance of other siblings cannot be ignored. The continual striving for superiority and mastery which has become such a part of their lives may suddenly come to a halt during hospitalisation. A complete change of activity and goals to be worked towards may, for the long-term patient, in time bring its own rewards, but possibly not without cost.

There must be considerable benefit in nursing children of similar ages and medical conditions in the same environment, so that the child can at least have a peer group to identify with and even compete with. It should be remembered that such a peer group emerges as a result of the similarities that its members share with each other in terms of the length of admission,

Fig. 14.1 Play is more than just having fun—it can help the child to express their fears and it can help health care professionals to gain insight into how the child views their predicament.

the nature of their illness (or surgery), or their similar predicaments (e.g. being confined to bed for a long period of time).

Except in cases of chronic disorders, these similarities will only be transient, and sooner or later the child will return to their home and school environment, and should not face too many problems of readjustment. Once again though, we need to exercise caution when making such assumptions without considering the length of stay, the condition they are being treated for, their psychological status on admission, and their relationships in the home environment.

THE EFFECT OF CHILDREN'S HOSPITALISATION ON PARENTS

The effects on the parents of a child's admission is an important factor when considering hospitalisation effects. The possible responses of the infant's mother have been briefly examined earlier in the chapter.

It seems likely that the response of parents to their child's hospitalisation will vary according to the reason for hospitalisation in the first place. In a study which investigated the parents of children with chronic disorders (Burke *et al.*, 1991) it was suggested that the basic psychosocial problem that affected the parents stemmed from so-called 'hazardous secrets', i.e. situations or people that are hazardous to the child.

Burke goes on to identify three categories of such secrets:

(1) Negative information when parents perceive that the carers are not telling them everything they know.
(2) Variations and/or omissions (in management), when parents notice that the treatment given varies amongst staff, and are not given a satisfactory explanation.

(3) Learning health care workers, if incompetent, may cause distress to the patient and parent.

The ways in which a parent will deal with these situations will, according to Burke, range from 'polite inquiry' to finally 'reluctantly taking charge' which may take several forms from seeking information to 'taking over' a task that the health care system is apparently unable to deal with. Perhaps more seriously, the researchers also identified behaviours such as 'negotiating rules' where the parent more openly challenged the system, even to the point of (to use Burke's own example) calling in another member of staff to start an intravenous infusion.

ADOLESCENCE

The adolescent may face problems in adjusting to hospitalisation, particularly if it is a prolonged and novel experience. Their search for identity which involves both a striving for independence and the group identity which they have with their peers puts them in a particularly vulnerable position when hospitalised.

Hospitalisation may again bring a fear of the unknown, but with it some apparently incompatible and unresolvable problems. At a time of illness parents will naturally be concerned for their offspring, and the adolescent, confronted with the unknown, may seek the security that they may be able to provide. Their striving for independence does not necessarily mean that 'I can do it without you' or 'I can't do it without you' but rather 'I can do it without you, but I may still need you'.

This strange dilemma may result in conflicts between the adolescent and their parents, and considerable care is needed when admitting the adolescent, in order that the parents (who are legally responsible until the adolescent is 16 years old) are involved, but the adolescent is involved in supplying answers whenever possible, as well as being involved in their own day-to-day management. It has been suggested (Collins, 1985) that a pre-visit questionnaire can be given to the adolescent which could form the basis of discussion between the adolescent and medical staff, and that such a questionnaire could contain the question of whether the adolescent wishes to have the parents present.

It is far preferable to look after the adolescent (if possible) in an adolescent unit where they may find others with similar fears, aspirations and qualities. A paediatric unit is most definitely not the place to care for an adolescent who is striving to make the painful transition into adulthood.

THE ADULT

Hospitalisation appears to be an anxiety-producing event in its own right, even for adults, and can be considered as a separate entity from illness and treatment. Once again, the theme of fear of the unknown prevails. The level of anxiety has also been correlated with a high neuroticism score on the Eysenck personality questionnaire (Wilson-Barnett and Carrigy, 1978) (see Chapter 2).

The preconceptions of the adult patient towards the hospital environment will naturally play an important part in how they view and anticipate their forthcoming experience. The hospital environment itself, to many people, suggests a loss of privacy and possibly a loss of control over their own lives, which leaves little scope for individuality (DiMatteo and Friedman, 1982).

TERRITORIAL CONSIDERATIONS

There are naturally times when the worst fears of the patient are realised when confronted with a situation where there is indeed little privacy, except for a curtain which may be drawn around the bed. It can therefore be seen that much of the problem may be architectural rather than to do with the professional care that the patient receives, and indeed this has been emphasised in research (Wainwright, 1985).

The fact that every individual requires their own interpersonal space has already been discussed in Chapter 5, and it is perhaps pertinent to this discussion to revisit this concept within the context of the matter in hand. Privacy may be maintained, at least in the visual sense, by drawing curtains around a bed, or even allowing the patient access to a quieter space where they may be alone for a while, but this may not be sufficient.

Drawing the curtains around a patient who is using a bedpan or commode does not prevent him from fearing that he will make a smell, or a noise when passing flatus. This can lead to considerable embarrassment, which only compounds the embarrassment that they may have felt when asking for assistance from a nurse in the first place. Drawing the curtains for privacy other than to fulfil bodily functions suggests that the individual wishes to be on their own, and they may be aware that instigating such action may lead to alienating those patients next to the bed.

The discussion in Chapter 2 led us to conclude that all individuals were different and indeed the variability between individuals with regard to how they socialise with others is vast. If we just take as an example the measures of introversion/extroversion and neuroticism, the level of anxiety has been correlated with a high neuroticism score on the Eysenck personality questionnaire (Wilson-Barnett and Carrigy, 1978) (see Chapter 2). There is considerable variance between human behaviour with regard to socialisation and therefore it must logically follow that some individuals will feel immensely uncomfortable when being confronted with the enforced socialisation of being a patient in a large ward full of patients. Indeed this phenomenon may even occur when put into a room with only one other patient.

The natural conclusion to emerge from the difficulties that arise through lack of privacy is that all hospitals should be built with private rooms and if they do not have them, they should be converted to take account of this. This would clearly constitute a considerable financial undertaking and in the short term at least, is just not possible, although other measures may be taken.

The recognition by health professionals that the patient may be anxious about a lack of privacy may help to make the patient feel more comfortable with a strange environment, and of course some control over their environment would be desirable. Naturally for a short-stay patient the situation is not quite so desperate, but for a long-stay patient some attempt at least to

Fig. 14.2 Having personal items near ensures that at least some individuality is maintained.

personalise their living space should be made, possibly by allowing personal items from home to be brought in.

Perhaps at this time a comparison between a patient in hospital and a guest entering a hotel would be useful. When going into a hotel room, even if it is only for a couple of days, most of us will tend to arrange things even in a minimal way in order to make us feel more comfortable. We may set out toiletries on the dressing table, perhaps move a chair or two and if we are alone may take pictures of loved ones and set them beside the bed. Such actions are quite automatic to many people, but the patient in hospital may not have the physical capacity to carry out such minor changes. Attempts must be made to ensure that they have all they need, but more especially, that they have those things at hand wherever possible that will make them feel more comfortable.

Once again, it should be stressed that all patients are individuals and there may indeed be some who prefer to mix with other patients and learn first-hand the possible progression, treatment, and implications of their own illness by observing others (Fagerhaugh and Strauss, 1977). The level of anxiety that the patient feels has been positively correlated with their view of the hospital environment, and indeed the individual's personality has its part to play (Lucente and Fleck, 1972). This appears to be separate from anxieties about the severity of their condition.

One further consideration is Erikson's assertion that intimacy is a key

EFFECTS OF HOSPITALISATION 275

aspect of the life of the young adult, and that sexual partners and colleagues in a competitive environment are the important relationships at this time. Prolonged hospitalisation may lead to feelings of isolation, and worries about work may compound their problems.

If we now return to our original point, that the patient may be suffering from a fear of the unknown when entering a hospital, it should be a logical step to conclude that as familiarity with the new environment increases then anxiety will be reduced, and this indeed appears to be the case (Johnston, 1980). However, previous hospital admissions are perhaps not as instrumental as it may at first be thought in reducing anxiety, as anxiety may actually be increased (Friedlander *et al.*, 1982) because of ideas of possible procedures and treatments.

COMMUNICATION

Adequate communication with the individual in hospital is essential if adverse effects of hospitalisation are to be avoided. It would appear that lack of information regarding treatment, hospital procedures, etc. are a major cause of patient dissatisfaction (see Chapter 12).

THE ELDERLY

Naturally, most of the anxieties facing the younger adult will also affect the elderly patient, and these may be compounded by other factors. As with any other age group, the potential problems facing the elderly will be seen to emerge from several different sources.

PAST EXPERIENCE

This first point to make is both obvious and straightforward, and yet it may cause considerable distress if it is ignored. It can best be illustrated by comparing the memories of a young person and an elderly person regarding hospitals. To the younger adult, memories of hospitalisation would be of modern purpose-built (or at least converted) surroundings. Childhood experiences of hospitalisation may of course leave their mark, but in this case it would appear that the important consideration is what a hospital represents. Not surprisingly, to the younger individual a hospital is just what it would appear to be. To the elderly patient however, hospital may be synonymous with 'workhouse', with all its implications, and hence is somewhere to be feared.

Hospitalisation is therefore an experience that may be feared by the elderly and may not always be beneficial (Salvage *et al.*, 1988). Previous experiences of hospitals (Ryan and Robinson-Smith, 1990) may be a significant factor in determining the individual's response to the experience, and an accurate and sensitive assessment of previous admissions (and those of spouses etc.) should be carried out.

TERRITORIAL CONSIDERATIONS

The elderly patient, particularly one entering hospital for the first time, may have concerns about the home that they are leaving, and may view the admission to hospital as being synonymous with losing their independence. They may feel that it will be decided that they can no longer cope on their own, and that they will not return to their home at all. Naturally, this is a highly individual problem, and few generalisations can be made, although the independence of the individual, however they perceive it, must always be handled with the greatest of care, and should be assessed with the patient's perceptions uppermost in mind.

CONCLUSIONS

Whenever we examine the possible effects of a particular experience on an individual, we can at best only generalise. As far as a particular subject is concerned, many factors could serve to temper some of the research findings. Amongst these could be the size of the hospital unit concerned, staffing levels, bed occupancy, staff training, and countless others. It is therefore interesting that many of the studies both on the individual's reactions to hospitalisation and to illness appear to highlight one vital component apparently overriding all others, and that is the lack of communication, which must invariably be linked with individual's reporting a 'fear of the unknown' when coming into hospital. Gooch (1988) observes that poor communication with a dying patient can cause more suffering than some of the symptoms of the terminal disease, and when considering the experience of family and friends, Gooch maintains that most of their complaints about care arise out of poor communication.

The individual, whether a parent of a child in hospital or patients themselves, could benefit considerably if the level of communication were to improve, but moreover if the level of communication was in line with their own understanding (see Chapter 5). Any assessment of the patient should include (their condition permitting of course) a full account of not only how much they already know, but also aspects of their stay that they have concerns about.

Certainly, not all fears can be laid entirely to rest, but aspects such as how much the individual (and even their families) can participate in care, who to obtain information from, as well as discussing such items as privacy and ward routine, should all reduce the fear of the unknown. Naturally, with very short-term admissions, this is particularly difficult to achieve in the ward environment. Hence it may be a good idea to commence the patient assessment at the out-patient department on their last visit prior to admission, or even by the use of a short self-assessment form sent to them shortly before admission.

It should be remembered that it is not only the lack of information that may cause distress, but also misconceptions. The elderly in particular may suffer considerable trauma if such matters are not corrected. This of course may not always be easy, but particularly when the stay is anticipated to be fairly lengthy, an in-depth assessment of their knowledge and beliefs may be carried out, usually in the course of ordinary conversation. Loneliness and justified concerns about home should also be addressed at the earliest opportunity.

SUMMARY

The infant relies on the recognition of behaviours/characteristics of the mother rather than the person. Within the hospital setting such behaviours may, for a time, be disrupted.

Further disruption may occur as a result of maternal anxiety.

Hospitalisation and separation may be synonymous for the pre-school child, and the effects are divided into three stages: protest, despair and detachment.

Bowlby's theory, although important, is by no means the last word on the subject, and researchers such as Michael Rutter, whilst accepting the importance of the maternal bond, also stress the significance of the care prior to the separation as well as the loss of familiar people and objects (Rutter, 1981).

Parke (1981) stressed the important role played by the father, and rejected Bowlby's relegation of the father to a secondary role.

Most of the difficulties that a child has with hospitalisation are with unfamiliar surroundings and unfamiliar people.

The use of pre-admission visits has been found to be of considerable use in recent years, although Goslin (1978) suggests that the younger children of this age group may not benefit greatly from the experience.

The experiences of school and the importance of other siblings cannot be ignored. The continual striving for superiority and mastery which has become such a part of their lives may suddenly come to a halt during hospitalisation.

The responses of the school child to hospitalisation are, in the younger members of this age group, similar to those of the pre-school child.

There must be considerable benefits in nursing children of similar ages and medical conditions in the same environment, so that the child can at least have a peer group to identify with and even compete with.

It is far preferable to look after the adolescent (if possible) in an adolescent unit where they may find others with similar fears, aspirations and qualities.

The hospital environment itself, to many adults, suggests a loss of privacy and possibly a loss of control over their own lives, which leaves little scope for individuality (DiMatteo and Friedman, 1982).

To the elderly patient, hospital may be synonymous with 'workhouse', with all its implications, and hence is somewhere to be feared.

REFERENCES

Bowlby, J., Robertson, J. and Rosenbluth, D. (1952) A toddler goes to hospital. *Psychoanal. Study Child* **7,** 82–94.

Burke, S.O., Kauffmann, E. and Costello, E.A. (1991) Hazardous secrets and reluctantly taking charge: parenting a child with repeated hospitalisations. *Image Journal of Nursing Scholarship* **23(1),** 39–45.

Clarke, A.M. and Clarke, A.D.B. (eds) (1976) *Early Experience.* Open Books, London.

Cohen, L.J. (1974) The operation and definition of attachment. *Psychol. Bulletin* **81,** 107–217.

Collins, E.W. (1985) Quality psychosocial care in ambulatory pediatric settings. In: Azarnoff, P. and Lindquist, P. (eds), *Psychological Abuse of Children in Health Care: The Issues.* Pediatric Projects Inc., Santa Monica.

DiMatteo, M.R. and Friedman, H. (1982) *Social Psychology and Medicine.* Oelgeschlager Gunn Hain, Cambridge, Mass.

Douglas, J.W.B. (1975) Early hospital admissions and later disturbances of behaviour and learning. *Developmental Medicine and Child Neurology* **17,** 456–480.

Fagerhaugh, S.Y. and Strauss, A. (1977) *The Politics of Pain Management: Staff Patient Interaction.* Addison-Wesley, California.

Friedlander, M.L., Steinhart, M.J., Daly, S.S. and Snyder, J. (1982) Demographic, cognitive and experimental predictors of presurgery anxiety. *Journal of Psychosomatic Research* **26(6),** 623–627. (Quoted in: Fitzpatrick, R. *et al.* (1984) *The Experience of Illness.* Tavistock, London.)

Glasper, A. and Burge, D. (1992) Developing family information leaflets. *Nursing Standard* **6(25),** 24–27.

Gooch, J. (1988) Dying in the ward. *Nursing Times* **84(21),** 38–39.

Goslin, H.H. (1978) Hospitalisation as a life crisis for the pre-school child: a critical review. *Journal of Community Health* **3(4),** 321–346.

Hahn, K. (1987) Therapeutic storytelling: helping children to learn and cope. *Pediatric Nursing*, May/June, Vol. 13, No. 3.

Hunsberger, M.M. (1989) Principles and skills adapted to the care of children. In: Foster, R.R., Hunsberger, M.M. and Anderson, J.J.T. *Family Centred Nursing Care of Children.* W.B. Saunders, Philadelphia.

Illich, I. (1977) *Limits to Medicine.* Pelican, Harmondsworth.

Johnston, M. (1980) Anxiety in surgical patients. *Psychological Medicine* **10,** 145–152.

Kent, G. and Dalgleish, M. (1986) *Psychology and Medical Care.* Baillière Tindall, London.

Kernaghan, S. (1985) Preadmission preparatory teaching: a promising option, but easier said than done. *Promoting Health* March–April, 6–8.

Lucente, F.E. and Fleck, S. (1972) A study of hospitalisation anxiety in 408 medical and surgical patients. *Psychosomatic Medicine* **34,** 304–312.

Morton, N.S. *et al.* (1991) Day case surgery for children. *Health Bulletin* **49(1)**, 54–61.

Quinton, D. and Rutter, M. (1976) Early hospital admissions and later disturbances of behaviour: an attempted replication of Douglas' findings. *Developmental Medicine and Child Neurology* **18(4)**, 477–479.

Parke, R.D. (1981) *Fathering.* Fontana.

Rutter, M. (1971) Parent–child separation: psychological effects on the children. *Joural. Child. Psychol. Psychiat.* **12,** 233–260.

Rutter, M. (1981) *Maternal Deprivation Reassessed.* Penguin, Harmondsworth.

Rutter, M. (1987) Psychosocial resilience and protective mechanisms. *American Journal of Orthopsychiatry* **57(3),** 316–331.

Ryan, M.C. and Robinson-Smith, G. (1990) What does it mean? Making sense of the hospital experience. *Journal of Gerontological Nursing* **16(8),** 17–20.

Salvage, A.V. *et al.* (1988) Attitudes to hospital care among a community sample of people aged 75 and older. *Age and Aging* **17,** 270–274.

Saylor, C.F., Pallmeyer, T.P., Finch, A.J., Eason, L., Treiber, F. and Folger, C. (1987) Predictors of psychological distress in hospitalised pediatric patients. *Journal of the American Academy of Child and Adolescent Psychiatry* 232–236.

Schepp, K.G. (1991) Factors influencing the coping effort of mothers of hospitalised children. *Nursing Research* **40(1),** 42–46.

Swartz, H.B., Albino, J.E. and Tedesco, L.A. (1983) Effects of psychological preparation on children hospitalised for dental operations. *Journal of Paediatrics* **102(4),** 634–638.

Wainwright, P. (1985) Impact of hospital architecture on the patient. In: Copp, L.A. (ed.), *Perspectives on Pain.* Churchill Livingstone, London. (Quoted in: Niven, N. (1989) *Health Psychology.* Churchill Livingstone, London.)

Wilson-Barnett, J. and Carrigy, A. (1978) Factors influencing patients' emotional reactions to hospitalization. *Journal of Advanced Nursing* **3,** 221–229.

SUGGESTED READING

Azarnoff, P. and Lindquist, P. (eds) (1985) *Psychological Abuse of Children in Health Care: The Issues.* Pediatric Projects Inc., Santa Monica. (The chapter entitled 'Quality Psychosocial Care in Ambulatory Settings' (p. 27) is a useful starting point when examining the plight of the child in hospital.)

Rutter, M. (1981) *Maternal Deprivation Reassessed.* Penguin, Harmondsworth. (This text, along with John Bowlby's *Child Care and the Growth of Love* (1965), are classics in their own right and are essential reading.)

CHAPTER 15

CONCLUSIONS

'And So To Bed'

SAMUEL PEPYS

Psychology is still a young science, and is still evolving. It would have been most convenient to have been able, at this stage, to have 'pulled together' all of the topics and theories discussed and to have produced a 'meaning of life'-type conclusion. In terms of some of the theories discussed, particularly those in the earlier chapters, this is not possible, although there has been discussion in later chapters on the possible applications.

In many cases, such as with the physiological aspects of behaviour, we have had a brief glimpse of a subject in which new data is being uncovered almost constantly, so that the assumptions of one year are becoming the history of the next.

Some attempt however will be made to discuss the general findings, and at times some of the underlying principles involved in order to gain an overall picture of how psychology can be applied to health care.

The assumption that the individual is largely the product of the influences which affected them in childhood has been revisited throughout the text, but in Chapter 1 the influence of upbringing on health was examined directly. Eating, smoking, and even the effects of depressed mothers was examined, and it was shown that the effects fell loosely into two categories. The first category was the effects that may result in possible adult behaviours, such as smoking, and the possible effects of role modelling.

As far as health education is concerned this is a serious consideration, and does appear on first inspection at least to be effective in some instances (as with non-smoking parents), although the effects of advertising are still far from clear. Certainly, advertising which is aimed at certain age groups does appear to have an effect, but peer group pressure could also be a contributing factor. Of course it is not beyond reason to assume that we may behave in a certain way precisely because our parents didn't (or vice versa)!

The second category, and perhaps the most worrying of the two, is the consequences of parental behaviours on our future health even if our behaviours change in later life. Probably the most obvious of these is our early eating habits which may set us on the road to a lifelong battle with obesity (see also Chapter 3).

Personality (see Chapter 2) will play a large part in how we behave, and the childhood influences are again emphasised by some theorists such as

Freud, Erikson, etc. Certainly much controversy surrounds virtually every personality theory ever written. The sexual theory of Freud in particular has been the subject of much heated and at times bitter discussion, but even here certain implications do emerge, even if the theoretical framework is questioned. The importance of toilet training and the possible effects of a rigid regime are just one example.

The view that we are all 'scientists' and that we are constantly forming theories about the world we live in (Kelly) is an interesting departure from other personality theories, and provides us with some clues as to why we behave in the ways we do. Certainly, one point that has been emphasised frequently is to provide the appropriate amount of information, and to communicate in such a way as to ensure that the individual understands. It makes sense that in order to form a theory about a situation, the individual should be in possession of all the facts. There are many occasions (see Chapters 12, 13 and 14) when this appears not to happen on a consistent basis in the health setting.

Information about the environment, the procedures and the illness may not only lead to a reduction in anxiety, but also to greater compliance with treatment. Perhaps it is appropriate for health professionals to ask the individual to describe their treatment, illness etc., in order to give a clear starting point for any explanations (Chapter 6). To describe the patient's problems in a form which has been dramatically changed from what they originally described could lead to confusion. The discussion in Chapter 5 looked at encoding and decoding, and to encode and then to record the results of such an encoding without any mention of the original problem as described by the patient is a serious error.

In this case, it is all too easy to treat the disease rather than the individual. The elderly lady who arrived in a hospital bed with a diagnosis of congestive cardiac failure has a whole set of problems that may have been worrying her, such as not being able to get her shoes on because of her swollen ankles, or having to stop to catch her breath when she goes shopping, or not being able to sleep at night because of her breathing. Congestive cardiac failure is the name that we may have given it, but her problems will require highly individualised attention if she is to be able to cope following discharge.

Individuality was one of the important concepts that was examined in Chapter 7, and Carl Rogers' assumption that no individual can ever hope to understand another provides us with a stark warning against making generalisations. The individual's reactions to illness, hospitalisation and even bereavement that have been discussed have all carried the warning against unwarranted predictions, although directions that reactions may take have been discussed. An analogy can be made here with an accident and emergency department. If a call is received from the ambulance control to expect a number of casualties from a road traffic accident, would we only get the equipment ready that was used to treat victims of the previous accident, or, put another way, would the physician only look for the injuries that previous victims had? Of course that would be absurd, and yet, although we are quite good at assessing the individual's physical status, how many of us can say the same about their psychological status?

Attitudes are perhaps one area where a series of conversations with the individual may reveal a lot of information regarding their beliefs and feelings, particularly those that may give them particular difficulties with coping with treatment and being in hospital. It may be, to return to an earlier point, that they need more information in order to be able to cope, or it may be that direct experience is necessary. Whichever way we look at it, we will all cope with situations in rather different ways, or at least cope in similar ways with rather different outcomes. Certainly, as was discussed in Chapter 9, one person's coping mechanism is another person's nightmare. Put this together with Rogers' assertion about individuality, and we can deduce that a process of facilitating the individual's coping responses rather than pushing them into thoughts and actions that are foreign to them, will result in a more satisfactory outcome.

It may be the case, as discussed in Chapter 12, that the individual is behaving in a manner that relatives may find odd or distressing, and that such behaviour is a direct result of their illness. Such concepts as the sick role can provide them with a time of evaluation, and can actually be useful, so it should not be assumed that it is a state that should be disposed with as quickly as possible in order to make the rest of us more comfortable. This is not to say that the onset of depression or inappropriate responses should not be dealt with, and hence, a continual monitoring of the individual's view of events and how they view their situation should be maintained.

The implications of life events was discussed in Chapter 9 in relation to health, and several links appear to be emerging. The possibilities that the stress produced by certain life events can cause physical and mental illness could lead us to ask the question: has the individual made the link, and if not, are they likely to continue with their lifestyle regardless of the consequences? This raises important questions as to the individual's perceptions of the possible causes of their disorder, and to whether they see that a solution (or even part of a solution) lies inside or outside their control. The individual's locus of control would appear to be of key importance when considering the possibility of self-care.

Having reviewed psychological phenomena, it is also important to consider the physiological aspects of behaviour, and even here, a great deal of individuality is involved. The discussion in eating in Chapter 3 focused on physiological controls, and the difficulties that some individuals will have in losing weight. It may be of use, in attempting to help individuals with an obesity problem, to consider their problem from this angle instead of from a purely psychological one, in order to understand some of the discomfort that may be felt, and that will lead to difficulties in losing weight. Sleeping was also discussed, and it was suggested that a more individualised approach was taken in its evaluation. The research currently being carried out into mental disorders may, in time, result in extraordinary changes, not only in the way we treat mentally ill individuals, but also in how society views them.

Another theme that ran through some of the chapters (e.g. Chapter 8) was that of the health professionals themselves. In terms of management practices, the needs of the individual, along with how job satisfaction is maintained, was discussed, and it emerged that a great deal of sensitivity is needed when caring for colleagues and junior staff. Also, as far as the health professional is concerned, attitudes were discussed in Chapter 13, and it was suggested that in certain areas in particular, patient care could and is being affected by the attitudes of those providing the care, and that in some cases, the key to remedying such situations could lie in education.

Psychology is a science which is essential to the understanding of any individual who is ill, or who works, or quite simply, who exists, and an understanding of mental processes is essential to the care that we give.

Glossary

Accommodation: The restructuring of mental organisations so that newly acquired information can be processed. (Piaget).

Acoustic code: In relation to memory, information which is represented as auditory features. Also called phonemic code.

Adaptation: An act of intelligence in which assimilation and accommodation are in balance. (Piaget)

Adipocytes: Fat storage cells.

Adipsia: Absence of drinking.

Adrenocorticotropic hormone (ACTH): Hormone secreted by the anterior pituitary gland which controls the release of glucocorticoids from the adrenal cortex. Released in response to stress.

Advanced organiser: In Reception Learning (Ausubel), introductory material that is presented ahead of the learning task and at a higher level of abstraction and inclusiveness than the learning task itself.

Altruism: Helping others without thought of personal gain.

Alzheimer's disease: Major type of senile dementia.

Amygdala: Brain structure thought to be involved in the consolidation of new memories. Located below the cerebral cortex.

Anima: The female set of feelings of males as represented by a woman figure. (Jung)

Animism: Occurs during the pre-operational stage when the child attributes many feelings, emotions and other qualities usually associated with humans and other animals, to inanimate objects.

Animus: The male set of feelings of females represented as a male figure. (Jung.

Anxiety: Broadly, a state of apprehension, worry and tension. There is wide variation between theorists as to the exact nature and types of anxiety.

Anxiety dreams: Wishful dreams which upon interpretation usually prove to be of a sexual nature, whose libido has been transformed into neurotic anxiety. (Freud)

Aphagia: Absence of eating.

Archaeopsychic: Still active ego states which were fixated in early childhood.

Archetypes: Jung places great emphasis on the existence of these ancestral remnants which, unlike the unique aspects of the personal unconscious, are common to many human beings. Jung proceeded to identify several archetypes which only become known to us in symbolic form.

Articulatory loop: In the 'working memory model', it holds the words we are about to say, and also acts as a rehearsal loop. It is used whenever we verbally repeat material in order to memorise it. It therefore deals with the articulation of verbal material and is considered as an 'inner voice'.

Assimilation: In Piaget's theory of cognitive development, the perception and interpretation of new information. Quite how new information is dealt with is dependent upon existing knowledge which may be very limited.

Attitude: 'A mental and neural state of readiness, organised through experience, exerting a directive or dynamic influence upon the individual's response to all objects and situations with which it is related'. (Allport, 1935)

Attribution: The process by which we try to explain the behaviour of others.

Avoidance coping style: Avoidance or denial of an emotional or threatening experience.

Bargaining: In the 'grieving process', the individual may attempt to change their behaviour in the hope that the inevitable may not happen. They may even be changing their behaviour in order to aid the return of a loved one who has died.

Basal ganglia: Brain structure which comprises the caudate nucleus, putamen and the globus pallidus.

Basic anxiety: The feeling of being alone in a threatening world, and comprises of helplessness, aggressiveness and detachment. (Horney)

B Motive: Concerned with growth. They are relatively independent of external factors, as they are concerned with the increase in pleasure drives such as curiosity. It can therefore be seen that B-motives come from within, and are unique to the individual.

B Love: Involves a relatively generous interchange of emotions, and generally thought of as more rewarding in the long term than D-love, although the satisfaction of the deficiency need is required in order for growth to take place.

Catecholamines: Hormones secreted from the adrenal medulla (adrenaline and noradrenaline) and formed from the amino acid tyrosine.

Cathexis: An amount of psychic energy invested in a mental representation of an object. (Freud)

Central executive: In the 'working memory model', the central executive stores information for short periods of time, can process information from sensory inputs in a variety of ways and is involved in tasks such as reading, writing, problem solving, mental arithmetic and learning. In other words, the central executive is involved whenever attention is demanded.

Chaining: A chain of two or more stimulus response connections. (Gagne')

Cholecystokinin: Hormone produced in the upper part of the small intestine, that has been found to be a powerful appetite suppressant in humans and other animals. Its exact action is unknown, but it is released in response to fatty acids in the bloodstream.

Classical conditioning: Originally described by Pavlov, the theory is concerned with reflexes, and attributes all learning to conditioning. Alternatively it can be described as responses to specific stimuli.

Claustral complex: An enduring effect on adult behaviour of natal frustations that includes passive dependency and a wish to return to a womblike state of security. (Murray)

Closure: In Gestalt Psychology, the grouping together of elements of a figure or for instance, learning material so as to complete the picture or subject.

Cognitive appraisal process: The individual's interpretation of an event in terms of its possible effect on their well-being. The individual's emotional response is therefore a function of this appraisal.

Cognitive dissonance: Cognitions regarding a situation or behaviour that are mutually exclusive.

Collective unconscious: According to Jung, that part of the psyche which contains the archaic remnants (archetypes).

Common trait: A trait shared to varying degrees by different individuals.

Component: The elementary processes which translate sensory input into mental conceptual representations. (Sternberg)

Concrete operational stage: According to Piaget, the stage of development in which the child becomes capable of logical thought. Conservation also occurs at this time. The final stage of the Concrete Operational Period.

Conditional positive regard: When significant, others only value the individual when their behaviour is seen as correct.

Conditioned reflexes: In classical conditioning, reflexes formed as a result of experience.

Conditioned stimulus: In classical conditioning, a previously neutral item which, through 'pairing' with an unconditioned stimulus, produces a new response.

Conditions of worth: The standards that the individual perceives must be attained in order to receive conditional positive regard from others. (Rogers)

Conscious: The component of the psyche that contains thoughts that we are aware of.

Conservation: The concept that certain properties do not alter whilst undergoing certain transformations. (Piaget)

Construct: A construct is basically a method of predicting future events and, depending on the outcome, behaviour will manifest accordingly. The usefulness of a construct is determined by the accuracy of the predictions we make from it. All constructs involve a contrast between two opposite poles e.g. hot–cold, and constructs arise when an individual construes two people, or objects, as sharing a common characteristic which differentiates them from a third. (Kelly)

Contiguity: Proximity.

Coping mechanism: A mechanism which attempts to reduce the gulf between the resources of the individual and the demands of the situation.

Core construct: A construct that will control an individual's identity and existence. (Kelly)

Corollaries: The corollaries (eleven in all) are designed to elaborate and clarify the nature of personal constructs. (Kelly)

Coordination of secondary schema: Occurring during the sensory motor period at about 9 to 12 months, the infant, having learned various skills in relation to certain problems, attempts to apply them to new problems and their activities become definitely intentional in nature.

Decoding: The process by which we translate words back into ideas.

D Motives: Concerned with the reduction of drives such as hunger and thirst, obtaining love and esteem from others, and of course safety. D-motives are largely dependent upon external individuals and objects to fulfil needs.

D Love: Selfish motivator that can have a rather unpleasant side as the individual resorts to somewhat devious strategies to achieve the tenderness and frequently the sexual satisfaction that is craved.

Defence mechanisms: Strategies used by the ego to eliminate or reduce anxiety.

Denial: A defence mechanism which prevents unpleasant and unacceptable thoughts into awareness.

Diencephalon: Part of the brain that contains the pituitary gland, hypothalamus, thalamus, subthalamus and the optic tracts.

Discovery learning: Learning which places emphasis on learner centred approaches, valued first hand experience, experimentation and the development of critical abilities.

Displacement: The directing of feelings and impulses towards 'safer objects' such as toys, or a less threatening person such as another child, or even ourselves ('turning against the self'), when it is dangerous, or we feel guilty about directing impulses and feelings towards the object of our frustration and anger.

Displacement activities: In terms of body language, displacement activities are 'small, seemingly irrelevant movements made during periods of inner conflict or frustration'. (Morris 1977)

Dopamine: An intermediate product in the synthesis of noradrenaline.

Ego: Spans the conscious, the pre-conscious and the unconscious. It is a part of the personality which is in constant touch with its surroundings, and provides the Id with more realistic objects of gratification. (Freud) The ego is described by Jung as being the centre of the personality, and is essentially conscious. Through the ego are channelled aspects of the wider 'self' which are unconscious to us in everyday life, but may manifest themselves through the imagination, dreams etc.

Egocentrism: Occurring during the pre-operational stage of development, it is when the child perceives the world from their own point of view only.

Ego-enhancement: Equivalent to self esteem, ego enhancement is strongly correlated to narcissism (self-love).

Ego-extension: The concept of 'mine' that emerges in the child, initially applied to parents, brothers and sisters, pets, as well as material possessions that they grow attached to. This, in turn, will normally lead to ego-extension in more abstract matters such as ideals (e.g. love of country), beliefs (e.g. religion) and values (e.g. career).

Ego states: Phenomenologically a coherent system of feelings. Operationally described as a set of behaviour patterns.

Elaborate code: A message which is imparted with detail as distinct from just a statement or command.

Emotion focused coping: The altering of our emotional response to a stressful situation. This can be done either behaviourally or cognitively.

Encoding: The process of converting an idea into symbols (words). In relation to memory; the transformation of physical information into memory codes via visual coding (transformation of the material into an image), acoustic coding (transformation of the material into the sound of the word) and semantic coding (transformation of the material into its meaning).

Endogenous depression: Term used by some practitioners to denote psychotic depression, although others consider it not to be a distinct type, but rather one end of a continuum, the other being exogenous or reactive depression.

Errorful learning: In discovery learning, trial and error strategies in which there is a high probability of errors and mistakes before an acceptable generalisation is possible.

Eros (life seeking): A major drive which directs the individual towards the engaging in pleasurable activities. (Freud)

Emotional dependency: A means for the individual to attain something (such as food, comfort, relief of pain, treatment of symptoms) for purely pleasurable ends.

Encopresis: Bed-soiling which occurs after bowel control has been established in childhood.

Enuresis: Bed-wetting after bladder control has been established in childhood.

Equity theory: An individual's motivation is largely influenced by how the individual feels he or she is being treated by those around him. The degree of equity is defined in terms of a ratio of an individual's input into a job to the outcomes from it, as compared to another person's.

Ergs: An innate and relatively permanent dynamic source trait. (Cattell)

Ethology: The comparative study of animal behaviour in the natural environment.

Exosystems: Setting in which the individual is not an active participant, but that will nevertheless have an effect upon him.

Exteropsychic: Ego states which resemble those of parental figures.

Extrinsic motivation: Involves the use of incentives which can be either positive or negative, and both are at best an artificial means of directing behaviour. The positive incentives revolve around such rewards as money, conditions of work, praise, encouragement etc. Negative incentives include punishment, fear of failure and anxiety.

Factor analysis: A statistical procedure which facilitates the computation of the minimum amount of factors required to account for the scores on a battery of tests.

Formal operational period: According to Piaget, the final period of cognitive development in which the individual is capable of abstract thought.

Gate control theory: The proposition that a 'gate' mechanism is located in the spinal cord, in the substratia gelatinosa of the dorsal horns (part of the grey matter), which is capable of 'closing', and hence preventing pain messages from reaching the brain.

General adaptation syndrome: According to Selye (1956), the body's response to stress can be divided into three separate stages: Alarm Reaction, Resistance and Exhaustion.

Glucocorticoids: Hormones of the adrenal cortex which influence protein, fat and carbohydrate metabolism i.e. cortisol, cortisone and corticosterone. See also ACTH.

Glucostatic theory: The theory that lowered blood glucose (and hence lower brain tissue utilisation of glucose), is the stimulus for the individual to eat, and vice versa. It is assumed that the blood glucose is detected by glucoreceptors located in the hypothalamus.

Hippocampus: Brain structure located on the medial wall of the temporal lobe. Associated with new memories, emotion and spatial orientation.

Humanistic psychology: An approach to psychology based on the subjective experiences and values of the individual, that emphasises the uniqueness of human beings.

Hydrocortisone: Cortisol.

Hyperinsulinaemia: Abnormally high levels of insulin.

Hyperphagia: Overeating usually associated with VMH (ventromedial hypothalamus) damage.

Hypothalamus: A brain structure which lies below the thalamus and forms the floor and part of the walls of the third ventricle. Plays an important role in homeostatic mechanisms, temperature regulation, eating, drinking, and emotion.

Hypothetico-deductive reasoning: The process of attempting to achieve a solution to a problem by attempting to identify all the possible variants involved as well as any possible combinations, and forming a hypothesis which will be tested. Described by Piaget as a feature of the formal operational period.

Ideal image: See 'Ideal self'.

Ideal self: The sort of person we would wish to be, as distinct from who we actually are (self image).

Identity: Encompasses four basic aspects of personality: Personal identity, continuity of personal character, the integration of biological development and social influences in the growth of the ego and solidarity with the ideals and identity of the peer group. (Erikson)

Identity crisis: According to Erikson, a part of development which leads either to the sense of identity or to inner fragmentation and role confusion (identity confusion).

Immanent justice: An accident or event that is purely spontaneous being observed by the child as a punishment for some misdemeanour on the part of the victim. (Piaget)

Induction: Taking particular instances and using them to devise a general case with a minimum of instruction. A component of discovery learning.

Inferiority complex: Exaggerated and pathological feelings of weakness, including the belief that one cannot overcome one's difficulties through appropriate effort. (Adler)

Instrumental dependency: A means for the individual to attain something (such as food, comfort, relief of pain, treatment of symptoms) which may not be achieved independently for one reason or another.

Insulin: Hormone secreted by the islets of Langerhans in the pancreas, and responsible for regulating the rate at which the body utilises carbohydrate.

Integrative reconciliation: In reception learning (Ausubel), the process of new ideas being consciously related to previously learned material (sub-sumers).

Intellectualisation: A defence mechanism in which the individual deals in detached intellectual terms with a threatening or upsetting situation.

Intrinsic motivation: Described as a drive from within. Curiosity and interest are the major intrinsic motivators, and this is seen perhaps within ourselves when we are learning.

Introversion–extroversion: Described by Jung and later by Eysenck; it is a dimension of personality that defines on the one hand the individual's inward orientation towards the self (introversion), or outwards to the outside world. The introvert is shy and withdrawn whilst the extrovert is outgoing and sociable.

Intuitive thought: Occurs in the latter part of the pre-operational stage of development, and is characterised by children becoming more capable of classifying than quantifying events and objects and applying and integrating them into their developing mental operations. As a result problem solving becomes more prevalent at this stage (4–7 years) but the child does not appear capable of explaining how he has solved the problems, hence the term intuitive. (Piaget)

Intelligence Quotient: The ratio between the mental (test score) and chronological age, and is calculated thus:

$$IQ = \frac{\text{Mental Age}}{\text{Chronological Age}} \times 100$$

Isolation: When feelings and emotions are separated from an experience or thought.

James–Lange theory: The theory that emotional feelings consist of the perception of the physiological changes initiated by the emotional stimulus. The awareness of these responses constitutes the experiencing of emotion.

Lateral hypothalamus: Part of the hypothalamus that has been associated with food intake.

Labelling: Categorising people according to a vast array of criteria, such as where they live, their profession, religion etc. 'Labelling' can be helpful, but often it leads to incorrect assumptions, and hence incorrect behaviour.

Libido: The psychic energy of the sexual instinct.

Lipostatic theory: The theory that the ventromedial hypothalamus (VMH) is responsible for the regulation of feeding according to whether there is a low level of fatty acids (resulting in feeding behaviour) or a high level (leading to inhibition of feeding).

Locus of control: The belief that we have control over our lives, or that external forces will rule our destiny. If we predominantly believe in the first statement then we are said to have an internal locus of control, whereas if we predominantly believe the second statement we are said to have an external locus of control (more commonly called 'internals' and 'externals').

Loading: The degree to which a particular factor is related to a test being demonstrated by the correlation between them.

Magical thinking: In childhood the explanation of events, past, future or present (or indeed the path to a resolution to a particular crisis) by often 'supernatural' factors.

Mammillary body: Part of the hypothalamus which projects into the anterior nucleus of the thalamus.

Mass sociogenic illness: The occurrence of symptoms within a group of people as a result of social factors rather than environmental or endogenous causes. Usually the result of a perceived rather than an actual health threat.

Maternal deprivation: Can refer to both the failure to form attachments with the mother/principal caregiver, or the disruption of an existing attachment.

Metaneeds: Growth ('B') values, which are usually only of importance to the older individual who has at least partially fulfilled the lower needs. Metaneeds are concerned with more nebulous needs such as 'goodness' and 'truth' and contribute to what Maslow terms as 'full humanness'.

Mesosystem: The interrelations among two or more settings in which the developing individual actively participates.

Microsystem: A pattern of activities, roles and interpersonal relations experienced by the developing person in a given setting with particular physical and material characteristics.

Mineralocorticoids: Hormones of the adrenal cortex (e.g. aldosterone), which affect the electrolytes of extracellular fluid, principally sodium, potassium and chloride.

Monoamines: Compounds which contain a single amine group, e.g. acetylcholine, serotonin, dopamine and noradrenaline.

Monozygotic twins: Twins which develop from the same egg.

Moral anxiety: A result of the conflict between the id and the superego and ego which is experienced as feelings of guilt and/or shame.

Multiple discrimination: Learning to discriminate between stimuli which resemble each other. (Gagne').

Narcissism: Self-love. (Freud)

Neopsychic: Ego states which are autonomously directed towards objective appraisal of reality.

Neurotic anxiety: Results from an unconscious conflict between id impulses (mainly sexual and aggressive) and the constraints enforced by the ego and the superego, and can take three main forms: apprehensiveness, phobias and panic.

Object permanence: The child's realisation that an object continues to exist even though it is out of sight. (Piaget)

Objective (or reality) anxiety: Considered by Freud to be synonymous with fear, and results from a perception of danger in the external world.

Oedipus complex: In male children, strong feelings for the opposite sexed parent, and resentment for the same sex parent who they see as a competitor.

Operant conditioning: Also known as Type 2 conditioning. Behaviour which is governed by the degree and direction of reinforcement given. (Skinner)

Operations: Acts such as combining, subtracting, adding within existing structures. (Piaget)

Peripheral construct: A Construct that can be changed without serious modification of the core structure. (Kelly)

Person permanence: The concept that a person may exist even when they are out of sight. Such a concept should be complete by about the age of two years.

Persona: A protective mask (symbolic) which prevents others from seeing our inner self and also prevents others from seeing our inner self and also creates a specific impression. This may be symbolized as a coat or covering of some description.

Personal traits: Traits which go to make up our true personality, which are entirely unique to the individual. (Allport)

Personal unconscious: According to Jung, that part of the psyche which contains material from personal experience that is not at the level of awareness.

Phenomenological: The individual's unique, subjective experience. See also Humanistic Psychology.

Pleasure principle: According to Freud, the goal of all people is to achieve pleasure and to avoid 'unpleasure' (pain).

Preconscious: The part of the psyche that contains material that can be readily brought to the conscious, although it is outside awareness until this occurs.

Primacy effect: Information which is imparted being remembered more than other material.

Primary organisation: To group information in terms of their relationships.

Progressive differentiation: In reception learning (Ausubel) it is the presentation of general ideas first (advanced organisers) followed by gradual increase in details and specificity.

Positive regard: Warmth, liking, respect, sympathy and acceptance from another person.

Positive self-regard: Liking and accepting oneself in the absence of specific contacts with others. A learned human need, derived from the need for positive regard. (Rogers)

Postulate (fundamental): A person's processes are psychologically channelled by the ways in which he anticipates events.

Prejudice: ' . . . an antipathy based on a faulty and inflexible generalisation directed towards a group as a whole or towards an individual because he is a member of that group.' (Allport, 1965).

Preoperational stage: The early part of the concrete operational period (2–7 years) in which the child can think in terms of symbols, but has yet to comprehend certain operations such as conservation.

Primary acoustic store: In the 'working memory model', the primary acoustic store is dependent upon the articulatory loop for the translation of visual information in an acoustic code, but deals with auditory information directly. This store can be used when reading and the printed matter can be 'heard' as we read. This store can be referred to as the 'inner ear'.

Primary appraisal: In terms of coping, an initial form of appraisal in which the individual is concerned with categorising the situation in terms of their own wellbeing.

Primary circular reactions: Occurring between 1 and 4 months during the sensory motor period, when activities are centred around and focused upon the infant's own body. When activities are discovered they are repeated continually. (Piaget)

Problem focused coping: Coping which is directed towards altering the relationship between the demands of the situation and the resources available. (Lazarus and Folkman)

Projection: Dangerous impulses that we may harbour can be unconsciously dealt with by attributing them to someone else. This projection can take on several forms, including the belief that someone wishes to harm us when, in reality, it is us that wishes to harm them.

Propriate striving: Intentions and goals that will give an overall purpose in life. Propriate striving first emerges during adolescence. (Allport)

Proprium: Describes those aspects which are private to us, and which contribute to our 'inward unity'. (Allport)

Psychic determinism: All mental activity has a cause, in other words, nothing in the psyche occurs by chance.

Psychosomatic (illness): A physically manifested illness with psychological causes.

Rapid eye movements (REM): Eye movements that usually indicate dreaming.

Rationalisation: Rationalisation is in many ways closely akin to intellectualisation insofar as we may reduce our feelings of guilt at having illicit feelings towards others by giving such feelings and impulses rational explanations in order to justify them.

Reaction formation: The replacement with opposite feelings and beliefs, when confronted with unpleasant feelings and urges. As such, reaction formation and repression will usually occur together, and both originate from the unconscious part of the ego.

Reality principle: Delay of immediate gratification in favour of long term gratification.

Reality testing: The experience of the child in comparing the images which the id creates, and the actual objects which exist in reality, that may satisfy his needs.

Re-appraisal: Following the primary and secondary appraisal of a stressful situation, re-appraisal involves the individual in continually reappraising the situation in the light of further information and perceptions and hence possibly changing their behaviour.

Recency effect: Information which is given at the beginning of the message may be lost to the individual in favour of the most recent information given.

Regression: Returning to an earlier (possibly safer) stage of development and response. May be a defence mechanism.

Reticular activating system: Originating in the brain stem recitular formation, an ascending system that arouses electrical activity in the cerebral cortex. Thought to have an important role in waking, sleeping and arousal.

Retrieval: The recovery of stored information from the memory.

Reversibility: According to Piaget, the realisation that objects that have had their shape changed may be restored to their original state.

Role construct repertory test: The method used to establish the basic construct which a person uses and the interrelationship between them. (Kelly)

Role identity: The development of an individual perspective and direction in preparation for approaching adulthood.

Role modelling: The adopting of a role from another individual.

Repression: A defence mechanism which prevents unpleasant or unacceptable memories from emerging into conscious awareness.

Restricted code: A message given without detail and with minimal or no explanation. Usually just a statement or command.

Schema: The organisation of new experiences in such a way as to classify them, not in the light of an individual experience occurring at a certain stage of development but rather as a contribution to a stage free cognitive structure which refers to a class of similar action sequences. (Piaget)

Secondary appraisal: Having ascertained that a situation is or is potentially threatening to their wellbeing the individual will then need to decide upon a course of action. The coping strategy that the individual will actually use should aim at reducing the gulf between the individual's resources and the demands placed upon it.

Secondary circular reactions: This stage of development occurs between 4 and 8 months during the sensory motor period and is characterised by the infant beginning to interact with its environment. The infant will return to play if interrupted and will look for objects that may have been dropped.

Random movements frequently initiate new behaviour patterns and show the beginnings of goal orientation of intentionality. (Piaget)

Secondary organisation: To remember information by categorical or associative means.

Self: Synonymous with the term self concept.

Self-actualisation: In humanistic psychology, the individuals' striving towards their maximum potential.

Self concept: Our attitude to and perception of ourself.

Self disclosure: The degree and manner in which an individual will reveal details about themselves to others.

Self-efficacy: The individual's belief in the possibility of achieving a particular goal.

Self-esteem: Develops from our self image and is essentially a judgement of aspects or the totality of our self image.

Self identity: Entails that there is no other person like us (uniqueness), that we are hence individuals (individuality), and that we continue to exist as such (continuity). Also our own personal experiences that we cannot share with other people (private experience), that further enhance our individuality and uniqueness, are included in the concept of self identity.

Self image: How we would describe ourselves, and includes the body image.

Sensory motor period: So called simply because the child is attempting to discover use and co-ordinate its motor abilities as well as perceptually exploring its environment. Takes place in the first two years of life. (Piaget)

Serotonin: Substance formed from the amino acid tryptophan, and thought to be a synaptic transmitter implicated in psychosis. Also known as 5-hydroxytryptamine (5HT).

Shadow: The unacceptable aspects of the self sometimes represented as a 'devil' figure. One of the archetypes described by Jung.

Signal learning: This is equivalent to Pavlov's conditioned response. (Gagne')

Social interest: A human being's innate aptitude to relate to other human beings.

Social shape: A structure inscribed around us as a result of our interaction with the communities in which we live.

Source trait: A basic element of personality. (Cattell)

Specificity theory: The theory that specific pathways transmit pain messages to a centre in the brain.

Stereotype: A usually overgeneralised abstract cognitive representation of the attributes of a class or group of people.

Stimulus privation: Deprived of stimulation. Term which is usually used when describing a child's environment which is for instance, deficient in communication from others as well as other stimuli essential for cognitive development.

Stimulus response learning: This is equivalent to Skinner's discriminated operant conditioning. (Gagne')

Storage: The retention of encoded information.

Stress: A particular relationship between the person and the environment that is appraised by the individual as taxing or exceeding his or her resources and endangering his or her wellbeing.

Sublimation: Modification of our innate instincts to other more socially acceptable outlets.

Substratia gelatinosa: Part of the grey matter in the spinal cord.

Superego: According to Freud, that part of the personality which represents the internalisation of society's values and morals. Sometimes referred to as the 'conscience'.

Superiority complex: False feelings of being superior to others are experienced, hence further preventing development by denying the inferiority that needs to be overcome. (Adler)

Tertiary circular reactions: Occurring between about 12 and 18 months during the sensory motor period, it is when the child begins to attempt to discover cause and effect (i.e. what results certain actions will bring), and will engage in trial and error activities.

Temperament trait: Trait that determines how an individual will reach a certain goal. (Cattell)

Thalamus: Brain structure (one on each hemisphere), located either side of the third ventricle. A major centre of neural integration.

Thanatos (death seeking): Thanatos endeavours to return the individual to the ultimate state of peace, namely death, and attempts are made by the individual to pull against Thanatos, and as a result, destructive behaviour is directed towards others. One of Freud's two major drives.

Thematic apperception test: Developed by Murray, this is a personality measure which requires the subject to make stories about relatively ambiguous pictures.

Trait: A predisposition to respond. In factor analysis; a first order factor.

Transactional analysis: The diagnosis of which ego state implemented a transactional stimulus and which one executed the transactional response.

Transductive reasoning: Centering on one salient element of an event, and proceeding to irreversibly draw as a conclusion from it some other, perceptually compelling, happening.

Type: A term used in the description of personality. Type theories propose that individuals can be categorised into discrete types that are quantitatively different from one another. In terms of factor analysis; a second order factor.

Uncanny emotions: Encompasses such emotions as horror, dread, awe and loathing. Anxiety, in its most extreme form, resembles such uncanny emotions and, as would be expected, underlies them.

Unconditional positive regard: To be valued by parents and others, regardless of whether our behaviour and attitudes have been ideal.

Unconditional positive self-regard: A 'utopian state of complete self acceptance, free from any conditions of worth'. (Rogers)

Unconditioned reflex: In classical conditioning theory, the normal response to an unconditioned stimulus such as food.

Unconscious: The part of the psyche which contains those memories and emotions which, in unaltered form, are not at the level of conscious thought.

Urethral complex: Traumatic effects associated with toilet training. Murray maintains that such effects endure into adult life as 'complexes', but only if extreme will abnormal behaviour emerge. Toilet training, if traumatic, may lead to a 'urethral complex' which is manifested by bedwetting (enuresis), or bedsoiling (encopresis).

Ventromedial hypothalamus: Area of the hypothalamus which has been found to be important in feeding behaviour. Sometimes referred to as the ventromedial nuclci.

Verbal association: Learning verbal chains. (Gagne').

Visual–spatial scratch pad: In the 'working memory model', this not only holds the words we are about to say, but also acts as a rehearsal loop similar to that in the Atkinson–Shiffrin model, and is used whenever we verbally repeat material in order to memorise it. It therefore deals with the articulation of verbal material and is considered as an 'inner voice'.

Wish fulfillment: The forming of mental images of objects by the id, that will provide satisfaction. (Freud)

Index